A HOLLYWOOD ENDING

ALSO BY YARON WEITZMAN

Tanking to the Top: The Philadelphia 76ers and the Most Audacious Process in the History of Professional Sports

A HOLLYWOOD ENDING

THE DREAMS AND DRAMA OF THE LeBRON LAKERS

YARON WEITZMAN

DOUBLEDAY · NEW YORK

FIRST DOUBLEDAY HARDCOVER EDITION 2025

Copyright © 2025 by Yaron Weitzman

Published by Doubleday, a division of Penguin Random House LLC, 1745 Broadway, New York, NY 10019.

Doubleday and the portrayal of an anchor with a dolphin are registered trademarks of Penguin Random House LLC.

Library of Congress Cataloging-in-Publication Data
Names: Weitzman, Yaron author
Title: A Hollywood ending : the dreams and drama of the LeBron Lakers / Yaron Weitzman.
Identifiers: LCCN 2025011342 (print) | LCCN 2025011343 (ebook) |
ISBN 9780385550222 hardcover | ISBN 9780385550253 ebook
Subjects: LCSH: Los Angeles Lakers (Basketball team)—History |
James, LeBron | Buss, Jeanie, 1961– | National Basketball Association—History
Classification: LCC GV885.52.L67 W44 2026 (print) |
LCC GV885.52.L67 (ebook) | DDC 796.323/640979494—dc23/eng/20250615
LC record available at https://lccn.loc.gov/2025011342
LC ebook record available at https://lccn.loc.gov/2025011343

penguinrandomhouse.com | doubleday.com

Printed in the United States of America
1st Printing

The authorized representative in the EU for product safety and compliance is Penguin Random House Ireland, Morrison Chambers, 32 Nassau Street, Dublin D02 YH68, Ireland, https://eu-contact.penguin.ie.

To Maayan, Lior, and Matan:
The wellspring of my life,
The light in my dark times,
The gift I didn't know I could never live without.

CONTENTS

AUTHOR'S NOTE

This book is primarily based on interviews I conducted with nearly three hundred people. A good chunk of those were done on the record, but most were not. I felt that giving sources the freedom to speak freely and without fear of retribution was the best way to tell this story in full. Because of that, you won't see much direct attribution in the pages ahead.

LeBron did not participate in this book and, through a representative, declined to take part in the fact-checking process. Most of the quotes attributed to him are pulled from press conferences and podcast appearances.

The Lakers did not participate either. Most of the quotes from members of the Buss family, especially those appearing in the book's early chapters, were pulled from the 2022 Hulu documentary *Legacy: The True Story of the LA Lakers,* for which Jeanie Buss served as an executive producer. I conducted two fact-checking sessions with Jeanie Buss early in my reporting process, but, in the spring of 2024, she and the Lakers enlisted famed defamation lawyer Marty Singer to represent them in their dealings with me. That June, Singer sent me a letter. It wasn't a cease-and-desist but more of a *we're watching you* type of thing. About a year later, before the book went to print, I sent the Lakers a lengthy fact-checking document containing the parts of my reporting that I wanted them to have the opportunity to address. In response, I received another letter from Singer, this one accusing me of writing "a salacious hit piece, targeting the Lakers and its executives with fabricated defamatory fiction" featuring "derogatory sexist innuendo" in order to "advance a misogynistic, sexist subtext."

"I want to be incredibly clear with you," Singer wrote. "There are many times when individuals threaten to sue with neither the reputations to stand up to scrutiny nor the resources to pursue a strong libel claim. Please have no doubt, neither of those issues applies here."

Singer's letter included numerous responses to my reporting. When applicable, those have been inserted into the text and attributed to a "representative" for the Lakers.

A HOLLYWOOD ENDING

PROLOGUE

LeBron James loves holding court. He doesn't need a big audience, just *an* audience, and on this night his audience consisted of Anthony Davis—his best friend on the Lakers—reserve forward Jarred Vanderbilt, and a few staffers. Everyone else had fled the locker room. The Lakers were in Miami and had the next day off, making it the perfect night to enjoy South Beach.

"Ain't nothing like that first one," LeBron said as he dried himself off with a towel. He was reminiscing about all the NBA contracts he'd signed. "That first one, where we come from . . ." He trailed off. He and Davis, sitting in a stall across the rectangular-shaped room, started breaking down all their NBA deals.

"It's crazy," LeBron said. "Because, like, we play a fucking game. Y'all paying me all this money to play ball."

"Well, then give it back then!" shouted a team staffer sitting next to him.

The half dozen or so people still milling around the locker room burst into laughter.

"No," LeBron said, trying to regain the group's attention. "Because on the other hand, on the other hand . . ."

The laughter continued.

"You know what, it's funny you say that," LeBron said, a little louder this time.

The chatter stopped. The King was speaking.

"Because on the other hand," LeBron continued, "I feel like I'm underpaid. I feel like I should be getting like—"

"Five-year, what?" Davis interrupted, referring to the maximum-length contract allowed under the NBA's collective bargaining agreement. "Five hundred?"

"Six trillion!" shouted the Lakers staffer.

More laughter followed.

LeBron jumped back in. "We shouldn't have a cap," he said. "It should be like baseball."*

"That shit'd be insane," Davis said.

"But then you don't have to worry about your players leaving," LeBron replied.

"Your five-year [contract] would be what?" Davis asked.

"Five years?" LeBron said, thinking out loud. "At least five hundred."

The staffer asked LeBron whether, looking back now, he felt like he deserved to make that much from every one of his NBA contracts.

"Well, fresh out of high school, I mean, I had to make my way, but when I came here," LeBron said, referring to when he signed with the Heat in 2010, "for real, that summer I could have did, like . . ."

"Twelve years," Davis began. LeBron countered that the most years a player changing teams could sign for is four years.†

"So four years, 450?" Davis asked.

"Yeah, when I came here, twenty-five years old," LeBron replied while lathering himself in lotion, "I should have got, like, four years, 450, something like that.‡

"And then when I went back home," LeBron continued, referencing his decision to leave Miami and return to Cleveland in July 2014, "I probably should have gotten like 500.

"And then, when I came to the Lakers the first time, I probably should have gotten like another 500 and then—"

"Oh my God," the staffer interjected, cutting off LeBron. The others laughed.

"Because it ain't just the basketball," LeBron continued, retaking

---

* Where players can sign for any amount, as opposed to the NBA, where the maximum a player can sign for is only 35 percent of the salary cap.

† This wasn't actually the case back when he joined the Heat. At that point, players could get six-year contracts with new teams if they changed teams via sign-and-trade, which is exactly what LeBron did. In exchange for some future draft capital, the Cleveland Cavaliers sent him to Miami on a six-year, $110.1 million contract that included an opt-out after four seasons, which LeBron exercised to return to Cleveland.

‡ This would have been nearly $383 million more than he actually earned in his four seasons with the Heat.

control of the room. He was fully dressed now, wearing perfectly tailored dark pants and a white graphic tee that probably cost more than some of his younger teammates were paying for rent in LA. "Like, you know, I'm helping the culture. I'm changing the culture, you know what I'm saying, I'm putting people in the seats." He didn't quote any of the studies that have shown the impact he'd had on the income and valuations of the teams for which he played,* but he certainly seemed to be aware of them.

He then brought the conversation back to a topic that he'd clearly been ruminating on all day. Earlier that morning, the Lakers practiced on a new Heat floor, which had the phrase HEAT CULTURE printed at center court and HARDEST WORKING. BEST CONDITIONED. MOST PROFESSIONAL. UNSELFISH. TOUGHEST. MEANEST. NASTIEST TEAM IN THE NBA. written in the paint. After practice, some local reporters had asked LeBron what he thought about the Heat's new branding campaign. In what ways, the reporters wanted to know, had Miami's culture impacted him?

At first, LeBron was complimentary. Even thankful.

"I learned a lot from being here," he said.

But the questions about Heat culture kept coming. Feeling like he'd received one too many, LeBron issued a clarification.

"I think I would still be at this level no matter if I would've came here or not," he said. "Let's not get it twisted."

Now, back in the comfort of the locker room, LeBron was elaborating, even if his audience was unaware of what had triggered this train of thought.

"It's more with me," he told Davis, Vanderbilt, and everyone else listening in. "Yeah, certain players, it's just basketball. With me, I come with everything, I change the whole shit. I win a championship in every city I've been in, every team I've played for, we won a championship. Every team.

---

* According to a 2017 report conducted by the American Enterprise Institute, the number of restaurants near Quicken Loans Arena in Cleveland spiked after LeBron's 2014 return to the Cavaliers, while the number of restaurants within a mile of Miami's American Airlines Arena started to slide. LeBron's presence, according to the study, boosted employment in these establishments by around 23.5 percent.

"Give me two years; I'm a two-year man."

Nobody was interrupting this time. There were no jokes, no questions.

All eyes were fixed on LeBron.

"Second year [in] Miami—championship.

"Second year back home—championship.

"Second year with the Lakers—championship.

"Give me two years," he said. "I'll figure it out."

•   •   •

This is a book about many things. It's a book about an American icon in the twilight of his career. It's a book about an iconic franchise trying to reclaim its throne. It's a book about the business of basketball and the ambitious people within that world and how they attempt to exert power. But at its heart, this is a book about the stories people tell. And, perhaps just as importantly, the ones they don't.

You have LeBron, in search of a fitting final chapter to the story of his career, one more arc to solidify his legacy as the greatest of all time; and you have one of his best friends, an agent looking to further solidify his standing as the king of an industry that had never before seen someone like him. And you have Jeanie Buss, daughter to perhaps the greatest mythmaker in the history of American sports, both desperate to add one last chapter to her father's story and, in doing so, write one of her own; and you have her most loyal executive, a self-described "storyteller" who'd earned Jeanie's trust in part by pledging fealty to the Lakers.

They all came together in July 2018. Two years later, they were celebrating the Lakers' 17th championship, feeling like they had accomplished everything they'd wanted.

Their stories, however, were not complete.

Because there was more to LeBron than the story he told about himself. And there was more to Jeanie and the Lakers than the stories they told about themselves. That's the thing about stories: Repeat them enough and you become blind to any reality breaking from the narrative. Invest enough resources in a narrative and any challenge will feel like a declaration of war.

That night in Miami, while he recounted the story of his career, everything LeBron said was true. He had revived the Lakers, or, as he had put it, "changed the whole shit." But that was just part of the story, the fairy-tale version. The full story of LeBron's Lakers tenure is far more complicated. It's one about ambitious people with competing agendas navigating complex times. That might not be the exact story that LeBron or the Lakers want told. But it is the kind through which legacies are made.

1

TOO MANY BUSS DRIVERS

He was seventy-seven years old, and still, Dr. Jerry Buss couldn't help but think about his team's future.

It was June 2010, and, once again, his Lakers were on top of the NBA world. Just about one week earlier, confetti had rained down from the ceiling of Staples Center as the team celebrated its latest championship, this one coming via a seven-game battle with the Boston Celtics. That night, euphoria had swept across Los Angeles, a town that, thanks to the brilliance of Dr. Buss, bled Lakers purple and gold. Not only had the Lakers been crowned champions for a second straight year, but the victory had also boosted their number of titles to 16, pulling them within one of the Celtics' NBA record.

Yet Buss wanted more. On this afternoon, he convened with his children—five of whom had roles within the organization—for lunch. The agenda was to lay out the team's offseason plans, but it didn't take long for talk to turn to the topic on the minds of the entire sporting world: the ongoing free agency of LeBron James, the two-time reigning MVP, who, after spending his entire professional career playing for the Cavaliers, appeared to be searching for a new home.

"It'd be good to know that guy," Joey Buss recalled his father saying. Dr. Buss added that he was thinking about setting up a call.*

LeBron, meanwhile, was also thinking about LA. That spring, he and David Geffen, the billionaire and record executive, had discussed the idea of Geffen buying the Los Angeles Clippers from the franchise's

---

* Through a representative, the Lakers described this quote, which was originally published in a July 2018 *Los Angeles Times* story, as "ridiculously phony" and an "outrageous smear of Dr. Buss, falsely making it appear that this legendary and highly respected team owner would intentionally engage in illegal tampering."

notoriously cheap, racist, and incompetent owner, Donald Sterling. LeBron would then sign as a free agent.

Sterling refused to sell, crossing the Clippers off the board for LeBron. As for the Lakers, they were coming off a title run and looking to spend the offseason bolstering the team, not revamping it. And LeBron, still just twenty-five years old, was looking to create his own legacy, not glom onto someone else's. Yet the seeds had been planted.

The night of the title, Earvin "Magic" Johnson, the former Lakers superstar, had accepted the championship trophy on behalf of the franchise. Upon addressing the raucous Lakers crowd, Magic congratulated "the greatest owner in the world in Dr. Buss," called head coach Phil Jackson "the greatest coach in the world," and boasted that "we do have the greatest player in the world in Kobe Bryant." The next day, in a story for ESPN.com, the acclaimed NBA analyst John Hollinger[*] ranked the Lakers as the top franchise in NBA history. "When it comes to superstars," Hollinger wrote, "the Lakers are so far out in front of everybody else it's not even funny."

Which is why no one could see the cracks forming in the foundation or notice that the whole structure was on the verge of collapse.

•　　•　　•

Jerry Buss's story was an American story, with an arc straight out of Hollywood.

Born during the Great Depression, Buss was raised by his mom and stepdad in the small mining and sheep ranching city of Kemmerer, Wyoming. Even as a kid he was a worker, taking whatever jobs he could get. Setting bowling pins. Shining shoes. Carrying guests' bags at a hotel, where he'd sometimes rig the lobby slot machines to get some extra cash. He was smart, too, especially in math and science, and earned a scholarship to the University of Wyoming, and then another one for graduate school to USC, where he received a master's and a PhD in physical chemistry. After that, Buss got a regular nine-to-five desk job at a Boston management consulting firm before moving back to California for a gig at a space laboratory.

In the late '50s, Buss and a friend started investing in Los Angeles

---

* Hollinger would later become an executive for the Memphis Grizzlies.

real estate, specializing in flipping buildings repossessed by banks. They made millions, and Buss, an avid sports fan, began looking for entry points into that world. In 1974, he founded the Los Angeles Strings, an indoor team tennis franchise. He wanted more, though, and in 1979, Lakers owner Jack Kent Cooke, looking for an infusion of cash following a divorce, reached out to Buss to see if he was interested in purchasing his LA sports teams. By this point, Buss had become a local celebrity, the rich guy with the long brown hair and thin mustache who'd be spotted around town—at clubs, at restaurants, at the Playboy Mansion—almost always with not-even-half-his-age women on his arms. At one point, he was offered the chance to play the Marlboro Man in an ad. He was exactly the sort of person who'd want to buy the Lakers, and after receiving Cooke's offer, Buss pounced.

It was a fraught time for the league. Drug use among players was rampant. Teams were hemorrhaging money. Ratings for games were so low that CBS would soon start showing finals games on tape delay. Yet, just like with all that real estate he'd flipped, Buss saw potential where others did not. He became one of the first sports owners to sell the naming rights to his arena. Recognizing that NBA games were about entertainment, he created the Laker Girls. He turned home games into a hot spot for Hollywood celebrities, most notably Jack Nicholson, because he knew they would be seen sitting courtside every time the Lakers were on TV.

"Dr. Buss was a legitimate genius," said Andy Roeser, a Clippers executive from 1984 to 2014.

Buss won a title in his first year with the Lakers and four more in the nine years after that. It was under his watch that Showtime—the team's fast-paced, freewheeling, fan-friendly style—was born. It was because of what he built that the Lakers transformed into not just the NBA's crown jewel but an organization synonymous with glitz and glamour and, most importantly, greatness. Seeing what the Lakers had become filled Buss with pride. The team was like another child to him, and his plan was for his family to take care of that child when he no longer could.

"The Lakers belong to my children," he told Fox Sports West in 2005, "and that's the way it's gonna be."

Doing so, he thought, would keep his family together.

Instead, the Lakers would become the thing that would drive them apart.

• • •

One day, when Jerry Buss was about twenty years old, his wife, JoAnn, approached him with some news: Jerry was going to be a father.

She was excited.

He was not.

A baby would derail his plans. He and JoAnn were about to move to LA. He was about to begin pursuing his PhD. There was no way he could do all that while caring for a child. He knew what it was like to be poor, and he knew that wasn't how he wanted to spend his life. It wasn't that he didn't want a family, he told JoAnn, it was just that this wasn't the right time.

In 1953, JoAnn gave birth to a baby girl.

She and Buss named her Marie.

They then gave her up for adoption.

"[I'm] too busy getting an advanced degree and [have] neither the time nor the finances to keep her," was the reason Buss listed on the adoption paperwork. JoAnn said that she "wanted to be a mother and keep [Marie] but went along with her husband's wishes."*

This was the first time Buss chose his career over his kids.

It wouldn't be the last.

• • •

Buss did keep his word to his wife. By the mid-'60s, he and JoAnn had filled their home with four children. First came two boys, Johnny and Jimmy. Then two girls, Jeanie and Janie. Buss loved them deeply. They'd play Monopoly and go swimming and take family trips to watch USC football. But he never changed who he was, never stopped prioritizing his businesses, never stopped putting his own desires before theirs.

"I remember asking a lot, 'Where's Dad?'" Janie said.

Buss and JoAnn separated in 1972. The kids remained with JoAnn in her Pacific Palisades home. Buss became more distant, showing up only

---

* Marie, who after being adopted was named Lee Klose, reached out to Jeanie in December 2018. Jeanie invited her to meet her and her siblings soon after. Dr. Buss had died five years earlier, but Lee did get to meet her birth mother. JoAnn died six months later.

in spurts. "It left us confused about who our father was," Johnny said. "We knew Dad only as the guy who came over on weekends and took us to McDonald's. I could never understand why he'd want to go to Las Vegas with the Playmate of the Year rather than take us to Disneyland."

Buss missed Little League games and Boy Scout events, dance recitals and graduations. On those rare occasions when he was around, "We'd vie for his attention," Jeanie said. This never-ceasing competition for paternal adoration left its mark, and, as the Buss kids grew older, their battles evolved. Attention was no longer the resource being fought over; their father's approval was. And, given the NBA's rules requiring each franchise to have one boss, they figured what better way to earn that approval than by proving capable of running their father's most prized possession.

•　　•　　•

Johnny was the oldest boy. He believed this alone qualified him to be his father's successor.

His résumé said otherwise.

Johnny had quit the high school football team on the first day of tryouts. He'd gotten kicked off the gymnastics team for not cutting his hair, and then out of school for cutting class. He had dropped out of Santa Monica College to spend more time with his then-girlfriend, the Strings' Australian tennis star Dianne Fromholtz, only to be dumped two years later.* He had enrolled in USC's drama department only to give that up early, too.

And yet, despite all that, Buss was still willing to give him a shot.

In 1982, Johnny was named president of his father's new Major Indoor Soccer League team, the Los Angeles Lazers.

"I think we were 8–40 that first season," Johnny recalled. Even worse: "We lost probably at least a half million dollars that first year, if not more."

Johnny quit after three years. After, he fell into a years-long depression. "Being the son of a famous man and being unable to find myself

---

* Though, to be fair, his father might have played a role in that by trading Fromholtz to the Indiana Loves. And yes, you read that correctly. Dr. Buss traded his son's LA-based girlfriend to a team two thousand miles away.

on my own," he'd tell *Sports Illustrated* years later, had been too much to bear. In the ensuing decades, he'd dip his toes back into sports here and there, most notably by running his father's WNBA team, the Los Angeles Sparks, from 1997 to 2006, a stretch that included two titles. But he bowed out of the competition to succeed his dad.

"I didn't like being in the limelight," he said.

With Johnny out of the picture, the battle was now between Jimmy and Jeanie.

Jimmy was older, but also more of a wild child, a charming and hard-partying former athlete with long blond hair and blue eyes who was popular with the girls but who, like Johnny, had never found himself after high school. Jeanie, on the other hand, was the golden child, the bubbly blonde who was named Miss Palisades in 1979 but knew how to hang with the guys, too. She read DC Comics. She played high school basketball. She served as the scorekeeper for the boys' team. She was also the most ambitious of the bunch, the one her siblings resented for, in Janie's words, "always trying to please my dad, entering beauty pageants, getting good grades." Asked by an interviewer in the '80s if she wanted to replace her father "at the top," she replied, "Yes, I already told him. He knows that. I think he's kind of surprised that his daughter would be saying that, wanting to fill his shoes, but I think I can do it."

At fourteen, Jeanie started accompanying her father to World Team-Tennis board meetings. At nineteen, despite being enrolled in USC—from where she'd eventually graduate with honors and a degree in business—Buss named her general manager of the Strings. "I want you to know what it feels like to do this job," he had told her, and so he gave her carte blanche. Jeanie chose whom to draft, whom to sign, and with whom to do business. Her acumen and enthusiasm impressed those around her. She took the job seriously, but not herself. She'd walk around with a smile and was affable and warm. On road trips, she'd sit with her team and laugh at the latest gossip from the tennis world. All the while—and taking a page out of her father's please-the-players playbook—making sure to provide the talent with top-notch travel accommodations, a far cry from some of their World TeamTennis peers.

"It was very much the minor leagues, especially compared to the Lakers, but she didn't treat it that way," John Lloyd, a player and coach for the Strings under Jeanie, said. "She took it very seriously."

Jeanie was fulfilling her dreams and doing what she had set out to, but she was looking for something more. In 1990, she married a gold-medal-winning volleyball player named Steve Timmons, whom she'd met at the Forum. (Buss showed up to the wedding reception with two dates.) Jeanie and Timmons moved to Italy, where Timmons was playing professionally, only for Jeanie to discover that, at that point, marriage wasn't for her. Or at least not a marriage that pulled her away from her father and the family business.

"I was homesick," Jeanie said. She'd fly back and forth to LA as often as she could, angering Timmons, who felt like she was choosing her family over their relationship. In 1993, the two got divorced, and Jeanie was back in LA. "I felt such a sense of relief," she said.

The Strings folded in 1993, but by then Jeanie had already both proven herself and outshined her siblings. She'd spent time steering her father's roller hockey and volleyball teams, with no qualms about the long hours or small staff, and had enticed tennis stars like John McEnroe,* Andre Agassi, and Jimmy Connors to come for exhibition matches with promises of limos and aggressive advertising campaigns. In 1995, Buss promoted Jeanie, just thirty-four years old, to Forum president and general manager. The job meant she ran the building and the two-hundred-plus events it hosted every year. He also named her an "alternate governor" of the Lakers. She began attending the NBA's ownership meetings, often alongside her father.

It was an exciting time, but also a difficult one. Many of Buss's colleagues didn't believe a woman belonged in those rooms. Some ignored her. Some just rolled their eyes. One went even further, grabbing her rear while waiting behind her at the buffet line.

"I didn't take it as much as a sexual advance but more, like, putting me in my place," Jeanie said years later. "You don't get a seat at the table. You're just a piece of ass."

Jeanie never told her father or brothers, nor did she ever name the culprit, and over two decades would pass before she'd share the story with the public. Her response was to do what she always did—put her head down and work. As the years went by, she grew more comfortable. She started speaking up more during meetings, and her approach—in particular, the way she prioritized the needs of the collective over those of the Lakers—endeared her to her peers.

---

* Whom she later dated for six months.

"With Jeanie, it was always, 'How can we do what's best for the league and stay close to the fans?'" Joe Maloof, who owned the Sacramento Kings with his brother from 1999 to 2013, said.

All the years of studying her father had paid off. And outside the family, there was zero doubt who among Dr. Buss's children was most equipped to be his heir.

"Jeanie has a complete knowledge of the interplay of sports marketing, building management, and TV," then–NBA commissioner David Stern told *Sports Illustrated* in 1998. "If she took over the Lakers from her father, I don't think anything would be lost in the transition."

• • •

But Jimmy still needed a home.

At times, his life appeared to be on the verge of spiraling out of control. He partied. He used drugs. He borrowed lots of money. He spent too much time in Las Vegas.

"Jimmy had some issues, and Dr. Buss had to keep bailing him out," said Ron Carter, a former Lakers player who later became Dr. Buss's close friend and business partner. "But he kept trying to find ways to keep him engaged."

After Johnny quit, Buss put Jimmy in charge of the Lazers. He reduced the team's annual losses but couldn't save them from folding, which they did in 1989. After that, Jimmy decided to give horse training a try. He took the reins—not literally, though he had attended jockey school—of some of Dr. Buss's thoroughbreds at the Hollywood Park Racetrack. It was located next door to his office. The two often got dinner together at the Forum Club—the legendary VIP spot Dr. Buss had opened inside the arena—where they'd party deep into the night.

"We were probably best friends more than father-son," Jimmy said.

By that point, Jimmy's life had been beset by tragedy. In 1981, his best friend was hit by a truck and killed while riding a moped in Hawaii alongside Jimmy. When Jimmy notified the friend's parents, "all they did was blame me for taking him to Hawaii," he said. Around six years later, a girlfriend of Jimmy's was decapitated while stepping out of a helicopter.

In 1997, after selling off his horses, Buss came up with a new idea: Jimmy would work for the Lakers, on the basketball side, directly under

Jerry West, where he'd get on-the-ground training so that he could one day take over as GM. Many in the building were shocked. "He sort of just catapulted into being the assistant GM," one person close to Dr. Buss said. But Jimmy was thrilled. *This* was a plan he could get on board with. The job was prestigious and fun and meant he could spend lots of time with his dad. And there was no doubt in his mind that he'd thrive.

"Evaluating basketball talent is not too difficult," Jimmy told *Sports Illustrated* soon after taking the job. "If you grabbed 10 fans out of a bar and asked them to rate prospects, their opinions would be pretty much identical to those of the pro scouts." In his view, the gig wasn't that different from his previous one at the racetrack. "With a colt, you watch his stride and how he pops to extension," he said. "I just have to learn the qualities to look for in humans." He was even willing to work with his sister. "I wouldn't mind Jeanie having control over Lakers finances," he said, "as long as I had ultimate say over player personnel."

By 2013, the succession plan was in place: Jeanie would run the business, Jimmy the basketball. "We all understood that, we all knew that, we were all for it," Johnny later told the *Los Angeles Times*. Dr. Buss had also fathered two more sons with another woman—Joey and Jesse— and assumed they would eventually inherit it all. "My dad just figured he'd last another 10 years and that Joey and Jesse would start taking over the basketball side and Jimmy would start retiring, and that would be it," Johnny added.

It was a logical, well-thought-out plan.

And it had no shot at success.

•   •   •

In 2011, Dr. Buss was diagnosed with prostate cancer. Later that year he was hospitalized with blood clots. His mind remained sharp, but his failing health prevented him from attending a single Lakers game during the 2011–12 season, a first for him since buying the team. In July 2012, he checked into Cedars-Sinai Medical Center in West Hollywood. His hope—and that of his kids—was that he'd make it out in time to attend opening night for the 2012–13 season, which was scheduled for October 30 at Staples Center. And for a few weeks, it looked like he might. But then came infections, and fluid in the lungs, and in

August he underwent another surgery. By September, the man known for being so full of life had grown despondent.

"I had never seen him like that," Jeanie recalled.

The only thing that seemed to cheer him up was talking about the Lakers, especially the players and coaches with whom he'd been closest. So the family invited them to the hospital. Jerry West came. So did Kareem Abdul-Jabbar. And Pat Riley. And Phil Jackson, who had been dating Jeanie since December 1999. Kobe visited him three times.

But the most emotional visit was with Magic Johnson.

Over the years, the relationship between the two had evolved into something like father and son. When Magic first arrived in LA as a nineteen-year-old out of Lansing, Michigan, it was Dr. Buss who'd taken him under his wing. He showed him around town, bringing him to restaurants and clubs and USC football games and, of course, the Playboy Mansion. He introduced him to contacts throughout the city, who provided a business education that helped Magic build his company into a $700 million empire. After Magic's HIV diagnosis in 1991, Buss stood by him—when Magic attempted to come back the following year, Buss gave him a one-year deal worth about $14 million, because, he said, he wanted to repay his former star for all the years when he wasn't the league's highest-paid player—and in 1994, he sold Magic a 4.5 percent stake in the Lakers.

"Without Dr. Buss, there is no Magic," Johnson once told the *Los Angeles Times*.

This was not a one-way relationship, either. It was Magic, with his electric play and magnetic style and Hall of Fame skills, who served as the catalyst for everything Dr. Buss became, who led Dr. Buss's teams to five titles in his first decade of ownership, who was the engine of Showtime, who perfectly personified the Laker mystique.

That day in the hospital they held hands. They laughed. They cried. They reminisced.

"I love you," Magic told Dr. Buss after about five hours together, "and I'll never forget you." He stood up and kissed him on the forehead.

Dr. Buss spent the next few months with family by his side. On January 27 of the new year, they all celebrated his eightieth birthday together in the hospital.

He died a few weeks later.

The children organized a memorial for him in the Nokia Theatre, across from Staples Center. Thousands of fans gathered in the plaza outside and left messages on boards laid out by the team. The service was televised. Johnny Buss spoke, and so did Kobe and Magic and Phil and Shaquille O'Neal, the latter of whom best captured the sentiment of the day and the legacy that Dr. Buss had left behind.

"He was a visionary; he saw the future before any of us did, and the future he saw brought people together," Shaq said at the service. "It brought people together to root for a team, a team that rallied around a city and redefined the merger of sports and entertainment."

The next day, in a private ceremony for family and close friends, Dr. Buss was buried at Forest Lawn Memorial Park in Hollywood Hills, beneath a bust of him clutching a trophy. Three words, chosen by his children, were engraved between his name and the dates of his birth and death: DEVOTED FAMILY MAN.

•   •   •

Before he died, Dr. Buss had placed the Lakers and all his holdings into a trust. It specified that each of his six children would inherit an equal share of his 66 percent ownership stake in the team, and that the franchise could not be sold unless at least four of the six siblings agreed. Beyond that, everyone understood that Jim—he was going by "Jim" in public now—was in charge of basketball while Jeanie was in charge of the business. What remained unclear, though, was who would be replacing Dr. Buss in the top chair.

"None of us really knew how things worked," Jesse Buss recalled years later. "When it was just my dad, he's going to be the final shot-caller. I was unaware who's going to be that person. Like, is it Jim? Is it Jeanie? Somebody else?"

Around a week after Dr. Buss's death, the family gathered for a meeting. There, Joe McCormack, the team's CFO, passed along the succession structure that Dr. Buss had left behind: Yes, Jim would be running basketball, but Jeanie would be the Lakers' boss.

Jim was stunned. As far as he understood it, the plan was for him and his sister to each have their respective domains, not for him to be reporting to her. "I think [Dr. Buss] kept it to himself in terms of the family because he may have been talked out of it or [thought] that there'd be objection," Jeanie said. "And he didn't want to have to deal with that."

Jim and Jeanie had been butting heads for years. It began in the mid-'80s, after Johnny quit the Lazers. Jeanie didn't like that their father had then-Jimmy in charge instead of her. Jimmy didn't like that Jeanie had taken issue with his getting the team, or the way Jeanie, while at the Forum and in control of all sorts of resources, had thumbed her nose at him and his group. From there, the resentment only grew. Sometimes Jimmy would get drunk at the Forum Club and tell associates that he was going to hire away all of Jeanie's staff.

The two never learned to trust each other, but they did learn how to work together. On occasions when the business and basketball divisions needed to consult, the two siblings did so without any problems.

Jeanie's relationship with Phil Jackson changed the equation. Jim was aghast when Jeanie first shared that she and Jackson were dating. "Are you kidding?" he said. Basketball was supposed to be his realm, and now, to him, it felt like Jeanie was encroaching. On top of that, Jim knew that Jackson didn't respect him. This wasn't unique to Jim—during Jackson's first season with the team, he had yelled at Jerry West, the Lakers icon and then–general manager, to "get the fuck out of my locker room," in front of the players—but that provided little solace when Jackson would do things like have the team plane leave without him.

There was nothing Jim could do while Jackson was still in LA. He was a living legend, the coach who had led the Lakers to five titles. But once Jackson informed the Buss family that the 2010–11 season would be his last—he'd been diagnosed with prostate cancer—Jim was able to assert more control. Especially given Dr. Buss's failing health.

"It wasn't public at the time, but everything in basketball operations was completely handed off to Jim," said someone close to the Buss family.

First, Jim replaced Jackson with recently fired Cavaliers head coach Mike Brown instead of Brian Shaw, a Jackson assistant and former Lakers player.

Next, Jim pulled off the sort of audacious trade for which his father had become known. In a three-team deal, he turned star big man Pau Gasol and reigning Sixth Man of the Year Lamar Odom into Chris Paul, a twenty-six-year-old All-Star point guard.[*] Paul had just one year remaining on his contract and had informed his team, the New Orleans Hornets, that he would not be re-signing. The Hornets didn't want to trade Paul, but they also didn't want to lose him for nothing. The deal was negotiated between Jim, Rockets general manager Daryl Morey, and Hornets general manager Dell Demps. All that was needed was sign-off from every team's owners.

There was just one problem.

The Hornets didn't have one.

In December 2010, the NBA had purchased the franchise from George Shinn, who no longer had the funds to serve as the majority owner. This meant that, until the league could find a buyer, NBA commissioner David Stern was the one who had final say on every one of their moves. After sharing the details of the deal with Stu Jackson, a former coach and general manager serving as the league's executive vice president of basketball operations, Stern decided to kill the trade. He and Jackson thought the Hornets could do better.

"I did it because I was protecting the Hornets," Stern told *Sports Illustrated* in 2018.

There were other factors at play, too. The league's owners had just spent nearly six months negotiating a new collective bargaining agreement—which had led to a 161-day lockout—where a key issue was leveling the playing field between the big- and small-market teams. A new revenue-sharing system, featuring harsher penalties for exuberant spending, was implemented. After going through all that, the league's small-market teams weren't about to allow the Lakers to have yet another star dropped into their lap without putting up a fight.

"It would be a travesty to allow the Lakers to acquire Chris Paul in the apparent trade being discussed," Cavaliers owner Dan Gilbert wrote

---

[*] The Lakers got Paul, and Gasol went to the Houston Rockets. The Rockets sent Luis Scola, Kevin Martin, Goran Dragić, and their 2012 first-round pick to the Hornets, who also got Odom.

in an email to Stern after news of the trade leaked.* "I cannot remember ever seeing a trade where a team got by far the best player in the trade and saved over $40 million in the process."†

Less than a week later, the Hornets found a different way to send Paul to Los Angeles. Except this trade was with the Clippers, a team that over the previous fourteen years had won just one playoff series. That Paul, a star entering the final year of his contract and therefore in control of his own future, was willing to sign off on a deal to play for LA's second-class team was a slap in the face to the Lakers and a signal of how far they'd fallen.

"Chris could have made it very clear that he'd opt out of his deal and leave if we traded for him, and, if he did, we never could have done that," a then–Clippers executive said. "This was the first time the Lakers wanted something and everyone else wasn't scared off and didn't just fall in line." The Lakers finished the 2011–12 season with the third-most wins in the Western Conference but were once again run off the floor in the second round of the playoffs, this time by the young and ascendant Oklahoma City Thunder. If it wasn't clear before, it was now: The title window for this Kobe-led core had closed.

"David Stern's decision fucked the franchise over the next ten years," a former Lakers executive said.

The second straight early postseason exit left Jim feeling desperate. Dr. Buss was still in the hospital at the time, living out the final months of his life, and making it clear to his kids how badly he wanted to see his Lakers win another title—matching the Celtics' record of seventeen—before he died. So in the offseason, Jim took two more big swings, bringing in Steve Nash, a two-time MVP point guard, via a sign-and-trade,‡ and Dwight Howard, a six-time All-Star center and three-time

* Nobody loves a strongly written letter more than Dan Gilbert.
† Gilbert noted that the Paul trade would have saved the Lakers $20 million in salaries over the next three years, and because of that, an additional $21 million in luxury-tax payments (which are distributed to non-taxpaying teams like the Cavs). It's worth pointing out here that, at that time, Dan Gilbert had a net worth of around $1.5 billion.
‡ The Lakers gave up first-round picks in 2013 and 2015 and second-round picks in 2013 and 2014.

Defensive Player of the Year who was widely considered one of the five best players in the league.*

Once again, it looked like Jim was on the verge of restoring the Lakers to glory. *Sports Illustrated* put a picture of Howard and Nash on the cover of its season-preview issue. "Now This Is Going to Be Fun" was the cover line.

Once again, the Lakers endured one of the most disappointing seasons in franchise history.

Nash missed 32 games. Howard, who had undergone back surgery the previous April, was limited during the offseason and training camp. Both players struggled acclimating to their surroundings. Nash was best when running the offense, which was difficult to do alongside Kobe. Howard was great rolling to the rim, which was difficult to do alongside Gasol. In addition to all that, Jim's choice at head coach had proven to be a disaster.

"I think Mike was in over his head," forward Matt Barnes later said.

Worried that the season was going off the rails, the Lakers fired Brown after a 1–4 start. Later that afternoon, a Friday, Jim called Linda Rambis, a Lakers business executive and one of Jeanie's closest friends. Linda's older sister was a Playboy Playmate who dated Dr. Buss in the '70s. He later gave Linda a sales job at the Forum, and she and Jeanie became close.

Where's Jeanie? Jim asked.

Linda told him that she was in her office.

I'll be right over, he said.

Jeanie knew what this meant. A few minutes later, Jim walked in. He apologized for hiring Brown and costing the team money. Then came the real reason he was there.

Do you think Phil would come back? Jeanie recalled him asking. Also,

---

* A four-team deal involving the Denver Nuggets, Orlando Magic, and Philadelphia 76ers. The Lakers sent All-Star center Andrew Bynum—whose career would be derailed by injuries—to Philly; the Sixers also got Jason Richardson. The Nuggets received Andre Iguodala. The Magic received Arron Afflalo, Al Harrington, Nikola Vučević, Moe Harkless, Josh McRoberts, Christian Eyenga, three first-round picks (one from the Lakers), and two second-round picks, one of which was conditional, from the Lakers.

Jim wanted to know, did Jeanie think he and Jackson could work together?

Jeanie said she wasn't sure how to answer those questions, that Jim had to ask Phil himself, that all she knew was that Phil was feeling great, that his prostate cancer was gone, that he'd recovered from knee replacement surgery, that he was in a great place.

Jim said he understood.

Jeanie felt better about her relationship with her brother than she had in years.

"I thought things would be different," she recalled. "Jim would want to hear what I had to say. And I, in turn, could support him."

That night, during the Lakers' blowout win over the Golden State Warriors, a "We want Phil!" chant broke out in Staples Center. The next morning, Jim called Jackson to set up a meeting. Later that day, he and Mitch Kupchak, the team's general manager, arrived at Jackson's Marina del Rey house. Jeanie left with her dog, a ten-pound Maltese named Princess Cujo, so the group could talk freely. They did so for ninety minutes, breaking down the roster. Jim told Phil that they were also considering Mike D'Antoni, a former Coach of the Year who'd previously coached Nash in Phoenix, and Mike Dunleavy Sr., an NBA lifer who'd coached the Lakers from 1990 to 1992 and was coming off a seven-year run with the Clippers. Jackson understood. Money was never discussed.

Beyond that, everyone has a different recollection of the meeting.

According to Jim and Kupchak, Jackson was willing to return, but it seemed like his heart wasn't in it. "He told us he didn't want to coach, but if we needed help to get through the year, he'd do it," Kupchak recalled. "We weren't looking for a coach to get through the season. I mean, that [didn't] help us." Jim would later say that Jackson told them he wanted to coach only home games.

Jackson, on the other hand, thought the meeting went great. He called Jeanie, telling her as much, and spent the weekend talking to his doctors about whether he could coach, to his family about whether he should coach, and to his friend and former assistant coach Kurt Rambis about how he would coach. He received sign-off from everybody, and on Sunday he told his agent to book a red-eye so they could meet the Lakers in LA on Monday. That evening, before cooking dinner for himself and Jeanie, he put on a Lakers-branded Hawaiian shirt that he'd often worn when he worked for the team.

"It was clear to me he was getting mentally ready to return," Jeanie recalled.

Jackson went to sleep that night thinking that the next day he'd be accepting an offer to return to his old job. Then, at 11:30 p.m., he was awoken by the phone ringing.

Hello, Jeanie heard him say. Then, just four words: *Okay. All right. Okay.*

He hung up and turned to Jeanie. It was Kupchak, he told her. The Lakers were hiring D'Antoni.

Jeanie was devastated. She felt played. And betrayed. And even more so when reports smearing Jackson began trickling out, claiming that he wanted an ownership stake, control over personnel decisions, and the freedom to skip some road games.

"I wonder where all that came from?" Jeanie sarcastically asked a reporter a few years later.

D'Antoni failed to revive the Lakers. The back surgery had sapped Howard's athleticism, the bedrock of his dominance, and left him out of shape. His lackadaisical style and off-court immaturity (he was known for his locker room farts* and eating the equivalent of twenty-four chocolate bars every day) clashed with Kobe's maniacal approach. Nash, meanwhile, fractured a bone in his leg in the second game of the season and never looked like himself again.

The Lakers hung in the playoff race by riding Kobe down the stretch. He moved to point guard, started guarding the opponents' best perimeter scorers, and rarely came out of games. The approach was working until an early April matchup with the Warriors when, with just over three minutes left in the game, he collapsed on the floor.

"Did you kick me?" he asked Matt Barnes, who was then playing for Golden State.

"No," Barnes replied.

"Fuck!" Kobe yelled as he clutched his left heel and played around with his shoe. It felt like his calf had slid down to his ankle.

A foul had been called. Kobe drilled two free throws. He then hobbled off the court to a standing ovation. The next day, the Lakers con-

---

* When Howard's Magic teammate Glen Davis was asked in 2012 what the team would miss most about Howard, his reply was, "A great farter. He can fart. He can fart loud—the loudest farts. Silent farts."

firmed what Kobe had suspected: He had a torn Achilles, one of the most devastating injuries an athlete can suffer. His season was over. No one knew if he'd ever return.

The Lakers squeezed into the playoffs but were discarded by the San Antonio Spurs in four games. It was a disappointing end to what was supposed to be an exciting season, but all wasn't lost. As long as they re-signed Howard, who was set to become a free agent that offseason, they'd still be in good shape.

In the lead-up to free agency, the Lakers put up several billboards throughout the city featuring the hashtag #StayD12, hoping that the message would go viral on social media, and wrangled celebrities for a video pitch, despite the responses being—in the words of a person involved in the process—"lukewarm." They then had both Nash and Kobe join for the in-person pitch at the Beverly Hills office of Howard's agent, Dan Fegan. Nash showed up in a crisp shirt and, after hearing Howard ask why his teammates had allowed him to become the scapegoat for the Lakers' failures the previous season, apologized.

Kobe, who arrived in basketball shorts and a T-shirt, took a different approach.

You have to learn how it's done, he told Howard. He spent most of the meeting chastising him.

The Lakers were still optimistic. Because NBA rules were designed so that players were incentivized to re-sign with their incumbent teams, they were able to offer Howard five years and $118 million, while others were limited to four years and $88 million. And yet, a few days after their meeting, Howard decided to sign with the Rockets. He was so desperate to leave the Lakers that he was willing to leave $30 million on the table.

It was an embarrassing outcome for the franchise, one that many Lakers fans believed would never have occurred if Dr. Buss was still running the team. Jeanie felt the same way. "They would've probably had a better relationship if my dad hadn't been sick," she said in a radio interview a month later. "When it came time to try to convince Dwight to stay, we lost the best closer in the business in Dr. Buss."

Just three years earlier, Magic Johnson had stood at center court to celebrate a Lakers title and boasted about them having the NBA's best owner, best player, and best coach. Now that owner was dead, that coach was gone, and that player's future was in jeopardy. Forget laying the groundwork to lure LeBron James—these Lakers couldn't even keep their own star center from leaving town.

In all the thirty-three years that Dr. Buss had owned the Lakers, things had never felt this bleak.

And it was all about to get worse.

2

KLUTCH TIME

Even in his earliest days as a pro, LeBron had his sights set on horizons beyond basketball. He never wanted to be just an athlete, and his plan was to empower those around him not only to execute his vision but to climb their own respective mountains.

The process started in 2005, when, at twenty years old, he fired his first NBA agent. Soon after, he set up a holding company, King James Inc., to take better control of his off-court business. In 2006, he launched the management company LRMR and put his close friend Maverick Carter in charge. One year later, LeBron and Carter formed a production venture, SpringHill Company, named after the housing complex in which LeBron grew up. Over time, LeBron and his inner circle collected a group of mentors who wouldn't look out of place as keynote speakers at Davos. Industry icons like music executive Jimmy Iovine. Renowned entrepreneurs like Marquis Jet CEO Jesse Itzler. Investment experts like Paul Wachter, whose client list included Arnold Schwarzenegger and Red Sox part-owner Tom Werner. Even Warren Buffett considered LeBron a friend.

"He tells me what socks to buy," Buffett said of LeBron in 2007, "and I tell him what stocks to pick."

By 2010, seven years into his NBA career, LeBron had two MVP awards, multiple seven-figure sponsorship deals (with prestigious companies like Coca-Cola and Upper Deck), and several signature Nike shoes. And, thanks to a strategy of seeking marketing deals that included equity, he was on a path toward becoming a billionaire. What he didn't have, though, was an NBA title, which was why, in the summer of 2010, he signed with the Heat. Miami was offering him the chance to play alongside fellow All-Stars Dwyane Wade and Chris Bosh. This, LeBron thought, was a way to guarantee himself multiple titles and a spot on the sport's Mount Rushmore.

At first, the move looked like a massive mistake. It started with the decision to create *The Decision,* the one-hour TV special during which LeBron announced that he was dumping his hometown team. The show, which aired on July 8, 2010, would be remembered as one of the biggest PR blunders in sports history. Everything about it was a disaster, from the stilted back-and-forth between LeBron and host Jim Gray (eighteen questions leading up to the announcement, including "Are you still a nail biter?"), to the language LeBron used to announce his decision ("I'm taking my talents to South Beach"), to LeBron's outfit (a purple gingham button-down with his undershirt peeking out).

The event transformed LeBron into a national villain. Words like "traitor" and "fraud" were tossed around. Cavs fans burned his jersey. NBA legends, including the normally sequestered Michael Jordan, mocked him. "There's no way, with hindsight, I would've ever called up Larry [Bird], called up Magic Johnson, and said, 'Hey, look, let's get together and play on one team,'" Jordan told reporters during a celebrity golf tournament a couple weeks later. Even *New York Times* opinion columnist Maureen Dowd got in on the action, using her space in the Gray Lady's renowned pages to describe LeBron as "narcissistic."

LeBron spent his first season with the Heat being booed by opposing fans. Those boos turned into laughs when he and the heavily favored Heat fell to the Dallas Mavericks in the finals, one of the biggest upsets in NBA playoff history.

And yet, despite all the off-court mockery and the on-court stumbles, LeBron had ushered in a new age, turning the tables on some of the most powerful people in the world.

First he had forced the billionaires to pitch *him.* Then he made them all wait for his answer. Then, in an unprecedented move, he convinced ESPN to hand over full control of its airwaves for an entire hour. He picked the host and reviewed the questions and sold the ads and donated the revenue to the national office of the Boys & Girls Club, and as much as people said they despised the whole thing, *The Decision* still drew just under ten million viewers, to this day ESPN's highest-rated studio program ever.

In June 2012, LeBron led the Heat back to the finals. They dropped Game 1 but won the next four. LeBron spent the final minutes of Game 5 on the sidelines, hopping with glee. Even viewers at home could see the weight he'd been carrying melt away.

"This right here is the happiest day of my life," he proclaimed that night.

He was no longer a punch line, no longer a heel. When appearing on David Letterman's late-night show a week later, he received a loud and lengthy standing ovation.

"Oh, wow," he said as he soaked it all in, clearly surprised.

With a title under his belt, LeBron was ready to think bigger. "When I'm done [playing] and I'm not around the media every day, I hope that somebody's continuing to fight off the narrative: 'You're the athlete? Can't have power, and can't be in control,'" he'd tell *Sports Illustrated* years later. "Because you can." What LeBron wanted was to take all that power he'd amassed and use it to reshape the power dynamics of professional sports. He was ready to break the system. And what better way to start than by leaving his Hollywood-based agency and handing over the reins of his NBA career to one of his closest friends?

•　　•　　•

It was the spring of 2002. LeBron, a junior in high school and just a few months removed from being billed "The Chosen One" by *Sports Illustrated,* was waiting to board a flight to Atlanta at Akron-Canton Airport when he spotted a man wearing a sky blue Houston Oilers jersey with Warren Moon's No. 1 on the front. LeBron loved throwbacks. He went over to find out where the jersey was from. The answer was an apparel store in Atlanta. LeBron said he planned on checking it out. The man told him to use his name. It was Rich Paul.

"The minute I met Rich, I knew he was different," LeBron once recalled. "He understood me from the jump." They both loved sports and music and fashion, but the connection ran deeper. Like LeBron, Paul grew up in a rough Northeast Ohio neighborhood. Like LeBron, Paul had attended a majority-white private school. Like LeBron, Paul was raised by just one parent.

LeBron's mom was sixteen when he was born; his dad was never in the picture. Paul's dad was, but his mother, who battled a crack cocaine addiction throughout his childhood, sometimes disappeared for months. Rich Sr. was married with kids when he started seeing Paul's mother, but he still took it upon himself to raise his son, setting up Paul and his mother in a two-bedroom apartment above the corner store he owned.

Paul's father was caring but stern. He knew life was tough, especially in the Glenville neighborhood where he was raising his kids, and he wanted them to be prepared. He gave them cash when they brought home good grades—$20 for every A, $10 for every B, $5 for every C—but their true classroom was his shop on the corner of 125th Street and Edmonton Avenue.

It was "way more than a store," Paul recalled in his memoir. It was "also a credit union, food pantry, taxi stand, community center, and more. Parents knew their kids were safe there buying penny candy and dropping quarters into the *Donkey Kong* game. You could get some bread and eggs there a couple days before your paycheck arrived . . . Guys who got locked up would use their one call from jail to ring the store pay phone and tell my dad to tell their people to bail them out."

Watching his father in the store, Paul learned how he read different people and different situations. Every customer was unique. Some needed money, some had plenty to spend. Some were respectful; some tried taking advantage of Rich Sr.'s generosity, telling him they'd pay him later with no intention of following through. Sometimes Rich Sr. would cave, sometimes he'd stand firm.

"He was a charmer, with a great sense of humor, but could instantly flip the switch if something went sideways," Paul wrote.

Paul spent most of his free hours working there. Otherwise, he was either gambling—his father ran a speakeasy in an apartment across from where Paul lived and taught Paul how to play dice when he was six—or obsessing over sports. Studying box scores. Staying up late to watch West Coast games. He was a good athlete, too, and played basketball for Benedictine, the private school across town that he attended.[*]

In 1999, during Paul's freshman year of college, Rich Sr. died from bladder cancer. The loss left Paul reeling. "I felt more alone than I ever had in my whole life," he recalled. By this point, Paul had started dealing drugs[†] and making solid money. He liked spending that cash on

---

[*] Rich Sr.'s brother, who worked for the post office, took out loans from his credit union and Rich Sr. made the payments.

[†] In October 2000, Paul was arrested on the corner outside the family store for possession of marijuana.

clothes and, in 2001, he took a trip to New York City to go shopping. There, he visited the NBA Store, and, while waiting in the checkout line, a couple throwbacks caught his eye: a royal blue No. 22 Lakers jersey (Elgin Baylor) and a forest green No. 1 Milwaukee Bucks jersey (Oscar Robertson). Paul bought both. The outfits were a hit back home. Paul googled "Hardwood Classics," the name on the labels, and found a store in Atlanta called Distant Replays. He dialed the listed number and placed an order with the store's owner, Andy Hyman, a process he repeated every week for the next two months.

Sensing a business opportunity, Paul asked Hyman if he could invest in the store. Hyman wasn't interested in another partner, but he told Paul to come down to Atlanta. "No one had ever approached me like that or was ever as aggressive as him," Hyman said. Paul was charming and inquisitive, and the two came up with a deal: If Paul worked in the store one weekend every month, Hyman would sell him jerseys at a rate just above wholesale, which Paul could then sell in Cleveland for profit.

Paul was in. He'd bring twenty-five or so back with him every month. He made good money off the gear but was growing tired of the hustle. He had recently become a father and was looking for a way to give himself and his family a better life.

One year after meeting LeBron in the airport, he was given his chance. LeBron was on the verge of entering the NBA and had just signed a record-setting $87 million deal with Nike. He was looking to secure his inner circle and decided that he wanted Paul around. He hired him to his company, King James Inc., and started him off with a salary of $48,000 per year.

At first, there wasn't much for Paul to do. Not that Paul minded. He was at the center of the sports world, working alongside one of the brightest young stars in the country. What could be better? But as the months went by, Paul grew dispirited. He wanted more. Organizing pay-to-attend parties and securing appearance fees for LeBron—which was how he was spending most of his time—wasn't enough to satisfy his ambitions.

"He was really stuck in a spot of, like, 'I want to do something. I don't want to just be a guy that's on LeBron's payroll, I want to have a purpose,'" Randy Mims, a longtime friend of LeBron's, recalled.

With the formation of LRMR in 2006, Paul initially believed he'd found his answer. After all, the name represented the first initials of the "Four Horsemen"—what the friends called themselves—who founded it: LeBron, Rich, Maverick, and Randy. Instead, LRMR became Carter's baby, forcing Paul to continue searching for a niche of his own. He asked Carter for advice. "He was in a lot of places, and he was trying to figure out what was right for him," Carter later recalled, "but he wasn't focused." Carter told Paul that he needed to pick a lane.

His opportunity came at CAA, which, two years earlier, had expanded into sports. The renowned Hollywood agency had bought the practice of Leon Rose, who was LeBron's agent, and also hired the hoops power broker William Wesley, as a consultant. Paul got along with Rose, but he and Wesley were especially close. The two first met around 2002. Wesley had relationships with numerous Cavaliers players and, during his many trips to Cleveland, took a liking to Paul. They had similar backgrounds, with Wesley's entry into the sports world coming from his sales job at a sneaker store in Cherry Hill, New Jersey. The spot was popular with local basketball stars, a group that included future NBA players like Milt Wagner and Billy Thompson. Wesley was captivating and charismatic and someone whom players both trusted and liked having around. By the late '90s, he had become the basketball world's premier connector, a role earning him the moniker "World Wide Wes."

Paul spoke with Rose and Wesley about joining CAA, and both urged higher-ups at the agency to bring him in. Not that anyone needed much convincing. Everyone knew about Paul's relationship with LeBron. Beyond that, CAA executives recognized that he was a dynamic personality who, they believed, could grow into a strong agent.

Paul spent his first few years at CAA learning parts of the business. He shadowed Rose. He recruited players. He attended meetings and retreats typically reserved for high-level executives. But as time went by, he once again began feeling restless. He wanted more and, despite his history with Rose and Wesley, no longer believed that they were truly invested in his growth. He grew especially wary of Wesley, who he believed considered him a threat.

"I learned nothing at CAA," Paul told *The New Yorker* in 2021. "There was no investment in me." Wesley and his CAA colleagues could feel his frustration, but it confused them. In their eyes, they'd opened all sorts of doors for Paul. Wesley had even introduced Paul to numerous coaches and trainers to help him build out a network.

By the summer of 2012, Paul was done. It was time, he decided, to follow in his dad's footsteps and start his own business. That August, while in London for the Summer Olympics, he met Rose and Wesley for lunch. The contract came up, and, after the meeting, Rose told colleagues that everything had gone well. Then, in the second week of September, about a month after the Olympics, Paul let Rose know he was leaving to start his own shop.

The next day, LeBron filed paperwork with the National Basketball Players Association terminating his relationship with CAA. He then signed with Klutch Sports Group, Paul's new agency.*

"I knew he had put in time. This is a dream we always talked about," LeBron recalled. "So it was that simple for me."

The previous night on Twitter, LeBron had outlined his goal.

"#THETAKEOVER," he wrote.

•   •   •

The attacks from other agents were immediate, scathing, and predictable. Paul and LeBron were trying to upend a system, and those who benefited from the existing structures weren't just going to hand over all their power, especially not to a young Black man entering the majority-white world of athlete representation. Paul was an easy target, too. He didn't have a law degree. He didn't have a college degree. He appeared to be the beneficiary of nepotism.

But the criticism was also condescending and, in the eyes of many, a result of Paul's race.

"I just hope we don't have another Master P situation on our hands," one agent told ESPN's Chris Broussard in 2012, referring to the rapper who had operated a sports agency in the late '90s only to famously run it into the ground.† Another agent asked Broussard, "How's he going

---

* How'd CAA take it? "Paul is a good guy who's starting a little four-person business," a "CAA insider" told Nikki Finke, the founder and editor in chief of *Deadline,* that week. "We wish him well."

† Mostly thanks to his advising his top client, star running back Ricky Williams, to sign an incentive-laden deal so bad that it caused the defection of Master P's other clients and the collapse of the agency, and became known as one of the worst contracts in the history of professional sports.

to walk into a Fortune 500 sports brand company and negotiate a deal? You can't give a dentist a scalpel and say, 'Go do heart surgery.'" Some agents asked the NBPA how it was possible for someone without a college degree to get certified.

In his first two years on his own, Paul did little to dispel these concerns. The college prospects he recruited failed to get drafted. Chris Paul, an All-Star point guard and close friend of LeBron's, had told Rich he planned to leave CAA for Klutch, news that Rich shared with multiple associates, only for Chris to later change his mind. On top of all that, in October 2012, just a month into Klutch's existence, the NCAA opened an investigation into Paul for allegedly providing improper benefits to University of Texas guard Myck Kabongo.*

But the low point came in the spring of 2014. Paul had spent months recruiting Jabari Parker, a Duke star projected to be one of the top picks in that summer's draft. He worked his contacts and met with Parker and his family multiple times, first in Durham and then back in Parker's hometown of Chicago. The two clicked.

Parker's father, however, was unsure. As a former college star and NBA player, Sonny Parker understood the terrain better than the parents of most recruits. He liked Paul but worried about his lack of experience.

"He was a really good person, but it was clear he was just starting out and trying to get things going," Sonny said years later. He wanted Jabari to sign with former Chicago Bulls guard BJ Armstrong, who was working as an agent at the Wasserman Media Group.

But Paul didn't let up. Landing a player of Parker's stature would help legitimize Klutch and serve as an announcement to the basketball world that he was more than just a LeBron lackey. Around May, Paul flew to Chicago and got a verbal commitment from Parker. Within a few days, the news had spread. The story was broken by Fox Sports' Bill Reiter.

---

* Paul later accused CAA of playing a role in the opening of the investigation. "A previous agency I was at, they leaked some stuff to the media," he said during an August 2022 appearance on former NFL tight end Darren Waller's podcast. After finding this quote, I reached out to CAA for comment. A CAA representative said the following: "Rich is a revisionist historian, who crafts tall tales to fit whatever narrative he is selling at the moment. He knows that CAA didn't leak this information. It just didn't happen."

"Huge get for that group," Reiter wrote on Twitter. "Top 3 pick, maybe even No 1."

But Parker was just nineteen years old, and NBPA rules dictated that players under the age of twenty-one could not sign with an agent unless they obtained consent from either a parent or a guardian. It didn't matter how close Paul and Parker became. Paul couldn't sign him until Parker's parents signed off, and Sonny refused.

"Every agent I talked to," Sonny Parker said years later, "at the beginning of the process, I told them that everything had to go through us."

Parker went with Wasserman. That June, the Milwaukee Bucks drafted him with the No. 2 pick.

•   •   •

Things for Klutch were looking bleak, but there was no time to wallow. LeBron was set to become a free agent. So was another Klutch client, Eric Bledsoe. For the first time since going out on his own, Paul was on the clock. These next few months, he knew, would be the most important of his professional life.

On June 24, after four seasons with the Heat, LeBron opted out of his contract. He was a free agent again, and five teams sent contingents to the Ritz-Carlton in downtown Cleveland to pitch their cases. This included the Lakers, who were represented by Kupchak and Tim Harris, the team's senior vice president of business operations. The meat of their pitch was simple: They were willing to hand LeBron the keys to the NBA's preeminent franchise.

LeBron's representatives were impressed with Kupchak and Harris's presentation. But, just like four years earlier, LeBron was looking for something the Lakers couldn't provide. For one, the Lakers were coming off a 27–55 season, and the previous year had given Kobe an enormous extension, limiting their financial flexibility. More than that, though, LeBron and his group wanted to remove the stain of *The Decision*. The only way to do so, they thought, would be by making amends with Cleveland.

On July 10, after talking it over with his family and inner circle, LeBron made his choice official. He announced the decision—no capitalization this time around—with a 942-word, first-person essay in

Sports Illustrated written with Lee Jenkins, the magazine's top NBA feature writer, who had profiled LeBron numerous times.

"I'm ready to accept the challenge," LeBron wrote. "I'm coming home."

The essay was widely praised. *Deadspin,* the typically irreverent sports and culture website, called it "an immaculately executed public relations coup." The letter, and the well-executed PR campaign, also helped conceal part of the reason LeBron was returning to Cleveland. Sure, the homecoming was nice, but what he really wanted was to run the show. He was never going to have that power in Miami, where Pat Riley was in charge. In Cleveland, though, things were different. LeBron could control everything, and he and his team recognized that the best way to do so would be by tweaking the structure of the typical star contract.

For this, the group turned to Mark Termini, a veteran agent enlisted by Paul to run Klutch's negotiations. A Cleveland native and the son of a high school and college basketball coach, Termini had starred on Case Western Reserve University's basketball team before getting a law degree from Cleveland State University in 1984. Two years later, at the urging of Flip Saunders, his close friend from Cleveland's basketball scene who was working as an assistant coach at the University of Minnesota, Termini set up his own agency. Soon after, he orchestrated successful holdouts for two of his first clients—Ron Harper and Rod Strickland—which put himself on the NBA map.

In 1992, Termini signed Jim Jackson, a star guard from Ohio State who would be drafted fourth by the Dallas Mavericks. Because his general manager had whiffed on a couple recent picks, the team's owner, Donald Carter, decided to take the reins and run the contract negotiations. He offered four years and $10.8 million, which was two years and nearly $10 million less than the Minnesota Timberwolves had handed Christian Laettner, that year's No. 3 pick.

"I said, 'Mr. Carter, no disrespect, but that's not my fault that they didn't work out,'" Jackson recalled, referring to the Mavericks' previous picks. "'I'm not going to take less than what my market value is.'"

The Mavericks pushed hard, offering Jackson a $1 million signing bonus to take the deal. Jackson rejected the offer and declined to report to the team. Both he and Termini were crushed in the press. "Take the Money and Run" was the headline of a column about Jackson in the December 15, 1992, edition of *USA Today.* The piece was penned by

Peter Vecsey, one of the country's most prominent and influential NBA voices. Two weeks later, Vecsey wrote a follow-up; the headline read, "This Guy's an Agent of Doom."

Despite all the noise, Jackson and Termini refused to back down. Deep into the holdout, Termini discovered that then–NBA commissioner David Stern had instructed teams to stop handing out lavish contracts to rookies. It was, to Termini, the textbook definition of collusion, and he made clear to the NBA that he was willing to take legal action.

"Finally, the Mavericks came in and signed me," Jackson said. "You know, they're hugging and kissing, and 'Hey, we're so glad,' but it was because of the [threat of the] lawsuit." Jackson received a six-year, $20 million contract. He was also paid for his entire rookie season, despite missing the first 54 games.

The win solidified Termini's reputation. Operating out of Cleveland limited his profile, but, within NBA circles, he became known as a fierce negotiator, someone who fought for every word on every page. He went to war over pay schedules. He insisted that contracts contain full death benefits for the families of his clients. He created a twenty-three-word clause that affirmed his players' freedom to engage in athletic activities—like pickup basketball—away from the team and without liability, which, despite frequent pushback from owners, was almost always inserted into contracts he negotiated. Executives and owners didn't love dealing with him, and behind closed doors some rolled their eyes. But Termini didn't care.

"In the NBA," he wrote in a book years later, "friends are good. Leverage is better."

All of which made him the perfect partner for Paul. After Paul had left CAA, a bunch of agents had reached out—working with him meant working with LeBron—but each had insisted on being the face of the operation. Termini was different. He wasn't trying to cozy up to LeBron. He wasn't interested in fame. All he insisted on was running point on contract negotiations. That meant he'd be the one devising negotiating strategies and discussing dollar amounts with NBA teams.

Paul was fine with all that. He recognized that, if Klutch was going to succeed, he needed help. "I knew what I didn't know," Paul said, "and I went and got someone who was able to fill that gap." He also figured that he could control the narrative and keep it so he'd be the one getting credit for his clients' deals. In December 2012, the two agreed to terms. Termini came on as an independent contractor in charge of contract negotiations. Klutch would pay him 25 percent of its gross fees on NBA contracts and marketing deals. And now, with LeBron a free agent for the first time in Klutch's existence, Termini had the chance to flex his muscles.

Unlike in 2010, when LeBron had taken a pay cut to help the Heat fill out the roster, this time around Termini told all suitors that LeBron would be signing for the max. On this, he said, there'd be no negotiations. The plan was also for LeBron to sign a "one-plus-one" deal: a one-year contract, with a second season tacked on in the form of a player option.

There were two reasons for this structure.

One was that it would give LeBron power over the Cavs. The threat of his leaving would force them to fully commit to winning, regardless of the cost.

The other was that the NBA was in the midst of negotiating new TV deals, which would kick in before the 2016–17 season and were projected to be worth at least double the previous ones, which would raise the league's salary cap.* LeBron could sign with Cleveland for four years and $88 million, or he could make $21 million in his first season, opt out and re-sign again on another one-plus-one in the summer of 2015 (the player option served as insurance against the potential of a catastrophic injury), then opt out again before the 2016 season and sign a new, even more lucrative contract, taking advantage of the projected cap spike.

After *Sports Illustrated* published LeBron's essay, Termini informed the Cavs of the particulars. The Cavs were annoyed that they were getting only a single guaranteed season, but, unless they planned on rejecting LeBron, they had no choice but to agree to those terms.

That October, the NBA announced its new media rights deals, which amounted to a total of $2.6 billion per season, nearly $2 billion more than the previous figure. Two years later, after that rights deal went into effect, LeBron re-signed with the Cavs on a two-plus-one with a start-

---

* Which would boost the max salary number, which is based off the cap, which is based off league revenue . . . Isn't NBA math fun?

ing salary of $31 million. The plan ended up earning LeBron an extra $20 million over four years.

"I'm not the beautiful mind over here," Termini said years later. "It was just math. I use my calculator and you talk to people that know that the cap's going up, so why would I want to tie up my player?"

With the LeBron negotiations done and most free agents off the board, the attention of the NBA world turned to the free agency of Bledsoe. A 6-foot-1 former first-round pick, Bledsoe was coming off a career year for the Phoenix Suns, one in which he had helped them win 48 games, nearly doubling their 2012–13 win total. The Suns wanted him back but didn't want to pay him like a top-flight point guard. He'd missed 39 games the previous season with shin and knee injuries, including a torn meniscus that required surgery. He was also a restricted free agent, meaning the Suns had the right to match any offer sheet he signed, a prospect that often scared away potential suitors.

The Suns had opened negotiations the previous year with a four-year, $32 million offer. Bledsoe turned that down. In July, the Suns upped their proposal to four years and $48 million, a contract similar to those recently signed by Jrue Holiday, Kyle Lowry, and Ty Lawson, all of whom were point guards seen to be in the same tier. Bledsoe rejected that offer, too.

Most people around the NBA were shocked. The Suns appeared to hold all the leverage. Sure, Bledsoe could roll the dice and sign a "qualifying offer" for one year and $3.7 million, which would allow him to become an unrestricted free agent the following summer, but doing so would mean leaving almost $45 million on the table and risk having an injury or a down season deflate his value.

Termini didn't see things that way. He believed there was a different way to frame the conversation around the qualifying offer; it didn't just represent a risk for Bledsoe, it also meant that, one year later, the Suns could lose their starting point guard and get nothing back in return.

Was that a risk *they* were willing to take?

"As long as I kept my client strong, I knew the team also had no place to go. I told them, 'If you can sign another All-Star point guard, go get him,'" Termini said years later. "That was my strategy, to turn the system against the teams when I had an indispensable player . . . and I took pride in proving that the right player with the right contract negotiator could pull it off."

By mid-July, the sides had reached a stalemate. "Bled felt antsy," Paul recalled. "When you grow up not knowing where your next meal is coming from, it's hard to turn down $48 million." Other players told him to take the Suns' offer. Rival executives and agents used the media to broadcast their disbelief in Klutch's stance.

"Eric Bledsoe and His Camp Need a Reality Check" was the headline of a July 18 *Arizona Republic* story by columnist Dan Bickley. "Nothing supports the notion that Bledsoe is worth that kind of money," Bickley wrote. A few weeks later, John Gambadoro, another Phoenix-area sports personality and someone known to be close to the Suns, published an open letter to Eric Bledsoe, which included the following line: "Memo to Eric Bledsoe—you need new representation. This Rich Paul is a joke and he is steering you down a slippery slope."

Yet throughout it all, Termini remained confident. So did Paul.

Sensing that confidence, Bledsoe held the line.

On September 19, with just eleven days until training camp and twelve until the deadline for Bledsoe to sign the qualifying offer, ESPN reported that the Timberwolves, a team run by Flip Saunders, Termini's close friend and client, were offering Bledsoe a four-year, $63 million max contract. That Minnesota couldn't actually sign him to such a deal (unless the Suns agreed to take back a bunch of overpaid players in a sign-and-trade) was irrelevant. All Termini needed was to boost the perception of Bledsoe's value, which, he believed, would spook Suns owner Robert Sarver.

That this leaked the week before Rosh Hashanah, the Jewish new year, was no coincidence, either. Sarver "doesn't do any work, not even pick up a telephone, and we knew [he] didn't want us to get an offer from another team during the holidays when he wouldn't be able to match it," Paul wrote. The holiday started at sundown on September 24. On his way into the office that day, Sarver, without notifying his front office, called Termini and upped the offer to five years and $70 million. Bledsoe accepted the deal. When Sarver arrived at work and shared the news, his executives were furious.

Two years after leaving CAA, Paul and his new agency had announced their arrival. "That was the first real money Klutch ever made," Paul wrote. "It sent a message to the entire NBA." When Paul first left CAA, LeBron had promised a takeover. Two years later, it was now underway.

3

THE MOTHER OF DRAGONS

In the summer of 2013, the Buss children gathered in a boardroom at the team's El Segundo facility for their yearly family meeting. It was their first since Dr. Buss's death, and the siblings—specifically Jeanie—wanted to hear how Jim planned to turn things around.

The Lakers were coming off a first-round playoff sweep and the roster was a mess. Dwight Howard, the player who was supposed to carry them into the future, was gone. Kobe was rehabbing from Achilles surgery. Steve Nash had never fully recovered from his leg injury.

Dr. Buss had been gone for only a few months and the fan base had already lost faith in his heir. Jeanie was losing patience, too.

When will we be back in the playoffs? she asked Jim that day. It was more of a challenge than a query, one she said she was issuing not as Jim's sister but as the team's president and governor.

Jim saw it differently. His younger sister had spent years second-guessing him, soaking up praise while the public dismissed him as the family fool. "Nobody understands the pressure I was under," he'd say years later. The job was more complex and demanding than any of his siblings could imagine, and the fact that Jeanie had dared to even ask this question was proof. When would they be back in the playoffs? It would take a week to break down all the various permutations and possibilities and come up with a reasonable target. So instead, Jim told his sister what he believed she wanted to hear.

"A year," he replied.

Everyone in the room was stunned. *Why would you say that?* Mitch Kupchak thought. Jesse Buss, the youngest sibling and then the team's director of scouting, laughed.

Jeanie, shocked, repeated Jim's answer as a matter of clarification.

"One year?" she asked.

"One year," Jim confirmed.

"There's no way that's going to happen," Jesse said.

Maybe, Jim conceded, his answer was a bit bold. But he still believed in himself and his abilities.

"Okay," he said. "Three years."

"Just so you know," Jeanie said, "if we're not back in the playoffs by then, I might have to make a change."

"If we're not back in the playoffs in three years," Jim replied, "I'll fire myself."

The two shook hands.

•　　•　　•

When Jim took over decision-making power around the start of the 2012–13 season, his goal was to follow in his father's footsteps. "You have to have a real superstar to have a credible franchise," Dr. Buss had once said, "especially in a city like Los Angeles." Jim and Kupchak's plan was to pounce in the summer of 2014. "Basically we put everything [into] that," Jim told *The Orange County Register*. LeBron and other A-listers like Carmelo Anthony and Dwyane Wade were set to hit free agency. Kobe's contract would also be expiring, and he'd previously hinted to reporters that he was considering retirement, which would free up even more cap space.

The summer of 2013 derailed those plans. Kobe wasn't going to let his final on-court image be one of him limping to the locker room, and took retirement off the table. Instead, he wanted a contract extension, and he told reporters he had no interest in taking a pay cut, either.

From a basketball standpoint, there was no way to justify giving Kobe another mega-deal. He was turning thirty-five in August—ancient in basketball years—and trying to come back from a devastating injury. But to Jeanie, on-court performance wasn't the only factor worth considering. "We never got an opportunity to do the farewell tour for Magic Johnson," she would later say in a television interview. "To have Kobe retire as a Laker, that to me is really important." Kobe also remained a box office draw, and, unlike many of the NBA's new owners—wealthy executives backed by multibillion-dollar corporations—the Buss family had no secondary source of income. Their business was the Lakers, meaning basketball decisions were often made for business reasons. "My God, we don't have Carnival Cruises behind us or Kohl's Department Stores . . . and Microsoft up in good, old Portland," Jim Buss once told a reporter. "This is it. If we lose money, we lose money."

The Lakers agreed to add two years and $48.5 million onto Kobe's contract. Despite his previous comments, Kobe did leave about $16 million on the table, but he remained the league's highest-paid player. The deal would keep him with the Lakers through the end of the 2015–16 season, which would be his twentieth and presumably his last. Jeanie had gotten what she wanted. But with it, the Lakers' hopes of landing two stars in the summer of 2014 had vanished. And not just because a chunk of their cap space was now gone. Dwight Howard's decision to bolt had sent a message across the league.

"I've had a lot of clients in the last five years, good players, who didn't want to play with Kobe," one agent later told *ESPN The Magazine*. "They see that his teammates become the chronic public whipping boys."

Kobe did battle back from his Achilles injury and, incredibly, returned to the court in December 2013, but after playing just six games, he suffered a fracture of the lateral tibial plateau in his left knee, ending his season. The Lakers limped to a franchise-worst 55 losses, leading to Mike D'Antoni's resignation. Still beholden to Kobe, they replaced D'Antoni with Byron Scott, a former Laker who despised analytics, believed modern players were soft, and, most importantly, had Kobe's approval. The results were disastrous. The team finished 21–61, missing the playoffs for a second straight year—something that hadn't happened since 1976. They were so bad the NBA flexed them out of multiple national TV slots. The main culprit was Kobe, who launched 20 shots per game despite shooting just 37 percent, making it one of the least efficient seasons in NBA history. But for Lakers fans and franchise insiders, it was easier to pin the blame on Dr. Buss's heir.

"Jim's trying to do it himself and trying to prove to everybody that this was the right decision that [his] dad gave [him] the reins," Magic said on ESPN's flagship daytime show, *First Take*. "He's not consulting anybody that can help him achieve his goals and dreams to win an NBA championship."

The worse Jim did, the more popular Jeanie became, despite being the one who had green-lit the Kobe contract. She was like the backup quarterback a city clamors for when the team's starter struggles, a role she seemed to relish. Unlike Jim, who rarely made public appearances, Jeanie walked around the arena before home games, chatting up employees and fans. She started doing tons of press, too. Whenever she was asked about the team's struggles, she'd say that the on-court product was Jim's domain. The tension between the two became so palpable that everyone in the organization was forced to pick a side.

"I never talked to Jeanie," Scott recalled. "It just felt like it'd be a betrayal of Mitch and Jim."

The lack of unity wasn't just bad for organizational morale; it was also holding the team back. This was on full display in the summer of 2015. Once again, management was trying to rebuild through free agency. The Lakers had missed out on LeBron, Anthony, and Wade, but now they had a meeting scheduled with LaMarcus Aldridge, a twenty-nine-year-old power forward and three-time All-Star. Aldridge was the best free agent on the market, and, unlike some of the recent star players the team had pursued, he actually wanted to be a Laker.

This is theirs to lose, he told his agent before the meeting.

The window for teams to talk to free agents opened on June 30 at 9 p.m. West Coast time. Not long after that, a large group of Lakers executives and employees marched into the LA offices of Wasserman Media Group, the agency representing Aldridge. Everyone settled in around a conference room table, while the team's Twitter account posted a picture of Maroon 5 front man Adam Levine wearing a customized Lakers jersey with Aldridge's name and number (12) on it, accompanied with the caption: "It's 9:01pm PT and Mitch Kupchak is walking in to meet with @aldridge_12 #LAtoLA." Aldridge's name began trending on Twitter.

The Lakers had spent weeks preparing, even enlisting the team's graphic design group to help build a pitch deck—a first for them. But they had misread their target, a fate they perhaps could have avoided had the basketball and business sides been capable of working together. There were NBA players who would have been excited to be getting social media shine. Aldridge, a laid-back Dallas native, wasn't one of them. "I don't give a shit about trending on Twitter," he'd say years later. He was more interested in hearing how Kobe envisioned the two of them fitting together on the court and how Jim and Kupchak planned on fixing the team. And yet the Lakers decided to have Tim Harris, someone with no connection to basketball operations, deliver the meat of the pitch.

A former UCLA soccer goalie whose influence had grown since Dr. Buss's death, Harris had met Jeanie while playing for the Lazers. The two dated for a few years and stayed close afterward. When Harris retired from professional soccer in the late '80s, he got a job in the Forum's marketing department, and his combination of intelligence, charisma, and ambition propelled him up the ranks. Harris was also a true believer in Lakers mystique. It was why, under his leadership, the Lakers were one of the last teams to create a department solely devoted to marketing. "He used to always say that our marketing is that we're the Lakers," said one former Lakers employee.[*]

In the Aldridge meeting, Harris's job was to lay out the benefits of the LA market. And he did. He talked about all the sponsorship and branding opportunities that would arise should Aldridge sign with the Lakers. Typical Lakers stuff. Only he kept going.

And going.

And going.

And going.

"You could see people around the room rolling their eyes," one attendee said.

The Lakers businesspeople weren't done. After Harris came a PR executive, who explained what it was like to play in a big market. A community relations director described the sort of work the team's foundation did and how Aldridge could fit in. Executives from Time Warner Cable, which televised Lakers games, and AEG, which owned a minority stake in the team, spoke, too.

"It was a miscalculation of me as a person," Aldridge later said.

That afternoon, reports trickled out saying that Aldridge would not be signing with the Lakers. One reason given was because of their botched pitch. ESPN's Ramona Shelburne then reported that the Lakers, who thought the meeting had gone great, were stunned. Later that week, Aldridge met with the San Antonio Spurs. The team's esteemed head coach, Gregg Popovich, showed up in jeans and a T-shirt. Spurs players wore sweats. The meeting took place on some couches. The con-

---

[*] The Lakers representative defended Harris's approach, saying the Lakers have "consistently been—in terms of both economic track record and industry-wide perception—one of the top marketing teams in the NBA and all of professional sports."

versation was free-flowing and centered on basketball. Aldridge signed with them soon after.

"The vibe of understanding who I was as a person," he said years later, "[it] was just, they get it."

•   •   •

This was the night everyone in LA had been waiting for. It was April 13, 2016, and Kobe's final game had finally arrived.

The season to that point had been a disaster. Kobe's November announcement that it would be his last had turned the team into something closer to a circus act, with his farewell tour taking center stage. Scott gave Kobe free rein, whether that meant firing off-balance, contested jumpers, or skipping practices altogether. "We were always waiting for him on the bus on the road because he was, like, drinking wine with the refs or opposing coaches," D'Angelo Russell, a 2015 Lakers draft pick, said. "He just really wasn't around the team that much. He kind of just showed up for the game, and we ran with it."

The season's laissez-faire atmosphere extended to the team's fans as well. Once, during a timeout, rookie Larry Nance Jr. felt a hand on his shoulder and assumed it belonged to a teammate. Then he turned around. "We break the huddle," Nance said, "and it's like, 'How the fuck did Samuel L. Jackson get in here?' He was in there a solid twenty-five seconds, just chilling, watching the play."

Yet on this night, Staples Center was buzzing. Nearly five hundred media credentials were issued. Celebrities—Jay-Z, Kanye West, Snoop Dogg, Shaq, David Beckham, and, of course, Jack Nicholson—filled the courtside seats. Kobe came out shooting, over and over and over and over. He missed more than he made, but no one seemed to care. With just over two and a half minutes left in the game, the Utah Jazz, the Lakers' opponents, led by 10. Kobe then hit a couple of free throws, trimming the lead to eight and giving him 49 points. Next time down, he floated the ball high off the glass for points 50 and 51. The crowd rose to its feet and applauded.

The lead was down to six.

The Lakers got another stop. Kobe, with the crowd chanting his name, split a double team and buried another stop-and-pop jumper from the right elbow.

Fifty-three points.

Four-point game.

Another stop. Another Kobe jumper, this time from behind the three-point arc.

"Got 'em all!" ESPN play-by-play announcer Mike Tirico shouted, over the cackling of his broadcast partner, Hubie Brown, an eighty-two-year-old basketball lifer.

Fifty-six points.

One-point game.

The building erupted as if it were Game 7 of the finals. ESPN's camera panned from Beckham to Kanye to Nicholson, all grinning and laughing like children.

The Jazz called timeout. Sitting alone on the bench, Kobe gasped for air.

The Jazz missed a shot coming out of the break. The Lakers got the ball into Kobe's hands. Everyone in the building stood up. Lakers forward Julius Randle sprinted and set a series of screens for Kobe. Kobe got to his spot on the right wing and rose up.

Fifty-eight points.

The Lakers led by one.

Two more free throws gave him 60.

With 4.1 seconds left, the Lakers took a five-point lead. The Jazz called timeout. A mix of ecstasy and shock swept through the building. Russell and Randle leapt into Kobe's arms. The electric opening chords of Guns N' Roses' "Welcome to the Jungle" blared out of the arena's speakers. More teammates surrounded Kobe. He swung by the sidelines to embrace Shaq, who was smiling in disbelief. The Lakers subbed Kobe out of the game for the last time.

The night had been something out of a Rocky movie. Kobe finished with 60 points. He'd taken 50 shots, the most in a game since 1967. He'd scored 15 of the Lakers' final 17 points and outscored the Jazz by himself in the fourth quarter, 23–21. And he'd done all this in a win, just the Lakers' 17th of the season.

After the game, Kobe addressed the crowd from halfcourt. He thanked his teammates. He thanked the fans. He thanked his wife, Vanessa, and their two daughters, Gianna and Natalia, all of whom were sitting courtside.

"What can I say?" he asked.

He paused.

"Mamba out."

He blew a kiss and put the mic down.

For one night, the Lakers had been reminded of everything they once were, of the greatness that had once graced their floor, of the way they'd once made people feel. For one night, they were once again the center of the sports world and all their problems had ceased to exist.

By the following morning, that was no longer the case.

For the Buss kids, there was no more hiding behind Kobe. They were on their own.

•　　　•　　　•

After being spurned by Jim Buss, Phil Jackson decided he wasn't ready to retire. He did some informal consulting for the Detroit Pistons and worked with an ownership group interested in bringing an NBA team back to Seattle. Then, in the winter of 2014, the New York Knicks came calling. They believed Jackson, who won two titles with the team as a player (in 1970 and 1973), could bring some of his magic to the Big Apple, and they were so desperate that they were willing to give him everything the Lakers wouldn't: control over personnel, a lighter schedule, and a five-year, $60 million contract. It was an offer too good to pass up, even if it meant that he and Jeanie, who had finally gotten engaged the previous Christmas after fifteen years together, would now have three thousand miles between them.

In March 2014, the Knicks introduced Jackson as their new president of basketball operations. Jeanie, who had grown up idolizing a man who prioritized his business over his family, remained in LA. She "was far too proud of her career [to move]," ESPN's Shelburne, a reporter known to be plugged into Jeanie's camp, would later write, "and she always saw the Lakers as a civic treasure for which she was responsible."

Just sixteen months after believing that they were on the verge of working in the same building once again, Jeanie and Jackson were now, in part because of Jim, living on opposite sides of the country. The relationship wasn't strong enough to withstand the distance. In

December 2016, Jeanie and Jackson announced that they had ended their engagement.

"The love of my life is the Los Angeles Lakers," Jeanie later wrote on Twitter. "I love Phil & will always. It's not fair to him or the Lakers to not have my undivided attention."

•   •   •

The one silver lining to all the losing was that it had allowed the Lakers to stock up on high draft picks. Julius Randle, whom they had drafted seventh overall in 2014, was coming off a season in which he averaged 11.3 points and 10.2 rebounds. D'Angelo Russell, drafted second overall in 2015, had struggled as a rookie but was still considered an intriguing prospect. And they had landed the No. 2 pick again in 2016, which they used on Brandon Ingram, a long-limbed, versatile scorer out of Duke.

The Lakers seemed to have the makings of an intriguing young core. What they needed next was a coach who could lead them forward. And they had their eyes on one candidate.

Luke Walton had grown up around the game. His father, Bill, was a basketball legend, first at UCLA, then in the NBA, and later in the broadcast booth. An avid Deadhead, Bill viewed basketball as much a spiritual exercise as a physical one.

Luke was the third of Bill's four boys. His childhood was, well, different. His parents separated when he was young, allowing Bill to turn his sprawling San Diego home into an upscale commune for the Dead and anyone embracing that lifestyle. The band often threw after-parties on his tennis court. Sometimes Luke would come down in the morning and be greeted by a naked Jerry Garcia. "People would walk in and go, 'Hey, what's up?'" Luke recalled. "And then [I'd] look at one of my brothers and [say], 'Who was that?' and they'd go, 'I don't fucking know.'"

Luke inherited his father's gregarious, fun-loving vibe. He also inherited Bill's basketball IQ and, by his senior year of high school, had shot up to 6-foot-8. He accepted a scholarship to the University of Arizona, where he spent four years starring on the basketball team but also relishing his time on campus. He'd drive around in a restored 1970 yellow Cadillac convertible, wearing cutoffs and tank tops. He had a deep voice and bushy light brown hair. The girls loved him. So did the professors and the team's fans. Luke knew how to have a good time, especially with Richard Jefferson, his teammate and roommate.

"If there was a recruit that Coach [Lute Olson] really wanted, he would put Richard and I on the job," Luke said.

In 2003, the Lakers drafted Walton with the second pick of the second round. He embraced his role as a reserve and spent nine-plus seasons in LA. He won two championships and became a fan favorite. He also found a mentor. "I think Phil [Jackson] saw a lot of himself in Luke, honestly," Kobe said once. When a back injury sidelined Walton for the majority of the 2009–10 season, Jackson invited him into the coaches' meetings and had him chart statistics from the bench. After he retired in 2013, Walton joined the coaching staff of the Los Angeles D-Fenders, the Lakers' D-League affiliate.

The players there loved him. "Being at that level is sort of this weird purgatory where you're trying to figure out your life and career and not making a lot of money," Brandon Costner, who played for the D-Fenders that season, said. "But you came in every day and saw Luke smiling and in a great mood, and it just lightened things in the locker room." Walton would blast Lynyrd Skynyrd and the Grateful Dead in the gym. He'd answer questions about the NBA and his experiences there. He'd run stations at practice, challenging players to beat him with their go-to moves.

"Guys would miss three, four, five times," Costner said. "And he'd go, 'Well, fuck. That doesn't seem like a go-to move.'"

The next year, Steve Kerr, a fellow Arizona alum who played for Jackson in Chicago, became the head coach of the Golden State Warriors. He hired Walton as an assistant. Walton connected well with the players and impressed the higher-ups with his ability to suggest adjustments on the fly. The Warriors won the 2015 title, but, during training camp the next season, a back issue forced Kerr to take an indefinite leave of absence. The Warriors named Walton interim head coach. When Kerr returned in January, the team was 39–4. Sure, Walton had inherited a roster that was coming off a championship and still running Kerr's system, but the record all but ensured that he'd soon be receiving a chance to coach his own team.

Less than two weeks after Kobe's final game, the Lakers fired Scott. They called Walton soon after. Jim and Kupchak laid out their plans.

They'd try to be opportunistic with free agents, they told Walton, but knew their recent draft picks were their future. Walton asked if they were willing to be patient and let the young players grow. They said they were. Walton told them he wanted to build a system and culture that could be sustained for a long time. That, they said, was exactly what they were looking for.

This was Walton's dream job. He was in. The Lakers were, too. They hired Walton—who, at thirty-six, became the youngest head coach in the NBA—without speaking to any other candidates. Jeanie was thrilled.

"I think he is our best free-agent signing in a few years," she told reporters.

The Lakers were better positioned than they'd been in half a decade. They'd finally turned the page on the Kobe Era. But Jim's pledge loomed over everything. He had promised a return to the playoffs within three years, and now, with just one season left in that window, it seemed he'd be falling short. Feeling the heat, he began scouring the market for potential upgrades to the roster. He and Kupchak homed in on Luol Deng, a thirty-one-year-old forward who'd spent the past two seasons in Miami.

Jim believed Deng could both mentor Ingram and start at small forward until Ingram was ready. Most of his staff disagreed. They told him that, while Deng was coming off a nice season, it was likely his best days were behind him, that he no longer had the quickness to play small forward, that his best stretch the previous season had come after the Heat had slid him up to the power forward slot, where he had more advantageous matchups and could spread the floor.

Well, he's going to be a small forward for us, Jim replied.

The Lakers began negotiating with Deng's representatives on the first night of free agency. While doing so, they learned that the Washington Wizards were also interested in him.

Jim upped his offer.

Deng accepted.

A few minutes later, Clay Moser, the team's director of basketball strategy and an assistant coach, entered the room.

We just got Deng. Four years, $72 million, he was told.

Why the fuck would we do that? Moser asked. Jim, infuriated, shot up from his seat and berated Moser, at one point even poking him in the chest. Word later got around the NBA that had the Lakers not made such an outlandish offer, Deng would have likely signed with the Wizards for three years and around $50 million. In other words, Jim had outbid the competition by more than $20 million. The Deng deal had also come just one day after the Lakers and Timofey Mozgov—a soon-to-be thirty-year-old center coming off an injury-plagued season for the Cavaliers that had led to his being benched for the majority of their playoff run—agreed to terms on a four-year, $65 million contract, meaning over the course of forty-eight hours, the Lakers had committed $139 million to a pair of role players on the back nine of their respective careers.

"Looking back at some of the decisions that Jimmy made," Jeanie said, "you think, 'Okay, was he making those decisions to undermine the organization and my authority to run a team, or was he just making poor decisions?'"

•　　•　　•

The first time Jeanie met Magic Johnson was in June 1979. She was seventeen years old and upstairs with Dr. Buss in his Bel-Air home when the doorbell rang. Magic, fresh off being drafted first overall by the Lakers, was outside with general manager Bill Sharman, ready to meet the team owner.

Offer them something to drink and I'll be down in a few minutes, Dr. Buss told Jeanie.

She went downstairs and opened the door. The image greeting her was one she'd never forget.

"It was this smile, it was blinding," Jeanie recalled. "There was, like, sparkles coming off his teeth."

The two, close in age, made small talk. Magic said he was excited to be a Laker. But, he added, his plan was to leave in three years—he wanted to play for his hometown Detroit Pistons.

Jeanie excused herself and ran upstairs.

You're not gonna believe what he said, she told Dr. Buss. *He's only going to stay for three years—he wants to go back home and play in Detroit.*

Dr. Buss told Jeanie to calm down.

As soon as he puts on a Lakers uniform, he said, *and sees that crowd and hears the cheers for him, he's never going to leave.*

Dr. Buss was right. Magic played his entire career for the Lakers, winning five titles and three MVPs. He became a Los Angeles icon. To Dr. Buss, Magic was part of the Lakers family, so to Jeanie, Magic *was* family. The two remained close throughout the years, and in December 2016, after hearing that Jeanie and Jackson had separated, Magic reached out.

A few weeks later, before a January game against the Denver Nuggets, they sat down for dinner at a restaurant inside Staples Center. Linda Rambis, a longtime Lakers executive and one of Jeanie's closest friends, joined, as did Lon Rosen, Magic's former agent and a former Buss family employee. The Lakers at the time were 15–30 and on a four-game losing streak, yet another tailspin in the midst of yet another lost season. Before long, talk around the table turned to the team. Jeanie said she was concerned about its future under Jim. She acknowledged that she was considering using the power her father had given her and making a change. She asked Magic what he thought about the team and what he'd do if he was in charge.

Running the Lakers was something Magic had thought about for years. The story he'd always told was that Dr. Buss had wanted him and Jeanie to do so together, but that he'd passed on the offer. "You have four boys," Magic claimed to have told Dr. Buss. "There's no way that's going to go over well." Magic sold his shares in the Lakers in 2010 for around $29 million and, two years later, became a minority owner of the Los Angeles Dodgers.

The story Magic had not told, however, was that he'd approached Dr. Buss about buying the Lakers, only for Dr. Buss to say no. Dr. Buss wanted his children to run the team, and while Magic was like a son to him, he wasn't one of his actual offspring. "It was a hard pill for Magic to swallow," a close confidant of Dr. Buss's said. In the aftermath, Magic made a rare business mistake. When he sold his Lakers shares in 2010, the team was valued by *Forbes* as being worth around $643 million. By 2015—thanks to new local and national media rights deals plus the NBA's new more team-friendly collective bargaining agreement—the value of the Lakers had skyrocketed to $2.6 *billion.* Yet even after selling his stake, Magic had never truly separated himself from the team.

"He's always cared about them as much as anyone," said a friend. "It affects him when the Lakers don't do well." They rarely did under Jim, and Magic became one of his most vocal critics.

"He always put[s] it on somebody else. Then he's mad at me 'cause I criticize him," Magic said during a February 2015 interview on *First Take*. "I'm telling the truth about the situation, trying to make us better, trying to get us to a winning situation, in terms of the Lakers getting back to being relevant and winning again. So you get mad at me when I tell the truth."

Jim had heard every barb and, in October 2015, punched back during an interview with *USA Today*. "Magic Johnson going nuts on me?" he told reporter Sam Amick. "It's like, 'Really, dude? My dad made you a billionaire, almost. Really? Where are you coming from?'"

Now, sitting at the dinner table with Jeanie, Magic wasn't going to change his tune. He outlined how he believed the Lakers could reclaim their glory. He shared what he thought the organization was missing. Jeanie agreed with every word, which she was certain was no coincidence.

"Earvin and I were basically raised by the same person," she later said. "We see things the same way." A few weeks later, at 10:30 a.m. on February 2, the Lakers announced that they'd hired Magic as an official advisor who would "report directly to Jeanie Buss."

With the trade deadline fast approaching, Jeanie told Jim and Kupchak that she wanted Magic brought in on all basketball discussions. The plan was for Magic to get a read on the situation, learn on the job, and lend Jim and Kupchak a hand wherever he could. Both would likely be phased out of their positions after the season, but, Jeanie thought, perhaps there was a way the trio could find harmony and continue working together moving forward.

But Jim and Kupchak kept Magic at arm's length. They held meetings without him. They didn't invite him to free-agent workouts. Magic would hear about calls with other teams only after they occurred. Word got back to Jeanie. She was furious but also concerned.

"I was worried that my brother was going to make trades that would put us further down and would take even longer to recover from," she said.

Later that month, Jeanie met Kobe for lunch at a poolside bungalow near his Newport Beach home. There, she laid everything out: why she didn't trust Jim, why she believed she needed to make a change, and why she believed she needed to do so immediately, but also the guilt weighing on her. After all, her father had wanted her and Jim to run the Lakers together.

"Go all in or don't do it at all," Kobe told her. He compared the situation to war, telling Jeanie she needed to be like the *Game of Thrones* character Daenerys Targaryen, the Mother of Dragons,* who begins the series meek and timid before growing into a cunning and powerful queen.† "If you play around," he told her, "they'll come back and kill you." Kobe told Jeanie to trust her instincts and all the years of work she'd put in, that no one knew what the Lakers needed more than her.

Jeanie decided that Tuesday, February 21, two days after the All-Star Game, would be the day. Instead of traveling to New Orleans for All-Star weekend,‡ she stayed in LA, huddling with close advisors and lawyers to finalize the plan. Dismissing Jim was a given, but Kupchak would go, too. Beyond being loyal to Jim, he was, in Jeanie's eyes, complicit in misleading Jackson during the 2012 coaching search. On Monday night, Daniel Grigsby, the team's general counsel, texted Kupchak asking to meet the next morning. Kupchak told him it would be tough with the impending trade deadline, which was on Thursday, but Grigsby insisted.

"That's when I knew something was up," Kupchak recalled.

Magic was at the gym Tuesday morning when his phone rang—the Lakers, he was told, needed him at the facility. He cut his workout short. At 10:01 a.m., the team released a statement: Magic was now

---

* Or, if we're using proper monikers: Kobe told Jeanie she needed to be like Daenerys Stormborn of House Targaryen, rightful heir to the Iron Throne, rightful Queen of the Andals and the First Men, Protector of the Seven Kingdoms, the Mother of Dragons, the Khaleesi of the Great Grass Sea, the Unburnt, the Breaker of Chains. Might also be worth pointing out that Daenerys showed no objection to her brother being executed.

† Daenerys also ended up becoming a (spoiler alert!) paranoid, homicidal maniac, but that didn't happen until the final season two years later, so we'll give Kobe the benefit of the doubt.

‡ This happened to be the first time the Lakers didn't have a player participating in the All-Star Game since 1996.

president of basketball operations, Kupchak had "been relieved of his duties, effective immediately," and Jim would "no longer hold his role as Lakers executive vice president of basketball operations."

Magic and the remaining front office spent the rest of the day working the phones. Not yet versed in the league's salary cap rules, he kept things simple and sought help when needed. Later that week, news broke that Jeanie had found a general manager to partner with Magic in her revamped front office—Rob Pelinka, Kobe's close friend and former agent.

Jeanie would now be flanked by people she trusted.

That night, for the first time in a long time, Jeanie could rest easy.

Unbeknownst to her, that moment of peace would be short-lived.

•   •   •

Jeanie was in her office in the Lakers' El Segundo facility the day after the deadline when the email arrived. It was a notice from Jim and Johnny to the Lakers' shareholders, notifying them that there'd be a meeting in ten days to elect a new board of directors.

Jeanie looked over the proposed ten-point agenda. To serve as the team's board of directors, Johnny had presented four names: himself; Jim; Dan Beckerman, the CEO of AEG, whose chairman, Philip Anschutz, already controlled two board seats; and an LA-based entrepreneur and investor named Romie Chaudhari.

Jim and Beckerman already had seats on the board, so there was nothing noteworthy about that. But two names were missing.

One was Joey Buss, the team's alternate governor, who had controlled one seat.

The other was Jeanie.

According to the Lakers' bylaws, only a member of the board of directors could be the governor. In other words, if Jeanie were no longer on the board, she could no longer serve as the team's controlling owner, allowing Johnny and Jim to seize control and potentially reinstall Jim at the top.

Besides the proposed board change, the agenda included a $25 million payout to be split among shareholders (meaning Johnny and Jim would each receive $5 million). Additionally, directors with a stake in the team—such as Johnny and Jim—would receive $10,000 per month, while non-shareholder directors would be paid $30,000 monthly, seemingly an attempt at incentivizing Beckerman and Chaudhari* to approve the proposal.

"We were trying to figure out if Jeanie's the absolute dictator of the Lakers," Johnny said. "It wasn't like we were trying to get rid of Jeanie as president of the Lakers. We wanted Jeanie to understand that Dad would not have wanted you to just take total control, hire and fire whoever you wanted, without the rest of us being involved." Jim said he and his brother were "just [making] sure there are checks and balances."

After receiving the email, Jeanie reached out to Adam Streisand, an LA-based lawyer who had represented Clippers owner Steve Ballmer in his 2014 court battle with former Clippers owner Donald Sterling over the sale of the franchise.

I'm going to propose to you a really risky and daring plan, Streisand told her after reviewing the Buss family trust documents. Fond of war analogies, he explained that he would go to court and launch a preemptive strike to remove Johnny and Jim for good. He assumed she'd reject the strategy or at least push back. Jeanie, however, was on board.

Streisand notified Johnny and Jim's lawyer, Robert Sacks, that he'd be filing a temporary restraining order against the pair, alleging they had breached their fiduciary duties as co-trustees of Dr. Buss's assets. The restraining order was meant to force Johnny and Jim into complying with the terms of the family trust, specifically the clause stating that "trustees shall take whatever actions are reasonably available to them to have Jeanie M. Buss appointed as the new Controlling Owner of The Los Angeles Lakers, Inc."

"They tried to disregard what their father wanted," Jeanie said years later. "That's a betrayal."

The threat spooked the brothers. Both signed a document that night reelecting Jeanie as the team's controlling owner.

The next morning, a week after Jeanie had received the notice, Strei-

---

* A lawyer for Chaudhari told ESPN at the time that "Mr. Chaudhari and Jim Buss met in connection with a non-basketball business transaction. He never agreed to be included as a candidate for the Lakers board of directors. In addition, Mr. Chaudhari made it very clear that he is not, nor has he ever been, interested in participating in a family dispute."

sand strode into room 629 of the Stanley Mosk Courthouse in Los Angeles—part of the Los Angeles County Superior Court—and filed both a restraining order and a lawsuit. In it, Jeanie accused her brothers of being "motivated by retaliation" and argued that an injunction was necessary "to prevent irreparable injury to the Lakers."

"Jim has already proven to be completely unfit even in an executive vice president of basketball operations role and I recently had to replace him," Jeanie said in the filing, adding, "I could not allow the damage being done to the franchise over the past few years to continue."

The judge scheduled a preliminary hearing for May 15, but Streisand, looking for a quicker resolution, approached Sacks in the courtroom hallway.

This is never going to happen again, he told Sacks. He then demanded the immediate resignations of Johnny and Jim. Sacks resisted, but Streisand had an ace up his sleeve: His team had uncovered that Jim was deep in debt, owing significant sums to various creditors, including loan sharks. Under California law, an insolvent individual could not legally serve as a trustee. If Jeanie didn't receive these resignations, Streisand implied that he'd make this information public.[*] As for Johnny, he went along with the whole thing, so Jeanie wanted him out, too.

The ploy worked. Jim resigned from the board and Jeanie was reelected alongside three loyalists: Joey Buss; Frank Mariani, a longtime Lakers executive, friend, and business partner to Jerry Buss; and Beckerman, who told ESPN in March 2017 that neither he nor Anschutz, whom he represented on the Lakers' board, had previous knowledge of Johnny and Jim's plans and that they "fully support Jeanie Buss as the controlling owner of the Lakers." Johnny remained, but without Jim, he was on an island. Jim also relinquished his position as a trustee and was replaced by Janie, Dr. Buss's youngest daughter and an ally of Jeanie's, ensuring Johnny would always be outnumbered.

The Lakers finished the 2016–17 season 26–56, the third-worst record in the league, but a nine-win jump from the year before. Ingram, after a slow start, had turned things around in the second half. Ivica Zubac, a seven-footer plucked in the second round the previous summer, looked like a steal. And Walton was growing into the job.

Most of all, things just felt different. Jim was gone. Jeanie was in

---

* Sacks, Jim Buss's lawyer, declined to comment.

charge. One rung beneath her was one of the most beloved Lakers of all time. One rung beneath him was the close friend of another franchise icon. The organization was also on the verge of a major upgrade, moving out of what *The Orange County Register* once called a "nondescript concrete bunker" and into the state-of-the-art, $80 million UCLA Health Training Facility just two blocks away. For the first time, the team's basketball and business operations would no longer be separated by a parking lot.

Back in March, after a press conference announcing their new leadership roles, Magic and Pelinka had walked across the parking lot to visit the team's business operations offices. They went desk to desk, introducing themselves to every employee, people who sold tickets and sponsorships and worked on community relations yet had long felt overlooked by the team's basketball executives. That, Magic and Pelinka assured them, was about to change.

"You're all essential to what we do," Pelinka told the staff, and, before leaving, Magic promised a return to greatness.

"I guarantee that the trophy is coming back," he told the group. A new era of Lakers basketball had arrived. And the NBA's biggest star was taking note.

4

CALL THE LAKERS

Following Jeanie's front-office shake-up, team higher-ups started using a new term around the facility: "Lakers 2.0." The phrase was coined by Tim Harris, who had been promoted to president of business operations and chief operating officer. The idea behind the campaign was simple. "It was basically, 'The losing is over,'" a then–Lakers staffer said. But the purpose of the reboot wasn't just to change the culture inside the building. It was also to broadcast to the outside world, including players around the NBA, that the Lakers were *back*. And there was one player in particular whom Magic and Pelinka had in mind.

"Everything," said a member of the Lakers front office, "became about chasing LeBron." The pursuit of LeBron even became water cooler fodder for employees at lower levels of the organization. "You'd hear things like, 'We cannot screw this up. If we do, the fan base is going to revolt,'" recalled one staffer.

The Lakers' hope was to pair LeBron with a second star. Their top target was Paul George, a four-time All-Star forward for the Indiana Pacers who'd grown up in LA idolizing Kobe. Like LeBron, George was also slated to become a free agent in July 2018. In fact, his agent had already been in touch with Pelinka about a potential partnership.* And so entering the 2017 offseason the Lakers had one goal: Create enough cap space to sign both players the following summer.

The draft would present them with their first opportunity to do so. For the third consecutive year, the Lakers landed the No. 2 pick, and the class was loaded with talent, especially at the top. There were highly

---

* Pelinka's overtures were so blatant that the Pacers filed a complaint with the league office, accusing the Lakers of violating the NBA's anti-tampering rule, which prohibits teams from communicating with other teams' players or their representatives. The league investigated and fined the Lakers $500,000.

touted point guards like Washington's Markelle Fultz and Kentucky's De'Aaron Fox, and Duke forward Jayson Tatum,* who grew up idolizing Kobe and dreamed of playing for the Lakers. Magic, however, had his sights set on someone else.

"It was Lonzo, Lonzo, Lonzo," said a member of the front office.

Lonzo was Lonzo Ball, a point guard out of UCLA who represented everything Magic was looking for in a franchise player. He was a great passer. He played fast. Because he was a Southern California native, he already had a strong following among Lakers fans.

He was also the most famous player in the draft. Much of that was thanks to his father, LaVar, a former low-level collegiate basketball player who talked like Ric Flair. LaVar was an expert at leveraging the media's need to fill hours of programming into attention for him and his family. He'd make ludicrous statements, once saying Lonzo would "be better than Steph Curry" and another time claiming, "Back in my heyday, I would kill Michael Jordan one-on-one." The resulting outrage would trigger cycles of media takes and debates, keeping the Ball family in the news.

"You may not like me. You may think I'm cocky or arrogant . . . but you will be thinking about me," LaVar told *ESPN The Magazine* in May 2017.

The Lakers were the only team Lonzo Ball agreed to work out for. In late June, Magic and Pelinka visited the Ball family's Chino Hills home, where they watched Lonzo sprint up hills with neighborhood kids, lift weights in a garage turned gym, and shoot on the backyard court LaVar had built. The Lakers' scouts had Fox ranked higher, but seeing Ball in his element and getting to know his family only strengthened Magic's conviction.

On draft night, the Lakers grabbed Ball. Magic was thrilled, though he was just as excited about the trade the team had pulled off before the draft even began. Believing Ball was now their point guard of the future, the Lakers used Russell to offload the bloated contract of

---

* "I always wanted to play for the Lakers," Tatum told an interviewer in November 2024. "For [the Lakers] to have the No. 2 pick, and it wasn't even a thought that I was going to get drafted [by them], that was kind of devastating. I never worked out for the Lakers. They never came to watch me work out."

Timofey Mozgov in a deal with the Brooklyn Nets. The move brought the franchise closer to its ultimate goal: creating two max salary slots for the following summer.

At a press conference the next night, Magic was asked why, with the Lakers whiffing on so many of their recent free-agent pursuits, he felt things would be different this time around.

"The tide has turned," Magic replied. "People want to play here again. It's exciting times for the LA Lakers. I wouldn't have made that move if I didn't think I could use that money."

•   •   •

While the Lakers and their revamped front office were laying down the groundwork to reel in a star, the Cavaliers' top decision-makers were looking for ways to hold on to theirs.

When LeBron had returned to Cleveland three years earlier, he made his mission clear: "My goal is still to win as many titles as possible, no question," he wrote in his *Sports Illustrated* essay. "But what's most important for me is bringing one trophy back to Northeast Ohio."

Two years later, he delivered, ending Cleveland's fifty-year title drought in historic fashion. The Cavaliers became the first team to ever rally from a 3–1 deficit in the finals, toppling a Warriors squad that had set a record with 73 regular-season wins. After the buzzer, LeBron collapsed onto the court and cried.

"This is what I came back for," he said moments later during the trophy presentation.

Having accomplished what he'd set out to do, LeBron was now thinking about leaving Cleveland once again, this time for LA. He'd started planting Hollywood roots in 2015, when he purchased a $21 million, ten-thousand-square-foot home in Brentwood. That same year, his production company, SpringHill Entertainment, had signed a deal with Warner Bros. Entertainment and set up shop in LA, too. Rich Paul and Maverick Carter had also moved out west.

The Cavs knew all this. They also knew that if they wanted to keep LeBron in Cleveland, they needed to upgrade their aging roster. The Warriors had responded to their heartbreaking 2016 defeat by signing Kevin Durant, one of the best players in the history of the game, an addition that made them virtually unbeatable. In 2017, they put together the most dominant postseason run ever, winning 16 of 17 games, with their only loss coming against the Cavs in the finals.

After that Game 5 defeat, LeBron retired to his Bay Area hotel suite with some teammates. Aware that reinforcements were needed, the group began tossing around names of players who could help close the talent gap.

How about PG? guard Dahntay Jones asked, referring to Paul George.

George was the perfect fit—a big, athletic, and dynamic wing but also a lockdown defender who could at least make Durant work. He had recently informed the Pacers that he planned to leave in free agency the following year, meaning their choice was to either trade him that summer or risk losing him for nothing. Everyone knew George was focused on LA. But the Lakers had decided to wait for George to reach free agency rather than give up assets in a trade, leaving an opening for another team to swoop in.

LeBron told Jones he loved the idea. Jones, who had played with George in Indiana, sent George some texts. A few days later, George, curious why Jones had reached out, followed up. Jones laid out the entire situation.

"He was selling like a motherfucker," George recalled.

George was unsure. He didn't have a relationship with LeBron. He was worried they wouldn't click.

You're both cool, both chill, both family-oriented, Jones assured him. *You just gotta get into the same room.*

A few days later, George met LeBron at his Brentwood home for a backyard lunch. The two hit it off. *I'm gonna try to make this happen,* LeBron told him.

Cleveland had already been in contact with the Pacers about a potential George deal, but they had competition. The Thunder were also in the mix, offering two promising young players—Domantas Sabonis and Victor Oladipo—a package that Kevin Pritchard, the Pacers' president of basketball operations, found more enticing. Pacers owner Herb Simon, however, was hesitant to take on the four years and $84 million remaining on Oladipo's contract, and so he went looking for another deal. He called a close friend, Denver Nuggets owner Stan Kroenke, and negotiated a separate three-team trade involving the Cavaliers. Under the proposed deal, the Cavs would land George, the Nuggets would acquire Kevin Love, and the Pacers would receive shooting guard Gary Harris along with draft picks. On June 30, just hours before the opening of free agency, the three teams agreed to terms.

The Cavs had landed their guy. Thrilled, they began mapping out ways to round out the roster. Pritchard, however, wasn't ready to give up on the Thunder's offer. He warned Simon that if George went to Cleveland, there was a good chance LeBron would then consider re-signing with the Cavs the following summer, which, as a fellow Eastern Conference team, would present a problem for the Pacers. Simon changed his mind, and the Pacers sent George to Oklahoma City.

"If they had gotten Paul George," one person close to LeBron would say years later, "there's a chance LeBron never leaves."

For the Cavs, it was back to the drawing board. But before they could gain traction on any new deals, they were hit with another blow. Kyrie Irving—their All-Star guard who had buried the championship-winning jumper in the 2016 finals—had grown tired of living in LeBron's shadow. On July 7, he spoke with Gilbert and demanded a trade.

Gilbert flew to Las Vegas, where the NBA's summer league was being held. He gathered his front office—which was now being led by Koby Altman, a thirty-four-year-old executive just five years removed from being assistant coach at Columbia University—in his suite and shared the news. Gilbert told the group that with Irving under contract for two more seasons, there was no need for them to acquiesce to his demand. After all, if they slow-played things, maybe Irving would change his mind.

LeBron, stunned by Irving's request, agreed. Confident he could convince Irving to stay, he urged the Cavs to hold off on any deals—partly because he mistakenly believed Irving's frustrations were with Gilbert and the organization, not with him.

Irving, however, was determined to leave. So much so that his agent, Jeff Wechsler, issued a threat: If Irving wasn't traded, he'd undergo a minor surgical procedure on his left knee that would sideline him for a significant portion of the season. Backed into a corner, Gilbert reconsidered his stance. Maybe, he thought, Irving's demand could be spun into an opportunity, one that could help prepare the Cavs for LeBron's possible departure in a year and free them from Klutch's influence.

Since LeBron's return in 2014, Gilbert—who had responded to *The Decision* in 2010 with a scathing, hate-tinged open letter in which he described LeBron as "narcissistic"—had given LeBron and his group everything they wanted. Jobs to friends. Above-market contracts to Klutch clients. Expensive rosters. LeBron had the power in the relationship, and the Cavs had no choice. But now, having won a title, Gilbert no longer felt the need to capitulate. And unlike the lead-up to 2010, he wasn't going to mortgage the team's future in a desperate bid to keep his star. LeBron, the Cavs figured, was likely leaving anyway, whether they kept Irving or not. So why not see if there was a way to remain a contender for one more year while also preparing for a post-LeBron future?

The Celtics were one of the few teams capable of giving Gilbert everything he was looking for. In exchange for Irving, they were willing to part with Isaiah Thomas, a 5-foot-9 point guard who finished third in scoring and fifth in MVP voting the previous season; 3-and-D* forward Jae Crowder; and also an unprotected 2018 first-round pick from the Nets, which they had received in a previous trade. Given Brooklyn's status as one of the worst teams in the league, the pick was widely considered one of the most valuable assets across the NBA. With this package, the Cavs would be able to fill the void left by Irving and also secure an asset to help protect their future.

By the afternoon of August 22, the two teams had nearly finalized a deal. LeBron was in Santa Monica at the time signing jerseys for a trading-card company when Cavaliers head coach Tyronn Lue, who was spending some time in California, showed up to share the news. He then put LeBron on the phone with Altman.

Do not trade Kyrie, LeBron told Altman. He especially didn't want his running mate sent to an Eastern Conference rival. After a brief discussion, Altman assured LeBron he'd hold off.

Minutes later, LeBron's friends showed him a tweet from ESPN's Adrian Wojnarowski: The Cavs, Wojnarowski was reporting, were sending Irving to the Celtics.

LeBron dropped his pen and slumped in his chair.

"At that point in time," LeBron would tell *The Athletic* one year later, "you realize that Koby's not the only one running the team."

Dan Gilbert was, and he was not someone LeBron wanted to be tied to for the rest of his career.

* "3" for three-point shooting, "D" for defense, meaning players who excel at both.

•   •   •

Entering the 2017–18 season, Lakers management made the team's mission clear.

"All I want us to do," Magic told reporters before training camp, "is to have a good season where free agents look and say, 'Oh, man. I can see myself in that lineup and with that team,' and we can step up to another level."

The Lakers, largely due to their success in the draft, were closer to that vision than many realized. Six of their recent picks—Jordan Clarkson, Brandon Ingram, Larry Nance Jr., Julius Randle, D'Angelo Russell, and Ivica Zubac—had already proven themselves to be NBA caliber. Meanwhile, most analysts considered their 2017 draft haul— Lonzo Ball, Kyle Kuzma, Josh Hart, and Thomas Bryant—one of the best of the night.

There was no single person responsible for this success. Kupchak had learned from Jerry West—widely considered one of the best talent evaluators in the history of the league—but had also become a respected scout in his own right. Bill Bertka, the NBA's first full-time scout and a Lakers fixture for over forty years, had a hand in every selection. Jerry West's son, Ryan, had been part of the scouting team since 2009 and became one of the group's most valued voices. Nick Mazzella had climbed the ranks from public relations intern to scout and general manager of the Lakers' D-League team. And in recent years Dr. Buss's two youngest sons, Jesse and Joey, had become key voices, too.

Dr. Buss had always intended for the two to succeed Jeanie when she could no longer run the franchise. Joey had been preparing by heading the Lakers' G League team, turning it into one of the NBA's most successful minor league operations. "He really took that program and made it his own," Coby Karl, who coached the team from 2016 to 2021, said. "He always did a really good job of building a culture there but also keeping it all connected with the Lakers." Jesse took a different path. A basketball fanatic with a seemingly photographic memory, he grew up in San Diego with his mother but spent countless hours talking about basketball with his dad. He officially joined the Lakers in 2006 as a teenager, was promoted to director of scouting in 2012, and became assistant general manager in 2015. Now, with Kupchak gone and the front office being led by a president and GM with no previous front-office experience, Jesse's role had expanded even further.

But there was a downside to all that draft success. The Lakers didn't have enough minutes to go around. Nance, Randle, Kuzma, Ingram, and Hart all played similar positions. "We were all kind of pitted against each other to a certain extent," Nance said. The internal competition took a toll. Practices often grew physical. "It's hard not to develop resentment in that situation. All you can see is, 'I'm fighting for my livelihood with this guy,'" Nance added. "None of us can really see that all of us were good guys just trying to survive. It was all cutthroat and not a really healthy environment."

Walton did his best to guide the group, but this was uncharted territory for him. "I think it may have surprised Luke how much you have to coax young players along to show them what habits are important to being a pro," one then–Lakers staffer said. Players frequently ignored their defensive assignments. Sometimes they'd simply forget them. Those on the bench often pouted. Frustrated, Walton would vent to his assistants.

"I can't talk any sense into these guys," he'd say, as the Lakers opened the season a disastrous 11–27.

Ball, in particular, proved to be more immature than expected. He showed flashes of the skills that had tantalized scouts, and he was well liked within the building, but his lack of professionalism irked his teammates. He blew so many defensive assignments that the coaching staff began to wonder if he was even reading his scouting reports.

One day, Lakers staffer Clay Moser decided to issue a test.

What can you tell me about Russell Westbrook? he asked Ball in the locker room before a game against the Thunder.

Ball began rambling but failed to mention the most critical detail—that Westbrook, despite being right-handed, preferred to drive left.

Moser pointed to the scouting report. *If you read it,* he told Ball, *then you'd know that.*

Ball said nothing.

Hand me your scouting report, Moser said.

Ball passed it over. Moser flipped to the back page. With every player watching, he pulled out the $100 that he'd taped to the back, returning the booklet to Ball. The room erupted in laughter.

• • •

The good news for the Lakers was that things in Cleveland weren't going much better.

The Irving trade had become a disaster. Thomas, it turned out, had been dealing with an injury to his right hip that wasn't healing properly,* and he missed the first three months of the season. LeBron had also convinced the Cavaliers to bring in Dwyane Wade on a one-year deal, a move that quickly backfired. Wade was a shell of himself on the court and struggled adapting to his new environment. "He came in and tried to flex his muscles a little bit and be outspoken, and it rubbed a lot of the guys the wrong way," said a Cavs assistant coach. "He was very willing to point out others' flaws and most of the players were thinking, 'Hey, this isn't Miami, you just got here, and you're also not the player you used to be.'"

Things only got worse when Thomas returned in January. His injury had sapped his quickness and burst, but he still played as if nothing had changed—seemingly hoisting shots every time he touched the ball. And yet that didn't stop him from openly criticizing the coaching staff and his teammates during media sessions. "He just rubbed everyone the wrong way," said a member of the Cavs' front office.

The team was spiraling, and LeBron, never one to hide his emotions, had clearly checked out. On defense, he stopped giving effort. On offense, he often strolled up the court behind the play.

Altman knew the Cavs needed help, and there was one team in particular eager to step in. The Lakers were the perfect trade partner, too. They were eager to unload Jordan Clarkson, whose contract† was blocking their free agency plans, and willing to take Thomas back. Altman understood that the deal would help the Lakers clear the necessary cap space to sign LeBron. "But in our view," said a member of the front office, "if LeBron and the Lakers wanted to make it happen, it was going to happen. So for us, it was just about getting the best players we could."

* Thomas was diagnosed with a femoroacetabular impingement and a torn labrum. No, I don't know what any of that means.
† $12.5 million in 2018–19 and $13.4 million in 2019–20.

Altman spent weeks working the phones. Then, in the twenty-four hours leading up to the deadline, he orchestrated three separate deals with the Lakers, Kings, and Jazz, sending out six players—including Wade, Thomas, and Crowder—along with two draft picks. In return, the Cavs received George Hill, a strong defender and knockdown shooter; Rodney Hood, a smooth reserve wing; Clarkson; and Nance, making them younger and more athletic.

"I think Koby did a heck of a job of understanding what our team needed," LeBron told reporters. The revamped roster reenergized him. His numbers surged after the trade deadline, and while the new pieces didn't fit together perfectly, the Cavs closed the season strong, going 19–10 after the deals.

LeBron wasn't the only one elated after the deadline. Across the country, Magic was celebrating, too. "This is what I came here to do," he told reporters during a post–trade deadline press conference. "To create flexibility for our organization so that one day we can have a superstar or two come to this organization with our incredible young talent that we have."

On top of all that, the Lakers had spent the year making inroads with Klutch. The process began the previous summer, when they signed Kentavious Caldwell-Pope—a Klutch client whose free-agency market had dried up—to a one-year, $18 million deal. Having Caldwell-Pope in the building allowed the team to lavish Rich Paul with perks. They invited him to practices, where he often sat beside Magic and Pelinka, and gave him courtside seats, which he often used for college recruits. "It felt like he was around us all the time," said a member of the team's coaching staff. "We all assumed he was scouting the situation for LeBron."

The signing also gave the Lakers a chance to demonstrate for Klutch just how player friendly they were willing to be. In late December, Caldwell-Pope was sentenced to twenty-five days in jail for violating the terms of his probation from a suspected DUI arrest the previous March. A local judge, however, ruled that he could participate in home games and practices under a work-release program. Most NBA teams would have declined the option. The Lakers not only let Caldwell-Pope continue to suit up for home games, they also allowed him to come into their facility early each morning so that he could get some extra sleep.

"I would get there at like 6 a.m. and crash on a couch just to get out of the other place," Caldwell-Pope said.

On the court, the Lakers had made progress, too. They won 35 games, their most in four years. Randle averaged a career-best 16 points per game on a career-high 55.8 percent shooting. Ingram nearly doubled his scoring output from his rookie year. Ball struggled shooting but excelled in every other facet of the game. Hart and Kuzma looked like two of the steals of the draft. And they were all buying into Walton's coaching, evidenced by the team finishing with the league's 13th-ranked defense.

The Lakers had done everything within their power to lure LeBron. All they could do now was sit back and wait.

The Cavs opened the playoffs against the Pacers. They dropped Game 1 and two more before grinding out a four-point win in a decisive Game 7, one in which LeBron scored 45 points. They then swept the Toronto Raptors* before surviving another grueling seven-game battle against the Celtics, setting up yet another finals matchup with the Warriors.

The Cavs entered the series as the biggest finals underdogs in sixteen seasons. Yet, thanks to LeBron putting on one of the greatest performances in NBA history, a 51-point, eight-rebound, eight-assist masterpiece in which he controlled the action from the opening tip, they entered the closing minutes of Game 1 with a chance to steal a win. Trailing by one with less than five seconds remaining, George Hill was fouled away from the ball, sending him to the free throw line for two shots. He had shot 82 percent from the line that season, and Cavs players assumed the game was theirs.

Hill sank the first but was short on the second.

J. R. Smith grabbed the offensive rebound—right under the basket, in perfect position for a putback.

Instead, thinking the Cavs were ahead, he dribbled out toward half-court to run out the clock.

---

* The third straight year LeBron's Cavs had knocked the Raptors out of the playoffs. As of February 2025, his career playoff record against the Raptors was 12–2. During the 2018 playoffs, ESPN announcer Mark Jones referred to the Raptors as "LeBronto."

A stunned LeBron, standing just feet away, jumped up and down, pointing frantically at the clock. By the time Smith realized his mistake and passed the ball back to Hill, the buzzer had sounded. LeBron glared in Smith's direction as he returned to the bench.

The game went into overtime. The Warriors won 124–114. LeBron stormed into the locker room after the final buzzer and punched a whiteboard, causing a deep bone contusion in his right hand. He still averaged 34 points, 8.5 rebounds, and 10 assists the rest of the series, but it wasn't enough to take down the Warriors. The Cavs fell in a four-game sweep.

During his press conference after the Game 4 loss, LeBron was asked if he felt he'd played his last game with Cleveland. "I don't have an answer for you now as far as that," he said. He added that, compared to 2010, things were different this time around, that there were other things for him to consider. But he did hint at how he was leaning.

"I came back because I felt like I had some unfinished business," he said. Later, Jason Lloyd of *The Athletic,* a reporter with whom LeBron had a good relationship, asked, "Does one championship finish that business?"

"I mean, that's a trick question, at the end of the day," LeBron replied. He cracked a smile. "And I'm not falling for that."

•　　•　　•

After the finals, LeBron spent two weeks at home in Cleveland, weighing his options with his closest advisors.

He could stay with the Cavs, but the prospect of remaining in Cleveland didn't excite his family. "His wife was ready to leave Ohio," a person close to LeBron said. LeBron was, too, but not for just any team. He'd grown up rooting for the Dallas Cowboys and the New York Yankees and had always been drawn to iconic franchises. "The only way he was ever going to leave the Cavs again," said a second confidant, "was if it was to play for one of the league's legacy teams." LeBron and his circle discussed the Philadelphia 76ers and Houston Rockets, but neither fit that bill. One team did.

In the middle of June, LeBron and his family left for a vacation in Anguilla. He stayed in a $75,000-a-week beach house and went cliff jumping with his kids. On the last Friday of the month, Paul formally notified the Cavs that LeBron would not be picking up his player option. The next day, LeBron's private plane landed at LA's Van Nuys Airport. At 9:01 p.m. PT, the start of free agency, he welcomed Magic into his Brentwood home.

For two hours, LeBron, Magic, and Paul sat in the living room, talking basketball and team-building. There was no PowerPoint presentation, no fancy meals, no bottles of wine. The three reviewed the roster. LeBron shared his own evaluations. Magic asked LeBron about his expectations. LeBron said he wanted to win but that he understood the Lakers' situation and that it would take time.

Our goal here is championships, Magic told him. *And we think you could be a big part of restoring our greatness.*

LeBron held his cards close, but his mind was already made up. The meeting was more of a final vetting than anything else. "I wanted to help Jeanie win championships, bring that [spark] back to the Lakers and see my family blossom in SoCal," he'd say years later. The next morning, he and his wife ate breakfast on the patio of a trendy Brentwood restaurant. Maria Shriver and Gavin Newsom, the latter then a candidate for governor of California, stopped by his table; Newsom asked about his free-agency plans, and Shriver pitched the Lakers. That afternoon, LeBron and his family boarded a private plane at Van Nuys Airport for a European vacation. Before taking off, LeBron spoke to Paul.

"Call the Lakers," he said.

There was no elaborate TV show this time around, and no first-person essay, either. Paul texted Jeanie one word: "Congratulations." She'd been expecting the news, but now that it was official, she became emotional.

"I just thought a lot about my dad, and you know, kind of how he would reflect on it," Jeanie recalled. "And he obviously, during his lifetime, made the Lakers great and, you know, always instilled the value of having a superstar on the team and what that would bring." She joined Magic and Pelinka on a conference call to celebrate. Klutch then posted a bare-bones press release it had prepared the previous week. It said that LeBron was signing a four-year, $154 million deal,* a longer

---

* The fourth year was a player option.

commitment than he'd given the Cavaliers upon his 2014 return and an indication that he believed he was entering a new phase of his career.

"I love the young guys that they have, and I'm not trying to force my hand in no way, shape, or form," he later told ESPN's Rachel Nichols. "I believe Rob and Magic and Jeanie have done an unbelievable job of reshaping what the organization should be, keeping Dr. Buss's dreams and what he was all about, to keep that going."

The news sent a wave of euphoria through Los Angeles. Celebrity Lakers fans from Snoop Dogg to Larry King tweeted welcome messages to LeBron. So did Eric Garcetti, the mayor of Los Angeles. Arnold Schwarzenegger posted a welcome video. Kobe did, too.

You have to have a superstar in order to have a credible franchise, Dr. Buss had often told Jeanie. Five years after his death, it looked like she now had both.

5

"LeBRON'S GONNA TRADE YOU"

A couple hundred media members had descended upon the Lakers' El Segundo practice facility on this September morning. There was a buzz in the room. "It was crazy," recalled Josh Hart. "I've never seen anything like that." Lakers Media Day had arrived, meaning LeBron would finally stand before the press and answer the questions Lakers fans, LA's media, and the sports world were dying to ask.

Because there was still so much that remained unknown. Three months had passed since he'd announced his decision, and he'd yet to take part in a press conference or offer much insight into what had drawn him to the Lakers or how he planned on approaching this next phase of his career.[*]

LeBron entered the gym a little after noon. He was greeted by more than a hundred cell phones thrust into the air. He settled behind a table, took hold of the mic, and, wearing a jersey so tight it looked like it was painted on, began answering questions as if he'd been forced to memorize talking points. He rarely smiled. His eyes were devoid of life. He spoke in a low monotone. He seemed surprised by many of the questions.

"How long have you been following me?" he replied when asked about the difficulty of juggling his business empire with his basketball career. He sounded annoyed.

"Apparently not long enough," the reporter answered.

"Apparently not long enough," LeBron replied.

This was not what the city had come to expect. For decades, the organization's leadership had pushed the notion of Lakers exceptional-

---

[*] He'd done one interview since signing—a sit-down with ESPN's Rachel Nichols in July—but the majority of the focus was on the opening of a new public school in Akron that was funded by his family foundation.

ism, the idea that the Lakers were special and the rest of the NBA was not. Many Lakers fans and even some local media had bought into this belief. In their minds, players were expected to pay tribute to the team's glorious past, to acknowledge that, unlike with other franchises in other cities, being a Laker was a symbiotic relationship, an opportunity where the stars benefited as much as the team. And yet here was LeBron, the one tasked with taking up the mantle Kobe had left behind, acting like a hostage who had been forced to sign a contract. It was a strange sight.

"He talked about adjusting to Los Angeles like it was less an adventure and more of a chore," was how *Los Angeles Times* columnist Bill Plaschke described the press conference in his column that evening. The piece was titled "LeBron James' First Public Appearance in a Lakers Uniform Is Exciting to Everyone but Himself."

A few days later, the Lakers traveled a hundred miles south to the Pechanga Indian Reservation, in what had become a yearly preseason tradition. They put on a clinic for local kids, invited Southern California–based service members to come hang with the team in a clinic called "Hoops for Troops," and on Sunday played a preseason game at Valley View Casino Center in nearby San Diego. The highlight, though, was always Saturday's casino night at Pechanga Resort Casino. "It's one of the most important appearances on the calendar," said a Lakers department manager. "Every player has to go." Not only was Pechanga Resort Casino one of the Lakers' biggest sponsors, but the team also invited premium ticket holders and top business partners to the event. The players didn't always like it—"A few times I did have to save a guy from being accosted by the wife of a sponsor who'd had too much to drink," said a longtime staffer—but it was understood that attendance was a must. Even Kobe had attended during his playing days.

"The meet-and-greet with the players was basically what the sponsors were paying for," the manager said.

Before the weekend, the entire team boarded a bus to ride down together. Everyone, that is, except LeBron. He elected to skip his first road trip with his new team and chopper down by himself on Saturday. That evening, a spot was cleared on the golf course for his pilot to land. There, Lakers staffers met LeBron; the plan was to escort him to casino night. Only now there was a problem: Ohio State's football team was facing Big 10 rival Penn State, and LeBron, an Ohio State fan, wanted to watch the game. He'd join the party after, he said.

By this point, the Lakers' guests were growing antsy. They'd come that evening to see the Lakers' prized free-agent signing, and yet two hours had gone by and LeBron was still nowhere to be found. Around 8 p.m., someone passed along to the event's DJ that LeBron would join them once the game ended, which the DJ shared with the room. All eyes turned to the casino's TVs as Ohio State completed a 12-point comeback. A cheer broke out when Buckeyes quarterback Dwayne Haskins Jr. took a knee one final time to secure a 27–26 win, signaling LeBron would be on his way.

He never showed up.

•   •   •

LeBron may not have yet felt comfortable off the court, but on it he began his Lakers tenure as locked in as ever. One of his goals early on was to show his new teammates, particularly the younger ones, all the work required to succeed.

He had spent years perfecting a training regimen, one that reportedly cost him seven figures per year. Along with his trainer, Mike Mancias, he mapped out every activity of every hour of every day, from his nonnegotiable eight to ten hours of sleep at night, to his midday nap, to every meal and snack. "We'll be in the middle of a photo shoot, and [Mancias] will bring out a small Tupperware filled with food and be like, 'It's time to fuel up,' " said Nathaniel Butler, a renowned NBA photographer. LeBron believed it was one reason why he'd avoided suffering a single significant injury throughout his career, despite always playing deep into the playoffs. If there was a proven therapy out there, he adopted it. If there was a machine that could aid with his recovery, he bought it. Teammates would see Mancias pop out in the middle of card games to massage LeBron and joke about his having access to secret trapdoors.

"Wherever LeBron is," said Michael Beasley, a longtime NBA player and friend of LeBron's, "there are always motherfuckers up in there like it's a NASCAR pit stop." LeBron brought this approach and Mancias, whom the Lakers put on their payroll, with him to LA. The two arrived at the facility before practices and stayed behind after. "For the people that hadn't been around him, everyone was pretty much in awe," said Coby Karl, then the coach of the Lakers' G League team, who also spent a few months during the 2009–10 season as LeBron's teammate in Cleveland. "He set the tone every day."

Sometimes that meant putting his strength on display, like when he'd do full, unassisted squats while balancing on an exercise ball, leaving onlookers in awe. Other times it meant treating training-camp pickup games like playoff battles. During one run, LeBron reeled off 10 straight baskets, a stretch that included back-to-back threes from halfcourt and a one-handed, between-the-legs slam that had Magic hollering from the sidelines. During another, LeBron posterized Johnathan Williams, an undrafted forward out of Gonzaga. "It was as bad as I've ever seen anyone dunked on in my life," said a then–Lakers assistant coach. Another time, LeBron had the ball on a fast break with nothing but Joel Berry, an undrafted rookie out of North Carolina, between him and the rim. Berry grew up watching LeBron and knew LeBron's favorite move in transition was a ferocious left-to-right spin. He'd fly down the court like a freight train, plant one foot, turn his back to the hoop, and drive his left shoulder into the defender's chest.

Stationed in the paint, Berry envisioned the sequence.

"I read the whole thing perfectly," he said.

It didn't matter. Berry was just six feet tall and 195 pounds. LeBron was 6-foot-9 and about 260. He dislodged Berry with his shoulder and laid the ball off the glass.

Berry landed on his rear under the basket. "It felt like a brick wall had run right at me," he said. He looked down; lying on the floor back where he drew the contact were his white Steph Curry Under Armour sneakers.

"That's what happens when you wear them Currys," LeBron, a loyal Nike man, shouted as he got back on defense. The next day, Berry was greeted with a gift in his locker: three pairs of Kevin Durant's signature Nike sneakers, courtesy of LeBron.

"He was trying to make clear the sort of focus and drive he expected at all times from his teammates," Karl said.

Which they all were fine with, until it became clear that LeBron wouldn't be holding himself to the same standard.

The Lakers opened the regular season on the road in Portland. They lost by nine. Two nights later, they returned to LA to face the Rockets in LeBron's home debut. The game, a Saturday-night affair, was broadcast on national TV. Fans donning LeBron's No. 23 jersey flooded Staples Center. Jack Nicholson, Kendall Jenner, Floyd Mayweather, and Adam Levine settled into VIP seats. A video narrated by Ice Cube paying tribute to LeBron played on the jumbotron before pregame introductions.* The Lakers issued so many media credentials that the only way for NBA photographer Andrew D. Bernstein to capture a picture of LeBron during the postgame press conferences was to climb a five-rung ladder.

With just over five minutes left and the Lakers trailing by one, chaos broke out. Brandon Ingram fouled Rockets star James Harden in the lane on a fast break and, frustrated from having taken just eight shots that night—a poor sign for where the former No. 2 pick now stood in the team's hierarchy—after the whistle shoved Harden in the back. The teams converged around the pair, and a few moments later, Rockets star Chris Paul and Rajon Rondo, a veteran point guard signed by the Lakers in the offseason, exchanged punches. Ingram rushed in and threw a haymaker, too. Paul later said that Rondo spit in his face; Rondo denied doing so and claimed that Paul had poked him in the eye. All three were ejected from the game, but what stuck out to Lakers players was how, during the skirmish, LeBron had shot over to and stood by Paul and not his teammates.

After the game, a 124–115 loss, Ingram was furious.

How am I the only one out here fighting? he vented to a staffer on his way out of the locker room. *I know he's got his guys out there, but we're supposed to be teammates.*

Years later, Ingram would come to understand LeBron's perspective. "He's the No. 1 player in the league—like, imagine him throwing a punch and being in the mix," he said. "He can't be out there fighting. He's gotta be there for the team, and he's got so much other shit to worry about.

"But back then, when I was twenty-one years old, the kind of person I am and where I come from, you stand up for your brothers, for the

---

* The Lakers might have been better off asking one of their famous fans to punch up the video's script. Here's a sampling: "With great respect to the legends that came before him, our new king ushers in a renewed promise of bringing Showtime back to LA." Doesn't exactly roll off the tongue.

people that go hard for you. So in that moment, yeah, I didn't think it was the right thing to do. I was like, 'Shit, yeah, I love Rondo and he's in there—what's Bron doing?'"

Two nights later, the Lakers returned to Staples Center, this time for a matchup with the San Antonio Spurs. With 1:10 remaining, they trailed by 10. The game seemed lost—until the Lakers ripped off five quick points. With 13 seconds left, Hart rebounded an errant Spurs jumper. A three would tie the game.

LeBron signaled for a timeout. Which would've made sense, but the Lakers were out of timeouts, meaning they'd lose possession of the ball and be hit with a technical foul. To see LeBron—widely considered the smartest player in the league—make this sort of mistake was shocking, and the only thing that saved him was that referees didn't notice.* No whistle was blown, and, realizing his error, LeBron dropped his hands, fielded a pass from Hart, pushed the ball up the floor, and, with 2.4 seconds left, drilled a deep three, tying the game.

The fans inside Staples Center went nuts. It was LeBron's first iconic moment as a Laker.

LeBron then ruined the moment by missing two free throws late in overtime, as well as a potential game-winning jumper at the buzzer, leading to a 143–142 loss. The defeat dropped the Lakers to 0–3. After the game, reporters asked LeBron how he felt being part of a winless team.

"I know what I got myself into," he said. "It's a process. I get it."

After the slow start, the Lakers righted the ship with a 16–6 stretch. It started with LeBron, who was playing at an MVP level. But he wasn't the only reason for the turnaround. Kuzma and Ingram grew as scorers. Rondo's veteran leadership proved to be invaluable. And Walton had the Lakers back to defending at an elite level.

"We had started to figure it out," said one of the team's coaches.

Thanks to LeBron's presence, the Lakers were once again slotted onto the NBA's all-important Christmas Day slate. They traveled to Oakland to face the Warriors and that evening came out playing their best ball

---

* When asked by reporters after the game about this gaffe, LeBron became defensive. "I wasn't calling a timeout," he insisted, despite there being video evidence that he had, indeed, brought his hands together to signal for a stop. "Nah. Just getting ready to go up there and try to make a game-tying shot. That's all."

of the season. Thanks to their suffocating defense, they entered half-time with a 15-point lead. Then, with a little over eight minutes left in the third quarter, LeBron tried corralling an errant dribble and felt a pop in his left groin. He left the game. An MRI confirmed a slight left groin strain, and LeBron was listed as day-to-day. As if that wasn't bad enough, Rondo tore a ligament in his right ring finger in that same game, an injury that would require surgery and sideline him for four to five weeks.

Walton, however, remained optimsitic.

"Our team is much better now than we were to start the season," he told reporters the next day. The Lakers' record backed up his claim; they were 20–14, good for fourth in the Western Conference. "So, it will get a lot more challenging for us if he misses some real time, but I'm also very confident in our group that they'll continue to step up and battle."

What he didn't know was that LeBron and Klutch had no intention of waiting for that group to do so.

• • •

In the summer of 2018, Anthony Davis was growing restless. A five-time All-Star and one of the highest-paid players in the league, he'd already accomplished more than he ever could have imagined. But one thing was missing: winning. He'd made the playoffs only twice in six NBA seasons and won only a single series. And now, coming off the best season of his career—a monster of a campaign in which he'd finished third in both MVP and Defensive Player of the Year voting—he was plotting out how to best address this problem.

A few years earlier, he became friendly with Kendrick Perkins, a journeyman center who at the time was playing for the New Orleans Pelicans. The two frequently ate together on the road, and during those meals, talk often turned to the greatness of LeBron, who played with Perkins in Cleveland and whom he had known since high school. Perkins retired three years later, but he and Davis remained friends, and, upon hearing that Davis was growing disillusioned with his situation, he introduced him to Rich Paul.

"I thought it was the best thing for AD," Perkins recalled. "I thought he needed to be around that type of greatness."

Davis loved the idea. LeBron was his favorite player as a kid. Davis wore his Nike shoes and, despite growing up in Chicago, spent his teenage years arguing with friends that LeBron—not Michael Jordan—was the true GOAT. He'd also known LeBron since attending his basketball camps as a high schooler, and the two enjoyed their time together while playing on Team USA at the 2012 Olympics. More importantly, LeBron had the career Davis wanted. And, Davis figured, who better to help him mimic that career than the man who'd ridden alongside LeBron the whole way?

That summer, Davis fired his agent, Thad Foucher, and hired Paul.

"We all knew what would happen next," a Pelicans coach said.

Soon after, Davis started fretting about the lack of talent around him. *When are you going to get me some help?* he'd ask head coach Alvin Gentry. Unlike most former top picks, Davis hadn't experienced much winning in his career, and his patience for losing was now wearing thin.

Davis grew up on the South Side of Chicago, in a sports-loving home with a twin sister and an older sister. He was drawn to basketball early on. Chicago at the time was known as a hotbed for the sport, with powerhouse high school programs like Simeon and Whitney Young renowned throughout the country. Games took place in packed gymnasiums on glistening courts in front of hundreds of fans and dozens of scouts.

Davis's high school experience was different. He attended a charter school, Perspectives, that played in a lower division. It had just a couple hundred students. There was no court on the grounds. "It was a school that had never been on my radar before," said Joe Henricksen, the editor of a Chicago-based recruiting publication. They held practices in a nearby church, on a gym floor full of holes. The team, not surprisingly, was no good.

"We were dogshit," Davis recalled.

When Davis entered high school, he was mostly known as the six-foot-tall, rail-thin, goggles-wearing guard who couldn't do much more than shoot threes from the corner. That he had a unibrow sprouting between his eyes only made things worse. "We used to crack all sorts of jokes on him," said Jamari Traylor, Davis's AAU teammate. "He was this tall, lanky, goofy-looking kid with big feet and crooked teeth."

But Davis kept working—he put up extra shots after every practice, sometimes making the bus that took the team back after practices wait—and, by the end of his sophomore year, he'd shot up to about 6-foot-4, too. Some Division II and III schools showed interest. Davis figured he'd play four years of college ball and then become a high school gym teacher and coach, until another growth spurt that summer changed everything.

"The first time I saw him after the break, I didn't even recognize him," his coach, Cortez Hale, said. "We were in the gym and he comes in and I asked my assistant, 'Who's that big-ass kid?'" Davis had shot up to 6 foot 10, all while maintaining his guard skills. And yet, despite joining one of the area's top AAU programs, MeanStreets Basketball—which had produced a number of pros—Davis continued to fly under the radar. His best scholarship offer was from Cleveland State, a mid-major Division I school.

Around that time, a Chicago-based scout named Daniel Poneman started getting calls from local sources. *There's this kid on MeanStreets that you have to see,* they'd say. Poneman was just nineteen years old but had covered the Chicago high school basketball scene for five years. He was considered an authority in the preps space. In the last week of April, he decided to make the ninety-minute drive from his home in Evanston to Merrillville, Indiana, to watch MeanStreets play. He arrived at halftime. It didn't take long for him to figure out that No. 41 was the kid he'd heard about. He was taller than everyone else and jumped higher, too. He seemed to swat any shot attempted within five feet of his reach. He could run the floor. He had a smooth shooting stroke.

"I'm like, 'I've never seen anything like this,'" Poneman said. "It was clear he was the best player in the state."

Poneman took out his 720p Flip video camera and began recording. That night, he uploaded the footage to Facebook and YouTube and sent the link to about thirty college coaches. By early the next morning, his phone was blowing up. A few months later, John Calipari, the head coach for Kentucky and the face of men's college basketball, was in Davis's Chicago living room pitching him and his family on the beauties of Lexington. "There must have been about fifteen of them in the room," Calipari said. In their meeting, Calipari was clear. He wasn't promising playing time or shots. What he was promising, though, was a chance to play alongside other elite talent and for a program coming off a trip to the Final Four.

"Coach, I don't care where you play me, how you play me," Calipari recalled Davis telling him. "I just want to win. I just want to be a part of some winning."

Davis's first few months at Kentucky proved to be a culture shock. In Chicago, he had towered over his competition; as a senior, he averaged a cartoonish 32 points, 22 rebounds, and seven blocks per game. In Kentucky, he no longer stood head and shoulders (both literally and in terms of talent) above everyone else. In some areas, he even lagged behind. He struggled bench-pressing more than 70 pounds. During his first practice with the team, while trying to post up a burlier defender, he got bumped off his spot and tossed up a brick while falling down. Calipari blew the whistle. *If we throw the ball to him in the post again, we're all running,* Calipari shouted. Davis was so embarrassed about his lack of strength that he asked assistant coach Kenny Payne if he could do his workouts in private.

But Davis was a fast learner, and he realized early on that he boasted the skills to control games, especially on defense. "He was so good that Cal changed how we played because of him," Sam Malone, who was a freshman at Kentucky with Davis, recalled. "We'd come out on shooters and pressure them like crazy just because we knew we had AD back there." As the season went on, Davis grew more comfortable around his teammates, too, often organizing team pranks and leading midnight pizza runs.

Davis was named the Naismith College Player of the Year—awarded to the country's top men's college basketball player—and the SEC Defensive Player of the Year. He led Kentucky to a 38–2 regular season and to the NCAA Tournament championship in New Orleans, where they faced Kansas. At halftime of that game, Kentucky entered the locker room with a 14-point lead, despite Davis being scoreless. Annoyed with himself, he stood up in front of the team. It was his first time doing so all season.

Look, guys, I can't make a shot tonight, he told the group, *so you guys score the ball, and I'll grab every rebound and block every shot.*

"You never hear a kid say something like that in the middle of a game," Payne said.

Davis finished the night with 16 rebounds, six blocks, and three steals, leading Kentucky to a 67–59 victory and its first NCAA title since 1998. He was so dominant that he was named the game's MVP, despite missing nine of his 10 shots and finishing with just six points.

Three months later, New Orleans[*] drafted Davis first overall. After experiencing his first season of winning basketball, he was once again joining a losing team. Unlike in high school, though, he was now expected to turn the whole thing around.

The Pelicans made the playoffs in Davis's third season. The Warriors swept them in the first round, but better times appeared to be on the horizon. Davis signed a five-year, $145 million contract extension, which would keep him in New Orleans through the 2019–20 season. Normally, this would mean that the Pelicans could operate with a long runway, that they could be patient and opportunistic with their moves and build something sustainable around Davis.

Pelicans general manager Dell Demps chose a different route.

He handed out lavish contracts to average players.[†] He traded first-round picks for veterans. The Pelicans backslid and missed the playoffs the next two years. They got back in 2018 and even won a series— the first in Davis's career—but the Warriors ran them off the floor in five games in the next round. The defeat broke Davis. "He just went underground after that loss," Calipari said. "We couldn't find him for a week—no one knew where he went." He was coming off the best year of his career and a dominant playoff run (30.1 points, 13.4 rebounds, 2.3 blocks per game), but in the end he felt only further from where he wanted to be.

"He just didn't think there was a way where we could be a championship team," Gentry said. "He didn't see it."

Gentry and others in the building tried selling Davis on the notion that he was the one who'd be driving the winning, but by then, Davis was checked out. And anyway, that wasn't how Davis was built. Even

---

[*] Though at that point they were the Hornets; they announced the change to Pelicans in 2013.

[†] Five years, $58 million to Ömer Aşık (retired in 2018 with career averages of 5.3 points and 7.1 rebounds per game). Four years, $50 million to Solomon Hill (retired from the NBA in 2022 with averages of 5.5 points and 3.1 rebounds per game). Four years, $20.2 million to Alexis Ajinça (retired from the NBA in 2017 with career averages of 5.3 points and 3.9 rebounds per game).

back during his AAU days, he wasn't the sort of player who threw the team on his back. He always played defense and always attacked the glass, but on offense he sometimes drifted into the background.

"I'd have to be, like, 'What are you waiting for? Take over,'" MeanStreets coach Jevon Mamon said. "But it wasn't a lack of confidence. He just knew we had a lot of good players on the team, and he liked playing with others." Payne described Davis as a "giver by nature. And when you're that kind of person and you want to please the people around you, then, yeah, sometimes we'd have to force him out of his shell."

The Pelicans won the first four games of their 2018–19 campaign. Then, a little over an hour before their fifth game, a matchup in Utah with the Jazz, they learned that Davis would be sitting out. He said he'd sprained his right elbow against the Nets the night before. It was the first time he had revealed the injury. The Pelicans lost by 21. They then dropped their next five games. The season had just begun and it already felt lost.

In mid-December, ESPN's Adrian Wojnarowski, the industry's top scoopster, had reported that the Lakers were interested in trading for Davis. That night, before a game in Brooklyn against the Nets, ESPN reporter Dave McMenamin approached LeBron at his locker.

McMenamin had covered LeBron the previous four years in Cleveland, and as far as reporters and subjects went, the two had grown close. Before and after games, McMenamin could often be found in the locker room speaking to LeBron, usually off the record. It was a relationship that benefited both. No one in the NBA was more adept at managing the media than LeBron, especially beat writers covering him daily. In Cleveland, he once referred to the three reporters assigned to cover him and the Cavs, a group that included McMenamin, as "my three wives away from my wife." LeBron both understood the job in a way most of his peers did not and was an expert in making sure that the reporters covering him every day saw things from his perspective. He was calculated in how he did so, too. Sometimes he pulled those reporters aside to share thoughts he wanted published. Sometimes he offered insight on background—meaning the information could be used, just not attributed to him—so that it could be passed along to the public to help shape a narrative. Other times he gossiped off the record. If McMenamin was quoting LeBron, it was because LeBron wanted to be quoted. Which was why the report McMenamin filed that night was so jarring; LeBron, it was clear, was sending a message.

"That would be amazing," LeBron told McMenamin of playing with Davis. "Like, duh. That would be incredible."

The comments infuriated the rest of the league. Executives, citing the tampering rules prohibiting the recruiting of players under contract, clamored for the NBA to step in.

"If these are the rules, enforce them," one Western Conference GM told ESPN's Wojnarowski in a story published three days later. "If you want to push Anthony Davis in LA, if you allow LeBron to interfere with teams, then just do it. Change the rules, and say, 'It's the wild, wild west and anything goes.' But give us a list of the rules that you're enforcing, and give us a list of the rules that you're going to ignore."

Davis tried downplaying the comments afterward, telling ESPN, "I don't really care. Obviously, it's cool to hear any high-caliber player say they want to play with me. But my job is to turn this team around." But no one, especially within the Pelicans organization, bought it. That skepticism only grew after reports surfaced that Davis had dinner with LeBron in LA two nights later, following a loss to the Lakers. The sense of betrayal within the Pelicans organization ran so deep that some questioned whether Davis's elbow sprain earlier that season was real or just an attempt to derail the season and pave the way for an exit.

In late January, Davis and Klutch laid their cards on the table. Paul informed the Pelicans that Davis wouldn't be re-signing with them and that he wished to be traded. He then shared the news with ESPN. "Anthony wants to be traded to a team that allows him a chance to win consistently and compete for a championship," Paul told Wojnarowski. "Anthony wanted to be honest and clear with his intentions, and that's the reason for informing them of this decision now. That's in the best interests of both Anthony's and the organization's future."

The NBA fined Davis $50,000—public trade requests were forbidden by the collective bargaining agreement—and the Pelicans did their best to project a position of strength. "We . . . have requested the League to strictly enforce the tampering rules associated with this transaction," they said in a statement, a clear shot at the Lakers. Davis was under contract for another eighteen months, meaning the Pelicans were under no obligation to acquiesce to his demands. The Pelicans were also headed by an ownership group that was new to the NBA but had spent years running the NFL's New Orleans Saints, a league in which the teams held all the power.

But basketball was a different sport, and the NBA was a different league. In this world, it was the players who ran things. If Anthony Davis wanted to be a Laker, it was going to happen, and there was nothing the Pelicans could do to stop it.

•　　•　　•

The strained groin that LeBron suffered on Christmas was supposed to be a minor injury. "Dodged a bullet!" he tweeted after receiving a clean MRI. He added the hashtag "#BackInNoTime." The injury wound up costing him 17 games, the longest absence of his career. The Lakers lost 11 of them, dropping their record to 26–25.

LeBron returned to the floor on Thursday, January 31, for a battle with the Clippers. A few hours before that, though, news broke that, with just over a week until the trade deadline and six weeks since LeBron's initial Davis comments, Magic and Pelicans general manager Dell Demps had initiated trade discussions. The Lakers, according to the *Los Angeles Times,* had emailed the Pelicans five different proposals, all built around their young core. Each featured two players from the grouping of Kuzma, Ingram, Zubac, and Hart in addition to a future first-round pick. The Pelicans, according to multiple reports, had yet to respond.

It didn't matter. The dam had broken.

The Lakers defeated the Clippers in overtime that night, but the potential of a Davis deal was all anyone cared about. Some Clippers fans seated near the Lakers' bench spent the night chanting "You're all getting traded" and "No one wants you" at Lakers players, who tried brushing it off but found doing so easier said than done. "We were all new to NBA life," Hart said. "The business side affected us on the court." Not only were Magic and the Lakers okay parting with them, but LeBron—their teammate and a player many of them idolized—was clearly pushing for it to happen.

"That part was a little weird," Ingram said.

The coaching staff was livid. Walton believed he and the group had been making progress with the young players before LeBron, despite promising patience before the year, had torpedoed the season with his comments. Some within the organization even wondered whether this move from him and Klutch was triggered by the team's strong play; if the Lakers had continued winning, it would have been difficult to justify blowing up the roster to go get Davis.

"Everything LeBron does is calculated," one Lakers coach said.

Hoping to prevent a spiral, Walton spoke to the group. He also met with some players one-on-one. The message was simple: Trade rumors were a part of being in the NBA.

Our jobs, as professionals, he told the players, *is to continue to come in to work, continue building what we're building, and control what you can control.*

A few days later, Magic and Demps spoke again. Magic said the Lakers were willing to include Ball, Ingram, and Kuzma, plus two first-round picks, plus three players on expiring deals, which would give the Pelicans more cap room moving forward. They were also willing to take Solomon Hill, an overpaid forward, off the Pelicans' hands. That night, Magic upped the Lakers' offer once more: He was okay parting with Ball, Kuzma, Ingram, Hart, Zubac, and Caldwell-Pope, plus two first-round picks in addition to taking back Hill.

Desperate for a deal before the deadline, Klutch decided to put its thumb on the scale. Paul knew that if the Pelicans waited until the summer, the Boston Celtics, a team known to want Davis, could enter the mix. The Celtics boasted an enticing combination of picks and young players but, due to a quirk in the collective bargaining agreement, couldn't trade for Davis until the offseason.[*] Never mind that Davis had no interest in playing in Boston. If the Pelicans held out until summer, they could use Boston's offers to drive up the price for the Lakers—potentially sabotaging LeBron and Davis's future title hopes.

---

[*] Boston couldn't trade for Davis until the summer due to a rule in the collective bargaining agreement at the time that prohibited teams from acquiring two players signed to designated rookie contract extensions, like Davis was. That tag was one that allowed teams to extend their previous draft picks for up to five years instead of four; it was meant to entice players to remain with their current teams and was one of the many rules implemented by the league's owners during the 2011 labor negotiations as pushback against the player empowerment era unleashed by LeBron. The Celtics had already traded for Kyrie Irving, who was playing under a designated rookie extension, so they couldn't trade for Davis until Irving's contract expired in the summer.

Klutch's plan was to leak a list of teams Davis would be willing to sign with long-term, hoping it would pressure the Pelicans into making a deal with the Lakers before the deadline and eliminate Boston from the equation. The list—featuring the Lakers, Clippers, Bucks, and Knicks, none of whom, other than the Lakers, had the necessary assets to land Davis—was delivered to the Pelicans and subsequently shared with various reporters.

But Demps and Pelicans ownership just dug in further. They didn't respond to the Lakers' proposals. Wojnarowski then tweeted that they were waiting for the Lakers to "overwhelm them [with] an historic haul of picks," including at least four future draft picks.

The next day, with a little over forty-eight hours until the trade deadline, ESPN and others reported that the Pelicans still hadn't responded to the Lakers' offer. About an hour later, Broderick Turner of the *Los Angeles Times*—a veteran LA-based NBA reporter and someone Magic trusted—reported that the Lakers had ended negotiations.

That was fine with the Pelicans. They were in no rush and figured the same offer would be available in the offseason. Also, the Celtics' president of basketball operations, Danny Ainge, spent the week urging Demps to wait for the summer, promising that he'd come with a big offer. Even with Davis and Paul specifying that Davis did not want to play in Boston long-term, Ainge was willing to roll the dice, convinced that Davis could change his mind after he arrived. And even if the Celtics weren't there as a possible landing spot, who knew what other possible suitors would emerge? The only parties that would benefit from a deal happening before the deadline were the Lakers and Davis, and the Pelicans weren't exactly burning to help either party.

That night, the Lakers faced the Pacers in Indianapolis. The crowd serenaded Ingram and Kuzma with chants of "LeBron's gonna trade you" when they shot free throws. With the Lakers down big in the fourth quarter, TV cameras homed in on LeBron seated alone at the end of the bench with three open seats separating him and the next-closest teammate.

The Lakers fell by 42 points. LeBron had never suffered a more lopsided loss, but that didn't stop him from posting a graphic to Instagram celebrating his moving into fifth place on the NBA's all-time scoring list.

"I know it has to be tough on a lot of our guys, especially our young guys," he said when asked about the trade rumors. "Right now, they've just never been a part of it, and they're hearing it every single day—and I know that the worst thing that you can do right now is be on social media. And I know all young guys love social media. So that definitely can't help."

As Thursday's 3 p.m. deadline approached, Ball and some teammates settled into the training room of Boston's TD Garden, where the Lakers were slated to take on the Celtics later that night. When the deadline passed, Ball put on Diddy's "Bad Boy for Life" and turned the volume all the way up. He then uploaded a video to Instagram featuring the chorus: "We ain't / going nowhere," rapped Diddy. "We ain't / going nowhere."

But LeBron wasn't done. Later that night, he and Giannis Antetokounmpo joined TNT's national pregame show to draft the rosters for the upcoming All-Star Game, a job handed to the top vote-getter from each conference. LeBron used one of his picks to select Davis.

"You sure you want him to be your teammate?" host Ernie Johnson quipped, fully aware of what he was implying.

"You know, yeah," LeBron said. "I'm very sure of that."

He laughed.

6

CAN YOU FEEL THE MAGIC?

In March 1994, two and a half years after an HIV diagnosis had forced him to retire, Magic Johnson received a call from Dr. Buss. The Lakers were in the midst of a second straight losing season and on the verge of missing the playoffs for the first time in eighteen years. Dr. Buss was ready to move on from his head coach, Randy Pfund. He wanted Magic to replace him.

Magic was reluctant. He didn't need the money. And with all his business ventures, he wasn't bored, either. But "Dr. Buss said, 'Can you do this for me?'" Magic recalled, "and when he hit me with that one, then I said, 'Yeah, okay.'"

The Lakers were 28–38 when Magic took over. Upon doing so, he told his players that things would be different with him in charge. "He was hard, man; he practiced the shit out of us," recalled James Worthy, one of five former teammates of Magic's on the roster. Worthy said that Magic ran practices like Pat Riley, who was notorious for his emphasis on fitness. The roster was young—nine players had less than four years of NBA experience—so Magic made a point of prioritizing culture and habits. "Teach the Lakers what it was like to be a Laker" was the phrase he used. Just thirty-five years old, sometimes he suited up in practice and ran with the veterans in scrimmages to illustrate his points.

At first, it all worked. Under Magic, the Lakers reeled off victories in five of their first six games to climb back into the playoff picture. "Magic Has Been Exactly What the Lakers Needed," proclaimed the *Los Angeles Daily News* in an April 5 headline. The first line of the story described him as a "smash hit." Fans welcomed him back with standing ovations during pregame introductions.

Then, on April 8, the Lakers lost at home to the Nuggets. They dropped the next two games, too. Magic grew frustrated, especially with his young players, who he felt cared more about themselves and their off-the-court endeavors than the team and its on-court performance. While at practice the morning after the third loss, he overheard some from this group talking about drag-racing their Porsches. He paused the session, called everyone over, and gave a lecture about the need to focus on basketball, especially during practice time.

When he was done, the players picked up the conversation where it had left off.

The next night, the Lakers lost to the Suns in Phoenix by 29 points. After the game, they flew back to LA. Magic told his players to be back for practice at 7 a.m. The following morning, he entered the locker room with Jerry West, the team's general manager. West went first, cursing out the entire team.

Then it was Magic's turn.

You motherfuckers enjoy driving around in your convertibles, looking up at the palm trees, wind in your face, calling bitches on your cell phones? he shouted. *Well, enjoy it now, because next year, it's gonna be someone else here in those jerseys.*

For twenty minutes, Magic ripped into and threatened his players.

The girls you all love? They're only interested in you because you're Lakers!

The party invitations you care about so much? Also just because you're Lakers!

That nice LA weather? Shit, you wait, you fucking guys will be in Cleveland!

Everything they cared about, he told them, would be gone.

Think I'm fucking with you? Try me!

Magic was on a roll when a succession of high-pitched beeps interrupted his rant. Someone's beeper was going off. The room was silent other than the noise. Furious, Magic hunted for the source. He zeroed in on Lakers center Vlade Divac, a former teammate. The beeping continued. Divac, whose wife was due to give birth to the couple's child any day, reached into his pocket and tried silencing the device. It was too late.

Magic reached out his hand.

Vlade, give me the beeper, he said.

Divac, shoulders slumped, handed it over.

Magic paused before firing the beeper against a wall. It shattered upon impact.

Two days later, Magic announced that he wasn't returning to coach the following season. He finished out the year, and the Lakers didn't win another game. They dropped their last 10 games.

"Everybody cares about me, I, I, I. 'Where's my minutes, where's my shots? What's wrong with my game? Why can't I get my game off?' So it's a lot of that now," Magic told reporters at the time. "And I don't like that."

Dr. Buss understood, but he also thought there was another reason Magic was stepping aside. "Coaching requires a tremendous commitment of time and energy," he said. "So with all that Earvin is trying to accomplish in his life, I readily understand his decision."

•   •   •

The first thing Magic did after being promoted in February 2017 to president of basketball operations was evaluate every department. "We're going to see if we have the best people," he said in his introductory press conference, "and hopefully we do in house, and if not, we just have to get the right people." After the All-Star break, he met with everyone. The coaching staff. The scouts. The medical staff. The training staff. And in each of the meetings the message was the same: Things would be different now, that he expected things to be done a certain way, the Magic way, and if they weren't done this way then changes would be made.

"I have 1,000 résumés sitting on my desk," he said during a summer 2017 all-hands meeting while pointing up toward his office. "Any of you can be replaced at any time." The sudden shift in Magic's tone shocked people in the room. "The speech was supposed to be a pep talk," said a staffer present for the meeting. "It had started as, like, a kumbaya moment."

It didn't take long for the team's basketball employees to realize that Magic's "all for one, one for all" talk was just talk, that he wasn't interested in creating a collaborative environment, that the charming, gregarious, vibrant person presented in public wasn't who he was behind closed doors.* "We'd joke to each other about how there was 'Magic,' and there was 'Earvin,'" said a Lakers assistant coach. "'Magic' was who you got when the cameras were on. 'Earvin' was who we saw."

---

* Through a spokesperson, Johnson declined to comment.

Magic frosted the floor-to-ceiling glass doors of his office so that no one could see inside. Instead of learning the names of lower-level employees he saw around the facility every day, he'd refer to them by nicknames, like calling a tall staffer "big guy" every time they passed each other in the hallway. The day before his first draft, he told his front office to wear the same black Lakers polo shirts the next night so that when the Lakers' in-house documentary crew came to capture the evening, they'd look like a team. "Everyone loved the idea," said a Lakers scout—until they arrived at the facility and found Magic and Pelinka dressed in white polos, separating themselves from the group.*

Magic wasn't interested in feedback from others, either, even when discussing subjects in which they held expertise and he did not. During one of his initial meetings with the training staff, he kept harping on body fat percentage. That, after all, was what Riley had always emphasized.

I want data on all the players, Magic said.

Tim DiFrancesco, the team's strength and conditioning coach, pointed out that from a medical perspective, body fat percentage was no longer viewed as the ultimate measure of fitness. *Different guys,* he said, *carry fat differently.* Never mind the fact that if a player was being asked to bang down in the paint, having a little extra meat on his bones could be beneficial.

The two went back and forth.

Magic then cut the conversation off.

I want it done, and I want it done by the end of the season, he said.

DiFrancesco resigned soon after, becoming one of the first of nearly thirty basketball operations staffers to depart the organization in the two years after Magic's promotion to president.

Other times, it didn't seem like Magic even wanted the job. Just five months after being named president he took three weeks off to sail the Mediterranean on a seventy-three-meter-long, $680,000-per-week yacht with Samuel L. Jackson, a yearly tradition for the two and their

---

* The Lakers representative said that "the reason Pelinka and Johnson were not wearing shirts that matched the black polos worn by the other Lakers employees is that they had not been told or asked to do so and they knew nothing about it. The fact that they each independently showed up wearing white Lakers' polos was merely coincidental."

wives. When he returned, he showed employees pictures on his phone and offered to help with restaurant recommendations.

"He was like, 'If you're ever in Italy and need a place to eat, just let me know. I've been going there for twenty years,'" a staffer recalled.

When Magic was in town, he'd come into the facility only one or two days a week. He had no desk or computer in his office, just a couch and TV. The theme songs to *Family Feud* and *The Andy Griffith Show* spin-off *Mayberry R.F.D.* were often heard coming from inside, as well as court shows like *Judge Mathis*. General managers of other teams had trouble getting him on the phone. "I never got the sense he knew what was going on," one said. "You bring up cap stuff or trade stuff, and he either didn't know the details or had to ask someone else."

Yet when it came to getting credit, he was quick to insert himself into the narrative. After the Lakers signed LeBron, Magic went on a press tour to celebrate the Lakers' resurrection. This included a visit to Jimmy Kimmel's late-night show, where Magic was eager to detail the role he played in recruiting LeBron.

"[Rich Paul] said LeBron would love to have a meeting with the Lakers," Magic told the prime-time audience, "but he wants to have it with Magic."

That night on *Kimmel,* and in numerous other interviews, Magic told the story of how he pulled up to LeBron's house an hour before free agency started and how once the clock struck 9:01 p.m. and he was allowed inside, the two connected over their similar histories. Magic, like LeBron, was a Hall of Famer born in the Midwest who used his on-court success to open doors to some of the world's most exclusive business and social corners, meaning he understood LeBron in a way that few did. This connection, Magic believed, was a major reason the Lakers were able to get LeBron.

It was not the case.

"LeBron was going there no matter what," said a person close to him. "It didn't matter if Magic was there. He had zero to do with it."

• • •

Throughout his career, LeBron's teams always performed best when he was surrounded with shooters. He was too good to guard with one defender, but too smart and sharp a passer to try attacking with double teams. When he joined the Lakers, it was assumed they'd emulate this blueprint.

Magic had other plans.

"You're not gonna out–Golden State Golden State," he said on ESPN during a mid-July broadcast of the NBA Summer League title game between the Lakers and the Portland Trail Blazers.

So what, exactly, was his plan?

While watching the playoffs, Magic said, two teams that stuck out to him were the Rockets and the Celtics, both of whom made their respective conference finals. What Houston had, Magic said, were "a lot of guys who can handle the basketball, and break the defenses down, and create their own shot." And what they and the Celtics both boasted, Magic believed, were lots of "tough guys." This, in Magic's mind, was not a coincidence.

"So what did I bring in?" Magic asked ESPN's announcers rhetorically. "Tough guys. So that's how I'm building it. I took a lot from watching Boston play, watching Houston play, then advancing, and they beat all the teams that had all the great shooters."

Which was true, but in part because they were *also* great shooting teams. The Rockets the previous season led the league in three-pointers made per game. The Celtics were seventh. LeBron's Cavs, who made the finals, finished third. The Warriors, the two-time defending champions, were one of the best shooting teams of all time.

On July 9, Pelinka met LeBron in LA to officially sign the contract. While they were together, he presented LeBron with a laminated packet illustrating the rationale for how he and Magic had approached the offseason.

"Just to kind of do a deep dive into sort of the lens Earvin and I had as we were building things out," he told him.

Pelinka flipped to the first page. It was titled "2018–19: CORE PILLARS." Five different attributes were listed underneath, each in all caps:

INCREDIBLY SMART BASKETBALL
ULTRA-COMPETITIVE MENTALITY
PIT BULL TOUGHNESS
IRON CLAD TEAM UNITY
VERSATILITY, SPEED, & DEPTH

Pelinka read each one out loud, explaining what they meant and why they were important.

"I think—and obviously you and Magic talked about this and the night you guys got together—but to try to play the Warriors at their own game, it's fool's gold, it's a trap," Pelinka added, echoing Magic's approach. "You can't beat them."

And so the Lakers brought in Lance Stephenson, a temperamental Coney Island legend best known for blowing in LeBron's ear four years earlier* while his Pacers and LeBron's Heat were battling in the conference finals. They signed Rajon Rondo, a four-time All-Star point guard but someone who had played for five teams in the previous four seasons and had the reputation of an irritant. They also added Michael Beasley, a former No. 2 pick who'd played for eight teams in ten years—including two in China—and had battled mental health issues throughout his career, and JaVale McGee, a seven-foot pogo stick who'd won titles with the Warriors the previous two seasons but was best known for his on-court antics (running back on defense when his team still had the ball, missing overambitious dunk attempts, taking popcorn from a fan sitting courtside) and being the starring character of the recurring "Shaq-tin' a Fool" segment during TNT's studio show.

"It was like the land of misfit toys," a Lakers assistant coach said.

None of those players were good shooters. And even worse was that Magic completed most of the signings without consulting Walton and his staff. Meanwhile, the moves for which Walton did advocate—like bringing back Brook Lopez, who had told the Lakers he wanted to return, and whose ability to space the floor on offense and protect the rim on defense made him an ideal fit alongside LeBron—were ignored.

On top of all that, the mix of players Magic had put together had created a tinberbox. In one corner the Lakers had all their young former lottery picks trying to secure their futures; in the other were their new veterans, all of whom were signed to one-year deals, meaning they were coming expecting to play and thirsty for minutes to help secure future paydays, putting Walton in a tough spot.

Would the goal be to prioritize winning or player development? Would it be possible to do both? How would he choose between Rondo and Ball as the point guard down the stretch? And between Hart and

---

* Yes, you read that correctly.

Kuzma and Stephenson and Caldwell-Pope and Beasley on the wings? What would happen if McGee lost minutes to Zubac at center? A locker room rebellion felt inevitable. Before the season, Magic preached patience. "As I was talking to Luke [with Pelinka], we said, 'Don't worry about if we get out to a bad start,'" he told reporters in September. "We have seen that with LeBron going to Miami, and we have seen that when he came back to Cleveland. He is going to struggle because there are so many new moving parts." But early on it became clear these were empty words.

On October 6, the Lakers lost in a preseason game to the Clippers. The game was a blowout, 103–87, but it was also an exhibition. LeBron didn't even suit up. Magic didn't care. The next morning, he stormed into the conference room where the coaches were reviewing the game and, in front of the staff, laced into Walton.

"It wasn't even anything technical," one coach recalled. "It was just like, 'This isn't the Lakers brand. This is embarrassing and not how we represent ourselves, and you better get your shit together or you're not going to be here very long.'"

The Lakers struggled out of the gate. On October 29, they fell to the Timberwolves in Minnesota, 124–120. It was their second straight defeat, dropping their record to 2–5. The next morning, back in LA, Magic summoned Walton to his office and berated him some more. He shouted and cursed and demanded that Walton implement a more structured offensive system, even though the Lakers boasted the league's seventh-best offensive rating. At one point, Walton tried speaking, only to be scolded for interrupting.

This time news of the confrontation leaked, with ESPN reporting four days later that Magic had "admonished" Walton "for the team's sluggish start to the season." The report added that Magic's "aggressive meeting tone circulated to individuals throughout the organization, including to principal owner Jeanie Buss."

Walton did his best to downplay the interaction. "I will tell you this: Magic, myself . . . are in constant communication, so this is no 'all of a sudden there's an emergency' meeting," he told reporters the next day. "This is something we do all the time." But the pressure was on. And for Magic, it was starting to look like a repeat of what happened the last time a member of the Buss family, in a time of desperation, had convinced him to return and save the team.

• • •

Almost all of Magic's offseason signings turned out to be busts. McGee put up solid numbers (12 points and 7.5 rebounds per game) but spent most of the season moping and forgetting defensive coverages. Stephenson hit just 42 percent of his shots—an awful mark—and logged more bloopers than memorable moments, like the time in November when he attempted a behind-the-back alley-oop pass to LeBron, only for the ball to sail out of bounds. Beasley never cracked the rotation and was depressed being so far away from his mom, who was battling cancer back in his hometown of Washington, DC. She died in December.

Magic's decision to ignore shooting proved to be particularly foolish. The Lakers had one of the league's worst offenses—unheard of for a LeBron-led team—and their inability to spread the floor (they ranked 26th in three-point efficiency) was the primary reason. Once it was clear Davis wasn't coming to LA, Magic and Pelinka decided to use the last few days before the trade deadline to address this issue.

First, they sent a second-round pick and the little-used Svi Mykhailiuk to the Detroit Pistons in exchange for Reggie Bullock, a 3-and-D wing. The next night, they came up with another idea. The Clippers had traded their leading scorer, Tobias Harris, to the Sixers earlier that day, and in return they received a package that included Mike Muscala, a veteran big with a solid three-point stroke. The front office thought Muscala, like Bullock, could provide a shooting boost, so Pelinka called up the Clippers and proposed a deal in which they'd receive Muscala in exchange for Zubac.

Sitting together in their war room, Clippers executives, a group that included Lakers legend Jerry West,* were stunned. Muscala was a slow-

---

* West's contract with the Golden State Warriors expired in July 2017. He indicated that he wanted to return to the Lakers. Jeanie, however, never truly considered him, mostly because she believed in Magic but also in part because she and West had never gotten along. West was always a vocal—and often profane—critic of her relationship with Phil Jackson. He didn't like Jackson, or the optics of his team's head coach dating the owner's much younger daughter (sixteen years younger, to be exact), or how it meant Jackson would likely always have ownership in his corner. "There's a fucking million women in this town," he once said to Jackson. "Why would you end up with Jeanie?" After the Lakers hired Magic and Pelinka, West joined the Clippers.

footed, twenty-seven-year-old forward averaging 7.4 points and 4.3 rebounds per game. At best, he topped out as a reserve. Zubac, on the other hand, was a skilled, not-even-twenty-two-year-old seven-footer who was already starting games.

That the Croatian native had reached that level at such a young age was a testament to his work ethic and skills. Zubac was just nineteen years old when the Lakers rolled the dice on him with a second-round pick in the 2016 draft, and he struggled in his first two seasons with the franchise. "He couldn't keep up with the pace of the guards," said Coby Karl, the Lakers' G League coach. But he worked hard and developed some touch and skills to complement his frame. He also trimmed his body fat from 19 percent to 8. Walton, in particular, became a huge fan, and Zubac's success became a badge of honor for the Lakers' scouting department and development groups.

Magic, however, felt differently. What he saw was a soft-spoken big man who was still learning how to deploy his size as a weapon. Watching Zubac frustrated him. He often heckled him during practices, calling him a pussy and accusing him of being soft.

"He'd be like, 'Man, you're a big guy; you gotta set the tone,'" a Lakers staffer said. "But at that point, Zubac just wasn't that guy."

The deal with the Clippers was finalized an hour before the deadline, with the Lakers adding Beasley to the package. The coaches and rest of the front office were shocked when they heard the news. West would later laugh at the Lakers with friends. Some people inside the building speculated that Muscala's 17-point barrage a few weeks earlier against the Lakers, a game that took place in LA and that Magic attended, had sparked the Lakers' interest. A similar theory circulated in the offseason after the Lakers signed Beasley, who in a game the previous season had torched them for 17 points in 14 minutes while playing for the Knicks.

Three days after the deadline, Magic flew to Philadelphia to speak with the team before a game against the Sixers. The goal was to provide a boost of confidence and inspire the group for a playoff push. Two months remained in the season, and the Lakers sat two and a half games out of a playoff spot.

The fact that you guys are still here shows just how much we value you, he told them.

This team has the talent to make the playoffs, he said.

It's time to come together, he added.

Soon after, he met with reporters. One asked him if he felt the Pelicans engaged in good-faith negotiations.

"No," Magic replied. His belief was that the Pelicans never intended to trade Davis and engaged in talks only so that, as payback, they could then leak the proposals and torpedo the Lakers' season. But, Magic added, he rejected the idea that players seeing their names appear in trade rumors was a problem.

"Quit making this about thinking these guys are babies because that's what you're treating them like," he told reporters. "They're professionals. All of them. And this is how this league works." He said he spoke to players individually and that everyone was now "heading all in the same direction." After the game, a 143–120 loss, reporters asked various Lakers how they felt about Magic's pep talk. Some, like Kuzma, expressed appreciation. "I mean, any time Magic Johnson, one of the greatest players in the game, comes to talk to you, you're always going to be all eyes and ears. Optimistic. That's just what Magic is. He's a guy that, when he walks into the room, [it] kind of electrifies. It's just who he is. You listen to what he says."

Others were less effusive.

"How am I supposed to answer that?" McGee asked reporters. "How did I feel? Tingly inside? I don't know."

On a conference call with reporters after the deadline, Pelinka compared the Lakers to the New England Patriots, who had just won the Super Bowl after starting the season 1–2, thanks in part to wide receiver Julian Edelman returning from a suspension.

"I almost look at Bullock and Muscala, my hope is, much like Edelman was," Pelinka said. "It's just one player, but that can have such a big impact on overall chemistry, and I hope those two guys can come in and have that impact."

The Lakers lost their next two games, dropping their record to 28–29. Heading into the All-Star break, they trailed the Sacramento Kings by two and a half games for the final playoff slot in the West. Even worse, they were under .500. It marked the first time since his rookie year that a LeBron-led team held a losing record that late in the season.

•   •   •

In their first game out of the break, the Lakers put on one of their most impressive performances of the season, erasing a 19-point second-half deficit and knocking off the high-octane Rockets 111–106. LeBron led the way with 29 points, 12 rebounds, and six assists. Ingram poured in 27 points. Kuzma added 18. Rondo dished out seven assists in just 19 minutes. Bullock drilled four threes. Their defense held the Rockets to 29 percent shooting from deep.

It was a nearly perfect performance, an example of what the Lakers could look like when everything clicked.

"Tonight was a step in the right direction," LeBron said after the game.

The good vibes didn't last.

Two nights later, the Lakers fell to the Pelicans in New Orleans, 128–115—despite Davis watching from the sidelines. LeBron was great again and Ingram was good, but the rest of the team was not, particularly on defense, where the Lakers allowed the Pelicans to hit more than half their shots. Speaking to reporters after the game, LeBron cited a lack of "urgency" as one of the team's problems that night and wasn't coy about whom he thought was to blame.

"How many know what's at stake if you've never been there?" he said of his teammates. By "there," he meant the playoffs. He added, "The last few years, everyone's so accustomed to the losses that I'm just not accustomed to. I'm not accustomed to it. I will never get comfortable with losing."

The Lakers flew to Memphis that night and were off the next day. But LeBron's teammates, having reached their boiling point, called a players-only meeting. They were sick of hearing LeBron criticize their effort but take possessions off, of hearing him talk about the importance of defending but then fall asleep on the backline ("This guy's supposed to be the best in the world, and he's not playing any fucking defense," one young player complained to a staffer after an early-season loss), of seeing him celebrate individual accomplishments on social media after losses, of his seeming indifference to their feelings, like how he showed up to the facility the day after the initial Davis reports sporting a big smile. "He was just sipping tea from this electronically heated mug and goes, 'What's everyone so down about? It's a beautiful day,'" a staffer recalled.

Some of LeBron's actions were understandable. Missing multiple weeks with an injury was something he'd never dealt with before. Neither was being surrounded by players ten-plus years younger. But LeBron's approach created an environment of distrust and, from there, finger-pointing. And in the eyes of his teammates, LeBron was too willing to lay the blame for the lost season at their feet.

That day in Memphis, the players met alone. Several spoke. Some called out LeBron for his body language during games, when cameras often caught him with his shoulders slumped or glaring at teammates.

"I tried to get LeBron to focus on his body language," Rondo later recalled. "Those young guys were looking at everything he did. If they missed four shots in a row and LeBron was making a face, it was crushing to them. He was their Michael Jordan. They didn't want to let him down. But if LeBron said one thing positive to Brandon Ingram or Kyle Kuzma, they immediately were back to their old selves."

LeBron seemed to take the criticism to heart, but it was too late. The Lakers lost 11 of their next 13 games. The damage—in the standings, but also in the locker room—was done. And it was about to claim two casualties.

• • •

When the Lakers first signed LeBron in the summer, Walton was ecstatic. That July afternoon, in the backyard of his Manhattan Beach home, Walton stepped away from his family barbecue and started reaching out to anyone he knew who had a history with LeBron or insight on how to coach a superstar. Walton was aware of how LeBron had clashed with Mike Brown in Cleveland; and how, early in his first season with the Heat, he had asked Pat Riley to replace Erik Spoelstra on the sideline; and how, in his return to Cleveland, he had tuned out David Blatt.

Walton spoke to Kobe. He spoke to Phil Jackson. He spoke to his dad, who happened to be at a concert with Grateful Dead drummer Mickey Hart. "The rhythm is the answer to everything in life," Hart shouted over and over.

Walton spoke to Spoelstra and, while in Las Vegas for summer league the next week, met with Tyronn Lue. Both gave similar advice. LeBron was demanding of those around him, had high standards, and asked a lot of questions. But he was also the hardest worker they'd ever seen and the smartest player they'd ever coached. They told Walton that if he put in the work and was able to explain the reasoning behind his decisions, he and LeBron would get along great.

Walton's first test came during training camp. At times, he'd be installing a scheme only for LeBron and Rondo to hijack the session. The two would spend ten minutes going back and forth about various counters while the rest of the team stood around struggling to keep up. "It was like watching two Rhodes scholars surrounded by a bunch of kids in kindergarten," said a Lakers coach. "We'd be trying to put in A, and they'd already be on L, M, N, O, P, and Q." Walton was happy to cede the floor. After all, why wouldn't he listen to what LeBron, one of the greatest players of all time, had to say? But some in the building felt like Walton was allowing LeBron to usurp his authority, an accusation that would plague him all season.

Two weeks into the season, after being admonished by Magic, Walton was already on thin ice. Even Magic's attempts at damage control hurt Walton's standing. "He's going to finish the year, unless something drastic happens, which it won't," Magic told the *Los Angeles Times* after the news of his berating Walton broke. That small window he had left open did not go unnoticed throughout the organization.

By November, Paul decided he was done with Walton, too. *I just didn't think he was a good coach,* he told an associate years later. Paul started telling anyone who'd listen that Walton needed to be replaced. Management. Reporters. Even NBA commissioner Adam Silver, whom he ran into during a lunch in November. When Silver asked who the right coach was for the team, Paul suggested Lue.

By January, the locker room was revolting. Players and people close to them started grousing to reporters. Walton's rotations, they said, were inconsistent. His offense, they said, was too simple. LeBron, they said, was allowed to do whatever he wanted. Walton had counters to all the attacks, which he shared with friends and reporters in private. The rotations were inconsistent because four key rotation players—Ball, Ingram, Rondo, and LeBron—had each missed at least 27 games with injuries. The offense was simple because new players were always being worked in and because so many of them were so young. He didn't challenge LeBron because, well, he was LeBron, maybe the greatest player in the history of the game. Also, that wasn't the sort of player-coach relationship Walton was looking to build. His goal was to form a partnership, one that would last long-term.

Every one of his points was valid. But they also didn't matter. Fair or not, he'd lost the team. And from that there was no coming back.

•   •   •

It was supposed to be a night of celebration.

On March 6, the Lakers welcomed the Nuggets to Los Angeles. Their season was on life support, but this night was going to provide a respite. LeBron was just 13 points away from passing Michael Jordan for fourth all-time in points scored. Moving ahead of Jordan, the player considered by many to be the greatest to ever play and someone LeBron had described as his idol, would be a momentous occasion. And it would give LeBron and Lakers fans something to celebrate together amid a lost season.

Except most Lakers fans didn't really care. They had no history with LeBron, and so far, all he'd given them was one of the more disappointing seasons they'd ever experienced. The relationship was icy from the start, too. Part of it was because LeBron was being compared to Kobe, whose fans were as defensive and emotional as any in American sports; after LeBron signed, some street murals celebrating the news were vandalized with pro-Kobe messages. But part of it was also because Lakers fans, like his teammates, felt that LeBron wasn't emotionally invested in them or the team.

That night against the Nuggets, the Lakers fell behind early in the first quarter. Then LeBron missed four straight free throws. The boos rained down, just like they had two nights earlier during a loss to the Clippers. When LeBron made the basket to pass Jordan—an and-one on the left side of the paint in the second quarter—the Lakers trailed by 18.

The reaction from Lakers fans inside Staples Center was subdued. It was "as if they were applauding an impromptu speech given by a distant uncle at an acquaintance's wedding," was how the *Los Angeles Times*' Plaschke described it in a column. During the next break in action, LeBron grabbed a seat on the bench and used a towel to wipe tears from his eyes. "For a kid from Akron, Ohio, that needed inspiration and needed some type of positive influence, MJ was that guy for me," he'd say after the game. "You guys have no idea what MJ did for me and my friends growing up, just in the sense of some days you don't even feel like you're going to make it to the next day where I grew up because of everything that's going on."

The Lakers lost 115–99, their fourth straight defeat and eighth in 10 games. Eleven days later, New York Knicks forward Mario Hezonja, a lead-footed wing on his way out of the league, swatted LeBron's potential game-winning, last-second shot at the rim, just his eighth block of the season. Five days after that, LeBron slipped and lost the ball out of bounds with 22.9 seconds remaining in the game and the Lakers trailing the Nets by three. That loss, a 111–106 defeat, eliminated the Lakers from playoff contention.

Few things had gone right during the season, but at the top of the list was their inability to score. The Lakers finished with the league's seventh-worst offense, and only the Suns connected on a lower percentage of their three-point attempts. Magic's offseason strategy had backfired spectacularly.

"That experiment?" LeBron asked, when asked by McMenamin before the Nets loss what he thought of management's decision to prioritize playmaking over shooting. LeBron paused, then "pursed his lips and stuck out his tongue as he trumpeted air out of his mouth," McMenamin would later write when describing the interaction, "making a raspberry sound. 'THBPBPTHPT!'"

One week later, with six games remaining, the Lakers shut LeBron down for the rest of the season.

From there, the spotlight shifted to Walton's future. He wanted to come back and had pitched his case to Jeanie during a team flight back from Milwaukee in mid-March. Jeanie remained a fan, but two weeks later she told an interviewer that, despite thinking that Walton had done "a terrific job . . . in terms of basketball decisions, I will always defer to Magic." Walton could read the writing on the wall. The Lakers, despite adding LeBron, had a nearly identical record to the previous season and would be missing the playoffs for the sixth straight year. He and Magic hadn't spoken in weeks. He'd also gotten wind that the front office was trying to pin its emphasis on signing playmakers over shooters on Walton's desire to play LeBron off the ball. "Luke knew he was getting fired," said a person close to him. He drove into work on April 9 for the Lakers' final game of the season, figuring it'd be his last time as the Lakers' coach, especially when he was told that he'd be meeting with Magic the next day. During his pregame press conference, in a Staples Center hallway outside the locker room, a reporter asked if he had "anxiety" about his future with the Lakers.

"No anxiety," Walton replied. "But call me later tonight, and the answer might be different."

A few feet away, Magic was chatting with ESPN's Rachel Nichols and a couple other reporters. "Just like we had done a bunch of times that season," Nichols recalled. "Nothing felt different." When Walton finished speaking with the media, Magic excused himself.

"I gotta go do something for a minute," he said.

He made his way over to the scrum, where most of the reporters were still lingering, and parked in front of the Lakers banner the team used as a backdrop for press conferences. "Well, now I'm gonna go," he said.

"We all sort of chuckled," Bill Oram, the Lakers beat reporter for *The Athletic,* recalled. "And then he just started talking."

The group figured he'd discuss the disappointing season and how he planned on getting things back on track. Instead, Magic opened by complimenting local broadcaster Jim Hill on an interview with LeBron that had aired on the local CBS affiliate the previous night. "I was riding here thinking about that incredible interview you had," he said. On that ride, he added, he also thought about all the "great meetings I've had with Jeanie the last couple of days. And I love her as a sister."

It was still unclear where this was heading. Until . . .

"So today, I'm going to step down as the president."

Everyone present was stunned.

"I just remember my jaw dropping," Nichols recalled.

The race to get the news onto Twitter began. Some began live streaming from their phones.

Magic, fighting back tears, explained his reasoning.

"I was like, 'Damn, I got a great life outside of this. What am I doing?'" he said.

He said he'd cried on the way over to the arena that night. He said he'd have "more fun" serving as a "big brother and ambassador to everybody." He said he'd recently received a call from Serena Williams asking him to "mentor me and be on my advisory board," and that those were the types of ventures to which he wanted to devote time. He said he didn't like all "the backstabbing and the whispering" and, when citing the people in the front office whom he enjoyed working with, didn't mention Pelinka. He said that "tomorrow, I'd have to affect someone's livelihood and their life," meaning his plan to fire Walton, and he'd realized that was a pain he didn't want to inflict.

"That's not fun for me," he said.

Most important of all, he said, he wanted to preserve his relationship with Jeanie, "my sister." Jeanie had wanted to keep Walton, and while Magic said she gave him permission to fire him, Magic was worried that the disagreement would be the first step in the fraying of their bond.

"I don't want to put her in the middle of us," he said.

Then came perhaps the most shocking revelation of the night.

"She doesn't know I'm standing here," Magic said. "Because I'd be crying like a baby in front of her."

He spotted Nichols in the crowd.

"Rachel! I'm free, my love," he said.

"Did you really not tell Jeanie yet?" she asked.

"No, I haven't," Magic replied. "I couldn't. I couldn't stand and tell her."

Listening in from the back of the scrum was Brian Shaw, Walton's associate head coach. After a few minutes, he scurried to the coaches' room, where he found Walton sitting with Tim Harris, the Lakers' president of business operations.

You guys knew Magic was stepping down and didn't say anything? Shaw said.

What are you talking about? Harris asked.

They turned on the TV and saw the news. Harris, in shock, rushed out of the room to call Jeanie. *I got a flat tire. I'm on my way, I'll be there soon,* she said before he could get in a word.

Turn around, Harris said. *Magic just quit.*

What are you talking about? Jeanie asked.

Harris passed along everything he knew. He told her to meet him at the office, where they'd lay out a plan for moving forward. Jeanie hung up and turned the radio on. Magic was still talking, and his press conference was being broadcast live.

Around the same time, Randy Mims, LeBron's chief of staff, found LeBron in the training room, where he was stretching.

Magic just stepped down, he said.

LeBron figured his friend was kidding. "I was like, 'Man, get the fuck out of my face, you bullshitting,'" he recalled. Then he pulled out his phone. It wasn't a joke.

"It was weird for him to just be like, 'I'm out of here,'" he'd later say.

Meanwhile, Magic was rolling. The longer he talked, the more loose he became. As the news had trickled out, the crowd surrounding Magic swelled. He spotted ESPN's Ramona Shelburne. "Ramona," he said, "you called me; what's up?" He spotted Lee Zeidman, the president of Staples Center. "Lee, thank you, man, for the suite, the tickets, the concerts." He shouted out the former players and Lakers broadcasters who'd swung by. He talked about how excited he was to go to Dodgers games.

More than forty minutes passed. A Lakers public relations official gave Magic a look.

"Yes?" he said.

"Wrap this up," the staffer said. Tip-off was less than an hour away.

Magic ended the session and went around hugging members of the media. He then went looking for Jeanie. After about fifteen minutes, he learned that she wasn't coming. He said goodbye to some lingering reporters and exited the building through a loading dock.

7

A ROB PELINKA-TYPE

With Magic gone, most people in and around the NBA assumed the Lakers would go searching for a replacement. Given how poorly the previous season had gone, the summer of 2019 would likely make or break LeBron's tenure with the team, and most assumed the Lakers would want a seasoned executive to lead them through the storm.

Jeanie, however, had a different view. In the wake of her brothers' attempted boardroom coup, what she wanted most was to be surrounded by people she could trust. And she already had two in place.

The first was Kurt Rambis, whom Jeanie had hired the year before as a senior advisor. A former Lakers player and coach, Rambis had worked alongside Phil Jackson for many years. He was also married to Linda, Jeanie's close friend. Jeanie trusted him. She believed he was as qualified as anyone to make basketball decisions. Rambis didn't receive an official promotion. But with Magic gone, his voice carried more weight.

Above him was general manager Rob Pelinka, Kobe's former agent. There were only a handful of people in the world whose opinions mattered to Jeanie as much as Kobe's, and if she couldn't convince him to take an official position with the franchise—which she'd tried in the years since his retirement—then in Pelinka, whom Kobe had pushed her to hire, she at least had the next best thing.

In May, the Lakers told ESPN's Ramona Shelburne that they would not be hiring someone to replace Magic.

The implication was clear: Pelinka was being handed the keys.

•   •   •

Pelinka's entire life had been geared toward reaching that moment.

The journey began on Chicago's North Shore, a cluster of affluent suburbs along Lake Michigan. Pelinka's father, Bob, was a beloved high school teacher and coach who prioritized faith and sports and pushed Rob, the younger of his two kids and his only son, in both. "He didn't yell at Rob or anything, and Rob never complained, but the vibe we all got was that his dad had high expectations for him," Stan Hickory, a childhood friend, said. By high school, Pelinka had developed the same expectations for himself. "He had a vision of what he wanted," said Ryan Trigg, a teammate of his at Lake Forest High School, and what Pelinka wanted was a Division I basketball scholarship to a top academic school. This, he decided, would be the only thing that mattered, and he'd orient his entire life around realizing that goal.

Pelinka gave up baseball so that he could focus on basketball. He pushed himself academically and even had a short story published by the school's literary magazine, which was edited by his classmate and future bestselling author Dave Eggers.* He skipped the usual weekend house parties—thrown in the mansion of whichever rich classmate's parents were out of town—so that he could get up early the next morning and shoot hundreds of jumpers with his dad in the school gym. He didn't date, and not because girls weren't interested. After all, Pelinka was a star athlete, tall, smart, and good-looking—later in life, he'd start bearing an uncanny resemblance to the actor Rob Lowe—who stood out with his Ralph Lauren clothes, but he had other priorities.

Pelinka grew to 6-foot-6, became a deadeye shooter, and, as a senior, averaged 30 points and nearly 10 rebounds per game. But the area's big-time programs weren't sure he had the athleticism to hang with top Division I athletes. It wasn't until a midseason 45-point outburst against St. Rita High School and their DePaul-bound star, Curtis Price, that Pelinka was able to change those minds.

In April 1988, Pelinka accepted a scholarship to Michigan. The Wolverines were coming off an NCAA Tournament appearance and boasted a loaded roster featuring six future NBA players. They won the championship in Pelinka's first year on campus, but the size and speed of the competition overwhelmed him. He spent most of the season on

---

* Eggers, who remains in contact with Pelinka today, declined to be interviewed for this book. Through a spokesperson, however, he described Pelinka's high school story as "very accomplished." What exactly does that mean? Eggers, through the spokesperson, declined to elaborate.

the bench, scoring just 29 points all year, but he didn't complain or mope. The way he carried himself impressed his teammates.

"He was always smiling and always encouraging us," Terry Mills, a star junior big man on that team, said. "When someone was having a bad day, he was the kind of guy who'd come and put his hand around you."

Pelinka redshirted his sophomore season to gain an extra year of eligibility. He figured the longer his college career lasted, the better the chances that he could crack the rotation. That plan was derailed when Michigan coach Steve Fisher landed the Fab Five, one of the best recruiting classes in college basketball history. The arrival of that group, led by future NBA players Chris Webber, Jalen Rose, and Juwan Howard, and the ensuing hype changed the landscape at Michigan. The Fab Five were the stars, the players around which everything revolved, relegating the upperclassmen, including Pelinka, to the background.

Some of the older players struggled to adjust. A few considered transferring. It took Pelinka some time, but he eventually found his place. He had other plans for his life, anyway. "He was one of the only guys on the team who seemed to know and understand what his goals were for after basketball," Michael Talley, a Michigan teammate, said. At the top of that list was receiving a law degree from a top school. To get there, Pelinka decided to re-create his high school routine. "He would go to practice and study, and that was it," Eric Riley, a center who spent four years with Pelinka at Michigan, said. "All the years I went to school with him, I never saw him at a frat party. He was more of a loner."

Pelinka read books on flights. He took meticulous notes in class and submitted twenty-page papers. He kept a diary. In his teammates' eyes, he came to represent his own category of a person: a "Rob Pelinka–type." They mocked him. But they also liked him. He went hard in practice and, as the best shooter on the team, gave the starters fits during scrimmages. Rose, whom he was often matched up against, would talk trash, calling him "white boy" and telling him to "get your ass back on the bench." But Pelinka didn't back down, and by his senior year he'd earned a spot in the rotation. He averaged nearly 16 minutes per game that season, with his dad making the five-hour drive east on I-94 for every home game. Pelinka had a few big moments, too, including drilling a pair of three-pointers in Michigan's 1993 championship game loss to UNC. That year, he received NCAA's highest academic honor, the NCAA Walter Byers Postgraduate Scholarship, an award given annually to two student-athletes.

After graduating, Pelinka enrolled in law school at the University of Michigan. There, he became close with a tax law professor named Douglas Kahn, who happened to be close to sports agent Arn Tellem, a Michigan Law graduate himself. Around 1998, Tellem told Kahn he was looking to add an additional lawyer to his group, which was on the verge of being purchased by SFX Entertainment and turned into SFX Sports. Khan recommended Pelinka, who at the time was working in the Chicago office of the white-shoe law firm Mayer Brown. Pelinka jumped at the opportunity and, in his rusty Jeep, made the move out to LA, where SFX's offices were based.

There, Pelinka thrived. He was smart and worked hard, and his writing on contracts and internal documents was clean, clear, and concise, something that Tellem, who earlier in his life had worked as a stringer for the *Philadelphia Bulletin,* valued. That Pelinka was a former player helped him connect with the athletes, too. Little by little, Tellem gave him more responsibility, including helping manage one of his top clients: Kobe Bryant.

Around two years after Pelinka arrived, Kobe proposed to his girlfriend, Vanessa Laine. The news infuriated Kobe's family. He was just twenty-one years old. Even worse in their eyes, Laine was an eighteen-year-old senior in high school who made money dancing in music videos. That she was Mexican American and not Black bothered them, too.

Bryant's family begged him to break off the engagement. He refused. They pleaded with him to push it off. He refused again. They urged him to sign a prenuptial agreement. So did Tellem, who'd represented Kobe since he declared for the NBA draft in 1996. Kobe didn't budge, and the arguments over Laine grew toxic. When Kobe and Vanessa got married in April 2001, none of his relatives attended.

Not long after, Tellem was promoted to CEO of SFX Sports. The added responsibility meant he had less time to run point for clients. He assigned Pelinka to Kobe. Pelinka was a talented agent who had gotten to know Kobe well. That he hadn't objected to Kobe's marriage—nor, like Tellem, had he pushed him to sign a prenup—made him a favorite of Vanessa's, too.

Pelinka started managing nearly everything for Kobe. Whether it was publicity inquiries or marketing deals or Lakers business or family affairs, it all went through him. "Rob became the gatekeeper," Sam Rines, Kobe's AAU coach, said. "He was the guy that kept control and handled everything." Kobe was a difficult client at the time, arrogant and stubborn and demanding, but Pelinka had the skills, patience, and, most of all, the desire to ride out the different moods. He didn't believe it was his place to push back on a client's wishes. In his view, the job was simple: "Service is the No. 1 thing we provide," he'd tell colleagues.

Whenever the Lakers called with an issue, Pelinka would come to Kobe's defense. When a sponsor or a brand pitched an idea, Pelinka would listen to Kobe's opinion before offering his own, which almost always echoed what Kobe had shared. And when Kobe was charged with one count of felony sexual assault in July 2003, a scandal that would temporarily turn him into a cultural pariah and cost him sponsorship deals with McDonald's and Coca-Cola, Pelinka stood by his side, his face visible in all the footage of Kobe entering and exiting the courthouse.

Being Kobe's Guy boosted Pelinka's profile. But, while he added several clients to his roster, he didn't go chasing fame. He mostly kept his name out of the media and showed no interest in building relationships with NBA reporters. He'd be cordial whenever one introduced themselves, take whatever business card he was handed, and then not return calls. He did, however, do one interview in March 2004 with *The Ann Arbor News*. When discussing why he'd become an agent, Pelinka said, "I looked at it as a challenge of going into that business and being a person of integrity." He added that he "was determined to make a difference in people's lives. I look at myself as being someone who has integrity and honesty, and I want to bring that to these relationships." At one point in the story, reporter John Heuser shared what Pelinka had recited as his favorite non-work activities. The list included pickup basketball, hiking in the mountains, and also "the theater" and "reading books such as Tolstoy's *War and Peace*."

A few months later, it was time for Pelinka to finalize an extension for Carlos Boozer, a second-round pick for the Cavaliers who, two years earlier, had emerged as one of the steals of the 2002 draft. Coming off a season in which he averaged a double-double while playing alongside LeBron, the twenty-two-year-old Boozer looked like a future All-Star.

But as a former second-round pick, he'd earned a total of only $913,000 in his first two years in the NBA, making him one of the league's most underpaid players. His contract included a team option for the following season, which, if picked up, would pay him a meager-by-NBA-standards $695,000. So in the lead-up to free agency, Boozer and the Cavs came to an agreement. The Cavs would decline the option and then, using their mid-level exception, re-sign Boozer, who'd be made a restricted free agent (meaning the Cavs would have the right to match any offer he received) to a six-year deal worth around $40 million, the most a team was permitted to hand one of its second-round picks. It was less than Boozer would be eligible to get in unrestricted free agency the following summer, but he'd be financially set for life and insured against a possible injury. The Cavs, meanwhile, would lock in a cornerstone at good value. It seemed like a win-win.

On July 1, the first day players and teams were allowed to negotiate, the Cavaliers declined Boozer's option. As soon as the news was announced, Pelinka called Boozer. "He was like, 'There are four teams drooling over you,'" Boozer recalled years later. The teams weren't just willing to beat the Cavs' number—they were throwing out offers that would surpass it by more than $20 million. Boozer wanted to stay in Cleveland but felt he had no choice. "What was I supposed to do?" he recalled. "Those kinds of numbers are not things you can turn down." On July 8, he agreed to sign a six-year, $68 million offer sheet with the Jazz, one Cleveland had no realistic means of matching.

Cavs owner Gordon Gund and general manager Jim Paxson were furious. So much so that, the following week, hours after Boozer signed the offer sheet, Gund posted a letter to the Cavs website explaining the team's side of the story.* "I decided to trust Carlos and show him the respect he asked for," Gund wrote. "He did not show that trust and respect in return." According to Gund, Boozer and Pelinka had first approached the Cavs about working out a long-term deal in December 2003. The two sides, Gund said, had multiple meetings over the next few months, culminating in a June 30 sit-down. Boozer, his wife, and Pelinka all attended, and according to Gund, he and Paxson had offered to not exercise that one-year, $695,000 option "if we had the

---

* Apparently this is the go-to move for Cavaliers owners after a player leaves in free agency.

understanding with [Boozer] that as soon as legally possible he would negotiate a contract with us for the maximum we could pay him under league rules."

According to Gund, Boozer, Boozer's wife, and Pelinka left the room to talk things over. Upon returning, Gund said, Pelinka relayed that "he had again explained everything to them so that they understood everything involved and said that their thinking had not changed."*

For the first time in his professional life, Pelinka was at the center of a controversy. Even worse, it was his integrity that was being questioned—the very thing he had told *The Ann Arbor News* that he valued most—and not just by the Cavaliers. Owners and executives across the league condemned Pelinka to each other and, anonymously, in the press. So did rival agents, never a timid group when presented an opportunity to tear down one of their own. "I'd resign immediately if a client wanted to renege on a deal, even a verbal one," one agent told ESPN's Chad Ford. "I still believe integrity in this business matters. If you agree on a deal, you have to live with it, no matter what else happens."

Years later, Pelinka would insist that he'd done nothing wrong. In fact, he'd say, he'd actually demonstrated integrity; before Boozer officially signed his new contract, Pelinka had terminated the partnership, costing himself a multimillion-dollar commission in the process. In Pelinka's retelling, he'd done nothing except fulfill his fiduciary responsibility of presenting his client with every offer on the table. If Boozer went back on *his* word, that was his decision to make—Pelinka's job was simply to facilitate his clients' desires and get them paid, and in Boozer's case, he'd done that. Others would later point out that Pelinka was far from the first agent to renege on a verbal agreement at their client's behest.

But it was one thing for a free agent to change his mind in the interregnum between a verbal agreement and putting pen to paper. What happened with Boozer was different. It wasn't a simple change of heart but, rather, an act of deception. The Jazz were only able to make their offer because Boozer and Pelinka had first verbally agreed to a separate deal with the Cavaliers. Had they not, the Cavaliers would never have

---

* I reached out to Jim Paxson to get his side. He replied that he and Gund "both agreed never to talk about it"—the Boozer negotiations—"publicly again."

let him out of his contract. Also, in his retelling of the story years later, Pelinka would leave out two key details: One was that, before he met with Gund and Paxson, Tellem told Pelinka that if he reached an agreement with the Cavs, he would have to honor it, even if other teams called with more lucrative offers. The other was that Pelinka had parted ways with Boozer only after Tellem, worried about SFX's reputation and wanting to make it known that he and his agency would not profit from unscrupulous behavior, had forced him to do so.

In January 2006, Tellem bought his agency back from SFX and sold it to Wasserman Media Group, a management and entertainment behemoth run by Casey Wasserman,* grandson of the famous movie mogul Lew Wasserman. During the sale, Wasserman met with all of Tellem's agents. Most of these meetings went well. His chat with Pelinka, who he felt came off as overly ambitious, did not. More damning, though, was what the other SFX agents had to say about Pelinka. They told Wasserman that he rarely collaborated on projects, that he didn't share information, that he didn't work well with others, that he cared only about himself. "Most people would pitch in on things regardless of whose name was on the certification," a former SFX agent said. "But Rob worked independently. He didn't want anyone getting near his clients."

Pelinka planned on going to Wasserman with his colleagues but wasn't offered a job. When Tellem's sale was completed, Pelinka remained at SFX. By this point, Kobe had regained his perch atop the basketball world. That January he'd scored 81 points in a game against the Raptors—the second most in a single game in NBA history—and he'd finish the season leading the league in scoring, his first time doing so. His legal troubles were behind him, too. The sexual assault charges were dropped in September 2004—his accuser refused to testify—and in March 2005 the two parties settled a civil case. All this paved the way for an image reset, one that sponsors were eager to embrace. That February, Nike ran its first-ever televised ad for Kobe.

The time was right for Pelinka to go out on his own. He launched

---

* "We had many breakfast meetings," Tellem told the Associated Press at the time, "but I told him"—Casey Wasserman—"he had me at the first bite of matzoh brei." I'm aware that the majority of readers won't have any idea what a matzoh brei is, but those who do will enjoy this.

Landmark Sports Agency. Kobe came along. Not only had Pelinka stuck by him after his arrest, but he also understood Kobe in a way most didn't. In many ways, they were similar, two loners who had sacrificed social lives in the pursuit of professional goals.

For Kobe, Pelinka was one of the few people he knew he could trust—and one of the fewer people whom Vanessa trusted, too.

For Pelinka, Kobe was one of the few people in the world for whom it was worth carving out time.

When Pelinka got married in 2005, Kobe and Vanessa read scripture at the wedding.

When Vanessa gave birth to the couple's second child a year later, they named Pelinka her godfather.

"Rob was as much a part of their family as anyone," said a former colleague of Pelinka's. "And whether it was swimming with sharks or random incursions, any harebrained idea that Kobe came up with Rob would be along for the ride."

Over the ensuing decade at Landmark, Pelinka recruited some of the league's biggest stars, including Kevin Durant and James Harden. He was good at connecting with players. "He just asked me about my life and told me about his,"* recalled Andre Iguodala, whom Pelinka recruited out of Arizona in 2004 and who went on to win four NBA titles. Iguodala's first meeting with Pelinka took place at a Ping-Pong table on campus. "It was the first time in the process of looking for an agent that I could just relax," he added. "He treated me like a human being and not a cash cow." When negotiating new deals for veterans, Pelinka made a point of involving them into the process, often having them speak directly to GMs.

But his rise in the industry put a target on his back. He never quite shook the accusations of dishonesty leveled against him from the Cavaliers, and the more he sat across the table from teams, the more that reputation grew. He became known as someone whose word could not

---

* I feel the need to point out here that my experiences with Pelinka were similar. The Lakers did not cooperate with this book, and there were people within the organization (from high-level executives down to a member of the PR staff) who were not shy in hiding their disdain for both me and this project. Yet every time I saw Pelinka—on the court before a game, in the hallway after a game, walking around the gym at a scouting event—he was friendly and inquisitive.

be trusted, an agent who'd say one thing in a meeting and then change his stance in a subsequent phone call.

"There were guys in the business who you could do a deal with at the [annual draft] combine in May and know that you're good until July," one former general manager said. "But Rob was never one of those." (The Lakers representative described this portrayal as "false" and "defamatory.")

The way Pelinka carried himself didn't help matters, either. Sure, he'd say hello to ushers at Lakers games and ask about their kids, but those weren't the stories that got passed around in gossipy league circles. He became known as someone who ignored lower-level team executives. He'd started regularly referring to his faith and quoting scripture, acts that many in and around the NBA found disingenuous. Same with all the SAT words he'd drop into casual conversations. Even some of his strengths were twisted into slights. His ability to connect with different people from different backgrounds was one of the skills that made him a successful agent, but it also led to people in the NBA world describing him as a "chameleon."

By the spring of 2016, Pelinka was thinking about making the transition to the team side of the business. The constant recruiting trips to college towns were grating on him, and, with Kobe retiring that season, there was nothing but money tying him to the job. The Lakers were the obvious target. "He was already looked at like a de facto executive," a rival general manager said. It had started back in 2004, when, during the team's search for a Phil Jackson replacement, Pelinka called up Duke head coach Mike Krzyzewski to gauge his interest. The closer Kobe grew to Jeanie, the closer she and Pelinka grew, too. After Kobe retired, the three often got together for lunch.

In January 2017, Jeanie began laying the groundwork for a front office shake-up. Around that time, rumors began circulating inside the Lakers' building that Pelinka was angling for the GM job. At the same time, he started asking his Landmark employees more pointed questions about the Lakers' salary cap situation and draft pick inventory. Not long after, Jeanie started recruiting him to work alongside Magic. "I need somebody who understands agents and trades and the collective bargaining agreement," she told him at one point. "Somebody like . . . you." Intrigued, Pelinka discussed the opportunity with Kobe over drinks in Newport Beach. "I know how you work. I know how locked in you are. I know you're a chess player," Pelinka recalled Kobe telling him. "I think you'll have the Lakers back winning the championship in two to three years." Pelinka was in—he just needed to ensure that he and Magic, who had no previous relationship, could get along.

A few weeks later, the two, both in New Orleans for the NBA's annual All-Star weekend, talked things over. The meeting went well, and on Sunday, Pelinka flew back to LA, skipping that night's game despite Harden, his most important client, being an All-Star starter for the first time. The next day, Pelinka asked his staff to meet him in the office at around 8 a.m. There, he shared that he was leaving for the Lakers. At 3:36 p.m. West Coast time, Wojnarowski broke the news. It wouldn't be official for a month, but, after nearly two decades representing players, Pelinka had switched sides. His life as an agent was over. His days of operating in the shadows were, too. He was now the general manager of the Los Angeles Lakers. And with that job came a spotlight that was bigger and brighter than any he'd ever been under.

• • •

Pelinka was formally introduced as the Lakers' new GM at a press conference on March 10. "This is truly [an] exciting day that I can finally know that my running mate is here," Magic proclaimed. Pelinka then spent the next ten minutes introducing himself. He talked about restoring the Lakers back to their "proper place of being the gold-standard franchise in all of sports." He quoted a verse from Jeremiah: "For I know the plans I have for you, plans to prosper you and not to harm you, plans to give you hope and a future." He name-checked every Lakers power broker, from Jeanie to Magic to Linda Rambis to Tim Harris to, of course, Kobe, who, alongside Vanessa, was in attendance.[*]

On the surface, the Magic-Pelinka pairing seemed like a perfect fit. Magic was a franchise legend with a big personality who would represent Jeanie's reset and could focus on big-picture items, like recruiting stars. Pelinka was a longtime agent with relationships across the league and experience running a business who, it was assumed, was familiar

---

[*] "What Michelangelo is to art, what Beethoven is to music, what Shakespeare is to words, you are to me as a friend, and you are to the Lakers, so thank you," Pelinka said of Kobe.

with the nitty-gritty of the NBA's collective bargaining agreement and salary cap rules.

The Lakers, it appeared, had turned over a new leaf. The days of infighting and ineptitude would be a thing of the past.

"When I thought about who I wanted to really start this journey with, and who could I pick that would complement my style and the way I am and also who is strong where I'm weak—it was no other than Rob," Magic said during the press conference. He added that he also wanted his GM to be "someone who understood the Lakers and what it means to represent the Lakers."

"Rob," he pointed out, "knows that better than anybody out here."

But the honeymoon phase didn't last long. Pelinka might have spent years running his own business, but Landmark was a small shop, one built around him and his whims. Being the general manager of an NBA team was entirely different. Pelinka was now the steward of an iconic franchise and charged with overseeing numerous departments and hundreds of employees. *I can't believe how many meetings I have to be in,* he told a friend shortly after taking the job.[*] When it came to making lower-ranking staffers feel seen, Pelinka excelled. He handed out T-shirts with slogans; volunteered for community relations initiatives, like the team's "Adopt a Laker" mentorship program; and sat with different staffers at lunch. But when it came to connecting with his underlings in the team's basketball operations department, it was a new chapter of the same story: Pelinka, the lifetime loner, unsure of how to work with others.

Only once in his first couple years on the job did he invite his scouts to a group lunch; when he did, he ordered his meal before anyone arrived and left shortly after they sat down. One time he led a game of icebreakers and the "fun fact" he shared about himself was that he once beat President Obama in a game of H-O-R-S-E, an anecdote that drew eye rolls; others had shared more mundane tidbits like their respective birth countries. He'd show up in the locker room before games—even after associate head coach Brian Shaw, who'd known Pelinka for

---

[*] "That is not something that [Pelinka] said or would say," the representative said. "He understood then and understands now that his job includes attending numerous meetings with his staff, Lakers management, players and agents, and others."

years, told him that most GMs steered clear of that area. He'd pop into coaches' meetings—even after Walton told him that no other GMs did.

He also became known around the building as someone whose word couldn't be trusted. Part of it was that he was different from most NBA lifers. "I'm a bit of a storyteller," was how he'd described himself in his introductory press conference, and in his first couple years in the job, he lived up to that billing. "I would venture to guess there's people in the room that are familiar with the stories in the book of Genesis," Pelinka told reporters at a press conference to announce the signing of Caldwell-Pope a few months later. "Where there was a time when the Israelites were wandering in the desert and, all of a sudden, bread came down from heaven.* That's kind of what today feels like for us, to have KCP join." During a 2018 press conference after signing LeBron, he put on reading glasses, took out a copy of the novel *The Alchemist*, and read a passage out loud: "But the young boy was able to understand one thing: making a decision was only the beginning of things. When someone makes a decision, he is really diving into a strong current that will carry him to places he had never dreamed of when he first made the decision." When trying to explain to reporters prior to the 2018–19 season what it was like for the Lakers' young players to learn from LeBron, Pelinka said, "I think of this story—I don't know if it's an ancient tale of old—of this young kitten that's running around in the jungle, and it sees a bobcat and it says, 'Oh, it's a bigger cat, it must be a lion.' So it starts mimicking the bobcat and thinks it's become the king of the jungle. A year later, along comes a male lion and the little cat says, 'Oh my gosh, I didn't realize that's what a lion's roar was until I saw and heard it, so now I know how to become a lion.'"

Yet the more time his colleagues, employees, and players spent with him, the more they began suspecting that he wasn't just telling tales but taking liberties with the truth. Like the time Pelinka told a story to the team about Kobe being wowed by Heath Ledger's performance in *The Dark Knight* and asking Pelinka to arrange a dinner with the actor, which Pelinka said he did—even though Ledger had died six months

---

* It's worth pointing out that this food, known as manna, appears in the books of Exodus, Numbers, and Deuteronomy, but never in Genesis.

before *The Dark Knight* was released.* And, the thinking went, if Pelinka was willing to fabricate and exaggerate when it came to more trivial matters, then when exactly could he be trusted? Walton became so wary of Pelinka that he began insisting that meetings with him include a third person. He'd either bring Shaw or make sure Jeanie attended.

"He kept feeling like he and Rob would discuss something and agree, and then Rob would go off in a completely different direction," a member of Walton's coaching staff said. "So Luke figured the only way to keep that from happening was having someone else in the room." Players had similar experiences. One example came during the first half of the 2017–18 season, when the Lakers waived veteran center Andrew Bogut four days before his contract became guaranteed. "The Lakers told me I'd be there the whole year," Bogut told the *Mercury News'* Mark Medina a year later. "They went against their word." (A Lakers representative denied this allegation, claiming that "no NBA player with an agent would ever sign a non-guaranteed contract if they had been told they were getting a guaranteed contract.")

Within a year, Pelinka and Magic were butting heads, too. Part of the problem was Magic's lackadaisical approach to the gig, which, given his fame and stature, became fodder for the NBA's insatiable gossip machine. Stories illustrating Magic's seeming indifference made the rounds. They'd eventually make their way back to Magic, who was told that his GM was the one spreading them. A favorite among league insiders was when Spurs executive R. C. Buford noticed, during a tour around the Lakers' new facility, that Magic's office didn't have a desk. Confused, he asked Pelinka about it.

"Earvin's not really a desk guy," Pelinka replied.† It was an attempt to cover for his boss, not bury him, but "Earvin's not really a desk guy" became a favorite line among those in NBA circles looking to mock Magic, and it was always attributed to Pelinka.

LeBron's first season with the Lakers being a disaster only com-

---

* Kobe would later say in an interview that Pelinka "got confused . . . I didn't go out to dinner in New York. I stayed in my room . . . I stayed up watching *Batman,* and watching Heath Ledger. And then I went and started researching about Heath Ledger, and how he got into character and how he just became all-consuming."

† This story was confirmed by multiple sources. When reached for comment, a Spurs spokesperson said, "R.C. has no knowledge of the anecdote."

pounded these issues. It was one of the most embarrassing seasons in franchise history—not only had they missed the playoffs, but they'd snapped LeBron's streak of eight straight finals appearances—and both Magic and Pelinka worked hard to pin the blame on others. Especially when speaking with Jeanie.

The poor play? That was all Walton's fault.

The negotiations for Anthony Davis, which had derailed the season? That was the media's fault, with Jeanie, taking the cue from her leadership group, at one point describing the reports about the negotiations as "fake news."[*]

Other missteps, like the decision to surround LeBron with creators instead of shooters, Pelinka laid at Magic's feet. Pelinka may not have had clients anymore, but that didn't mean his days of catering to people were over. He still had a boss. The only difference now was that it was an owner, not a player, whom he was trying to keep happy.

One move Pelinka made was empowering Linda Rambis, Jeanie's close friend, in a way no Lakers basketball executive ever had. He looped her in on basketball discussions and had her join him on late-night conference calls with agents. (The Lakers representative said, "No such calls ever took place.") He green-lit the hiring of Gunnar Peterson, a trainer to the stars and friend of the Rambis family, as the team's new director of strength and endurance training. Peterson had trained elite athletes like Tom Brady and Pete Sampras but was known best for his work with celebrities like Sylvester Stallone and Kim Kardashian.

"Kurt and Linda had been pushing the Lakers to hire him for years," a person familiar with the Lakers' inner workings said. "Rob was the first executive to say yes."[†]

And so when it came time to replace Magic at the top of the organi-

---

[*] "[That] we were supposedly trading our entire roster for a certain player . . . is completely not true," Jeanie said on a panel at the 2019 MIT Sloan Sports Analytics Conference. Technically, she was right. The Lakers had offered only half their roster to the Pelicans.

[†] The Lakers representative said Linda Rambis "had nothing to do with [Peterson] being hired" and that she had "no input into the decision" to do so. The representative added that "although Gunnar Peterson had been an acquaintance of Rambis's years earlier, he was by no means a 'family friend' or anything close to it." Given this response, I feel that it's worth mentioning that Peterson has told at least one person that Kurt Rambis is the godfather to his oldest son.

zation, it was clear to Jeanie that Pelinka was the one for the job. She'd heard the stories about him but believed them to be part of a smear campaign executed by rival agents still scarred from their recruiting battles with Pelinka and jealous of his success. And anyway, Pelinka had basically spent the past couple of years acting as team president. He was the executive calling other teams and speaking to agents and scheduling meetings and mapping out future strategies. Why not just make it official?

·   ·   ·

After the 2019 season, and in light of Magic's resignation, LeBron and Rich Paul met with Jeanie and Linda Rambis to discuss the state of the franchise. As part of that, they shared their thoughts on Walton.

"The message was, 'No offense to him, but what are we doing here?'" a person familiar with the meeting recalled. Soon after, the Lakers announced in a press release that a "mutual decision" had been made between them and Walton and that the two sides were parting ways.

With Magic gone, it was now up to Pelinka to run the team's coaching search. At Jeanie's behest, he enlisted Kurt Rambis, and the two put together a list of potential candidates. It included Jason Kidd, a Hall of Fame point guard coming off a four-year run as the head coach of the Milwaukee Bucks; Monty Williams, a widely respected former player and 76ers assistant who had previously coached the Hornets/Pelicans; and Miami Heat assistant (and Pelinka's former college teammate) Juwan Howard.

But one candidate among the group stood out.

Tyronn Lue was everything the Lakers were looking for in a head coach. He won two rings with the Lakers as a player and one with Cleveland as LeBron's coach. He was genial and fun—during the NBA's annual summer league in Las Vegas, he could often be found holding court at a craps table in an upscale casino—and a brilliant tactician, serious about his work and craft. He was beloved around the NBA and, most of all, by LeBron, who respected the way Lue challenged him. One time in 2016, not long after Lue had taken over for the fired David Blatt, LeBron tried hijacking a mid-game huddle, a regular occurrence during Blatt's stint, only to be told by Lue, "Shut the fuck up, I got this."

Later that season, with the Cavs trailing by seven at halftime of Game 7 of the finals, Lue, frustrated with LeBron's passive play on offense and lazy defense on Warriors forward Draymond Green, scolded him in front of the team. The Cavs went on to win the game and the title.

Lue, who had been let go by the Cavs at the beginning of their post-LeBron rebuild, was interested in the job, too. The day after parting ways with Walton, the Lakers reached out to Lue's representatives. Five days later, Lue met with Pelinka for ninety minutes in Newport Beach, where Pelinka lived. The next week Lue spoke on the phone with LeBron, who wanted Lue to get the job. Lue then did a formal interview at the Lakers' facility, where he illustrated to Pelinka, Kurt and Linda Rambis, Jeanie, Jesse and Joey Buss, and Tim Harris how he'd succeeded with LeBron in the past. He believed LeBron was at *his* best when playing within a structured offense and that LeBron's teams were at *their* best when others on the floor were given room to thrive. He pointed out as an example that during the 2016–17 season, Kyrie Irving had actually led the Cavs in shots per game.

Lue's pitch impressed the Lakers, but they figured dragging things out could help in contract negotiations. They were also wary of the optics; they didn't want it to appear like they were just capitulating to LeBron.

The equation changed on the morning of May 3 when Williams, the only other candidate the Lakers had interviewed twice, was hired by the Suns. Around that time, both Magic (who had recently told TMZ that, despite quitting his job with the Lakers just a few weeks earlier, he still talked to Jeanie "almost every day") and Phil Jackson (another man with whom Jeanie had a complicated relationship and yet from whom she still sought out advice) had told Jeanie to hire Lue.

That Friday, after learning about Williams's decision, the Lakers reached out to Lue's representatives. The two sides began discussing a contract, and the news leaked to the press. Most people around the league assumed that the negotiations would go smoothly and be completed quickly and that Lue would soon be back at the helm of a LeBron-lead team. After all, it was hard to imagine a more ideal match.

The Lakers, however, decided to take a different approach. They liked Lue, but not enough to pay him a market rate. They refused to offer anything more than a three-year, $18 million contract, a shockingly low figure for a coach with a title on his résumé. Williams, who had never made it to the finals as a coach, had just received a five-year deal from the Suns.

This fiscal approach wasn't out of character for the Lakers, who, under Jeanie, had developed a reputation for penny-pinching. Wages for entry-level staffers were so low that some had to work second jobs to make ends meet. Staffers sometimes paid for their own travel to summer league.* Mid-level members of the front office weren't immune, either. In 2019, Antawn Jamison, a two-time All-Star who had been working as a Lakers scout, informed management that the Wizards had offered him a better and higher-paying job. He told the Lakers he wanted to stay, as long as they matched the deal. "And they told him, 'We don't feel like we need to match because you made so much money as a player,'" a person familiar with the inner workings of the Lakers' front office said. Jamison disagreed with that logic and left.

These accusations of stinginess infuriated Jeanie. Sometimes she'd deny the charges. "We paid a luxury tax the last few years," she told an interviewer in the fall of 2023, referring to a mechanism instituted by the league to promote competitive balance by penalizing high-spending teams. "Like, how does that equate to how the Lakers operate, except that someone's trying to create a false narrative about me doing things on the cheap?"† Sometimes she'd lament that no one had seemed to care when her father had made cost-cutting moves. But the most revealing responses came whenever she or a surrogate attempted to explain the

---

* "Not covering expenses for personnel who have not been asked to attend or work at summer leagues and other events and who are nonessential but who have nevertheless chosen to attend for their own purposes is not 'penny-pinching,'" the Lakers representative said.

† So, funny story: In this case, that someone "trying to create a false narrative" was me. This quote came from a 2023 interview Jeanie did with a reporter named Graham Bensinger. Bensinger was complimenting her for "not nickel-and-diming players" (Frost-Nixon, this was not), and Jeanie's response was, "There's somebody that's out there writing a book, and he said to me that I have a reputation of running a bare-bones organization." I had been told by Jeanie that our conversations were off the record, but since she referenced me in an on-the-record interview, I figured why not provide the full context here? Also, don't blame the messenger; all I was doing was relaying the reputation and giving her a chance to respond.

Lakers' approach. "If you want to call this [a] bare[-bones] organization, I like to think that we're efficient," Jeanie said in that same 2023 interview. "We don't have a lot of waste and are not gonna spend needlessly." The negotiations with Jamison were a perfect example. "One person believing he ought to get paid more does not evidence 'penny-pinching,'" the Lakers representative said. "It merely evidences . . . perhaps why the Lakers valued this individual's contributions less than he valued himself."

This was the essence of Jeanie's philosophy. She was willing to spend, but only on people and things that she and her inner circle deemed worthy. Some coaches might have fallen into that category. Lue, in their view, did not.

As negotiations with Lue's representatives progressed, the Lakers made a number of additional demands. One was that Pelinka and Kurt Rambis would have final say on Lue's coaching staff, with Rambis at one point asking how Lue would feel about having him on his bench. The Lakers also insisted that Lue hire Kidd, who had impressed Pelinka and Rambis during his interview, as an assistant.

"Since Lue had experienced a medical situation in Cleveland the prior year and had ended up missing a good portion of the season it was important to make sure that there would be seasoned coaches on the bench if that recurred," the Lakers representative said, even though Lue's medical absence had occurred two seasons earlier and even though he'd missed only nine games that season. After he experienced multiple episodes of chest pain in March 2018, doctors recommended that Lue take time off. He did, but he returned less than three weeks later and led the Cavs to a title. The Lakers representative added that Kidd was merely "recommended," not "insisted upon."

Lue was angry and offended. Championship-winning head coaches were almost never treated this way. But the Lakers refused to budge. For one, Rambis, who had coached Lue in LA nearly twenty years earlier, believed Lue's success in Cleveland had more to do with the talent of those Cavs teams than his ability as a coach. Jeanie, meanwhile, believed the Lakers held the power and that if Lue truly believed in his ability as a coach, he should take the job, win, and earn an extension. And Pelinka, still new to the job, wasn't going to push back on either opinion.

"Coaching for the Lakers is a uniquely special opportunity—as well as a uniquely challenging assignment—and the Lakers routinely give coaches three-year deals to see if the match is right," the team representative said. "There is nothing wrong with that. The inference that Lue was treated less favorably than other candidates is inaccurate, and the suggestion that he should have been treated more favorably than other candidates is not in keeping with the Lakers' ethics or organizational values."

On the afternoon of May 8, five days after the two sides had begun negotiations, Lue's representatives informed the Lakers that they were done. Multiple reporters were told as well. The Lakers tried getting ahead of the news, telling the *Los Angeles Times* that they had decided to move on, but it seemed clear what had occurred.

Furious, LeBron called Lue.

"He said, 'What do I gotta do? You want this?'" Lue recalled. "And I said, 'No, I want them to respect me, I don't want to have to go to you to get my deal done. If they don't respect me like I should be respected, then it's okay.'"

• • •

With Lue out, the Lakers added a few new candidates to their search and quickly homed in on former Indiana Pacers and Orlando Magic head coach Frank Vogel. An NBA lifer, Vogel got his big break in the summer of '94, when, after three years of playing point guard for Division III Juniata College, he convinced Kentucky—then led by head coach Rick Pitino, a future Hall of Famer—to bring him on as a student manager. Vogel endeared himself to Pitino and his staff by volunteering for everything and doing whatever was asked, whether it was cutting up film, playing point guard for the junior varsity team, or teaching assistant coach Jim O'Brien how to use the school's new digital editing system despite not knowing how to use computers himself.

In May 1997, Pitino left Kentucky for the Celtics. He brought both O'Brien and Vogel with him—O'Brien as an assistant and Vogel to be a video coordinator. Vogel remained in Boston until 2004, when he left with O'Brien, whom the Sixers hired as their head coach. Vogel then followed O'Brien to Indiana in 2007. In 2011, in the midst of a disappointing 17–27 campaign, the Pacers fired O'Brien and named Vogel interim head coach. Vogel led them to the playoffs that season, ending a four-year drought.

Vogel built the Pacers in a specific image. Defense was emphasized, often in meticulous, multi-hour film sessions. He preached physicality. Sometimes he asked his big men to put on weight. *A team might beat us,* he'd tell his players. *But if they do, it's gonna be while we're beating them up.*

Where he separated himself, though, was with his ability to combine this old-school approach with a fun-loving, energetic attitude. He had a soft spot for goofball comedies like *Airplane* and *Spaceballs,* and he'd often splice clips into film sessions. He believed in building players up as opposed to tearing them down. "Even when he chewed us out," Pacers forward David West said, "he'd do so in a way that would give us confidence. It would be like, 'I can't believe you don't see that you're better than everyone out on that court.'" It was how, despite being just thirty-nine years old and having no playing background, Vogel was able to earn the respect of a veteran-heavy group. He led the Pacers to the playoffs in four straight seasons, and in 2013, Indiana nearly knocked off the LeBron-led Heat in the Eastern Conference finals, pushing the defending champions to seven games.

Vogel lasted six seasons in Indiana before Larry Bird, the Pacers' president of basketball operations—who had long believed that most coaches lose their standing within the locker room after three years—let him go. His plan was to take the year off. Then he received an offer from the Magic. The gig wasn't a good one. Orlando had missed the playoffs in four straight seasons and had a roster full of overpaid veterans and busted draft prospects. Yet Vogel felt like he couldn't say no. "Frank has a real humility about these sorts of things," said a coaching friend of his. "His view is that there are only thirty of those jobs, and so if someone calls and gives you the chance to take their team over, you better fucking do it." The Magic went 29–53 in Vogel's first season, leading to the firing of general manager Rob Hennigan, who had hired Vogel. One year later, Vogel was out, too. He spent the 2018–19 season visiting with different coaches throughout the league and was on the verge of being hired to serve as one of Lue's top assistants when the negotiations between Lue and the Lakers fell through.

Vogel had impressed Pelinka and Rambis in his interview. And they liked his playoff experience. Even better, though, was that he was willing to take whatever they were offering.

Three-year deal?

Fine with him.

Have his staff chosen for him?

All good.

Name Kidd his lead assistant, even though most assumed Kidd would soon be gunning for his job?

Fine with him.

Either I'm going to end up in the Hall of Fame, Vogel told a friend, *or I'm going to get fired in two years.*

The two sides agreed to a deal on May 11. An introductory press conference was called for May 20. The plan was to celebrate Vogel's arrival, talk about how excited everyone was, and spit out some upbeat bromides signifying a new day.

That morning, as the Lakers were preparing for the press conference, the TVs in the facility were tuned to ESPN. At around 7:30, staffers saw Magic Johnson appear onscreen. It was his first public appearance since quitting.

"Let's get right to it," ESPN's Stephen A. Smith said as soon as Magic found his seat. "What the hell happened? Why did you resign from the Los Angeles Lakers?"

"Well, there was a couple of reasons," Magic said. But first, he wanted to provide some context. He explained why and how he'd originally taken the job. He talked about the cap-clearing moves he'd made, and the drafting of Ball and Hart, and how he'd set the Lakers up to sign LeBron.

"Things got going in the right direction [during my first season]," Magic said.

Preamble finished, he was now ready to unload.

"And then I started hearing, 'Magic, you're not working hard enough; Magic's not in the office,' " he said.

Then came the kicker.

"People around the Laker office was telling me," Magic said, "Rob was saying [these] things." Later, he added, "When I took the job, you know how many agents called me and said, 'You've got to watch out for him'?"

Magic wasn't only there to talk about Pelinka. He had thoughts on every key Lakers executive.

Joey and Jesse Buss?

"I had to monitor the brothers," Magic said. "[They] wanted more involvement, more power."

Tim Harris?

"I didn't like that Tim Harris was too involved in basketball. He's supposed to run the Laker business, but he was trying to come over to our side. Jeanie's gotta stop that."

Jeanie?

"Jeanie will always make the final decisions, but she huddles up with Linda Rambis, and probably now, I think Phil Jackson advises her a little bit, and now Kurt Rambis is home . . . you've got to empower somebody. And then have everybody who has a role with the Lakers stay in that role."

It was a wild interview, and with a press conference scheduled for later that day, the Lakers were left scrambling. Vogel was no longer the story. Pelinka and the *Game of Thrones*–like nature of the Lakers' front office was. Before heading out to greet the media, Pelinka, who was set to join Vogel on the dais, pulled his new head coach aside.

I'm gonna get all these questions, he told Vogel. *If you get asked, just say you're focused on your role here.*

Back in the media room, Lakers beat reporters huddled. There were so many questions to ask, most of which had nothing to do with Vogel being named head coach, and the group wanted to make sure they were all on the same page. Soon after, Pelinka and Vogel took their seats at the dais. LeBron, who had come to watch, found a spot in the back of the room. Pelinka introduced Vogel. He listed the qualities that had impressed him and Rambis. Vogel explained what excited him about the job and how he planned to approach it. The Lakers opened the floor to questions. The first three were softballs ("How surprised are you to be sitting here today?" "How emotional a day is this for you and your family?" and a question about his emphasis on defense), which Vogel handled with ease. Then the mic was handed to Tania Ganguli, a no-nonsense reporter from the *Los Angeles Times*.

"Rob, Magic Johnson did an interview this morning in which he said that he felt like you betrayed him when you guys were working together," she said as Pelinka nodded along. "What was your reaction to him saying that, and do you believe that's a fair assessment of your relationship?"

Next up was ESPN's Dave McMenamin. "Frank, congrats and welcome to LA," he said.

"Thank you," Vogel replied.

"Rob, question for you, though," McMenamin said. He brought up Lue and Williams. "All due respect to Frank," he said, "but there were other people you intended to hire before him."

The next two questions were for Vogel. Then *The Athletic*'s Bill Oram took the mic. "Can you please explain the front office structure?" he asked Pelinka. "And then can you explain Kurt Rambis's role?" One reporter asked Pelinka if he was worried that Magic's characterization of the Lakers might scare away potential free agents. Another asked Pelinka whether, in the wake of Magic's comments, he was concerned about his reputation taking a hit around the league. Another asked whose decision it was the previous year to ignore Luke Walton's advice and let Randle and Lopez walk in free agency. The *Los Angeles Times'* Plaschke wanted to know about "the chain of command" and where Linda Rambis "fit into the equation."

Nine minutes passed without Vogel receiving a question. He put on a good face, occasionally smiling, sometimes nodding. Pelinka, visibly annoyed, tried steering things back to his new head coach—"First and foremost, we do want today to be about Coach Vogel," he said in his response to one of the questions—but the media and Lakers fans were more concerned with the internal dynamics of the team's front office.

Pelinka spent the press conference downplaying the issues Magic described. He said Magic was an "unbelievable person to work with" and that it was "saddening and disheartening to think he believes things are a misperception." He claimed that Vogel had always been one of the team's coaching candidates and added that "he's the right guy for this job." He said it was great having Kurt Rambis around and described him as a "valuable resource." As for who was in charge? "When it comes to a basketball decision," Pelinka said, "I collaborate with the staff . . . and then I make a recommendation to Jeanie, and she blesses that or not."

He also acknowledged that the only way for the team to shift the focus away from off-court drama was to "do what the Lakers do . . . win."

Before that, though, he and the Lakers were confronted with more controversy. Eight days after the press conference, ESPN published a story by reporter Baxter Holmes illustrating the depths of the Lakers' dysfunction. According to Holmes, an "ex-Lakers star," when talking about the team with a confidant, had said, "It's fucking crazy over there." The piece depicted Rich Paul as a meddling agent who'd spent the year burying Walton. And, citing "multiple Lakers staffers," Holmes wrote that Pelinka's penchant for " 'storytelling' . . . is viewed as disingenuous—at best." He relayed Pelinka's concocted Heath Ledger story, which went viral.

And yet, despite it all, Pelinka and the franchise still had LeBron. As long as he was there, they'd have a shot. All they needed now was to find his wingman.

•　　•　　•

Anthony Davis may have ended the 2018–19 season in a Pelicans uniform, but that didn't mean he'd changed his tune: His feelings were once again made clear when he showed up to the final game of the season in a white T-shirt with three words on the front: "That's all, folks!"*

The Pelicans, who had fired general manager Dell Demps in February, were now being led by David Griffin, the former general manager of the Cavaliers. Griffin knew Paul well from his time in Cleveland and hoped that relationship would give him a chance to change Davis's mind. The Pelicans had also won the draft lottery, meaning they now had the No. 1 pick. "We can hold on to [Davis] and let him see what we really are," Griffin told ESPN's Zach Lowe after the lottery. They could use it to take Duke star Zion Williamson, the most hyped prospect since LeBron, or trade the pick and get Davis some help.

Davis didn't care. He didn't take any of Griffin's calls; all communication from the Pelicans was funneled to Paul. Sensing that there was

---

* When he was asked about the shirt later that night, Davis said, "I actually didn't choose it. It was hanging for me already when I put my clothes on . . . Every night, Big Shot"—apparently the nickname of one of Davis's friends—"lays out what I'm gonna wear to the game. I have no control over that. I just put it on." I don't know about you, but I'm sure sold.

nothing else to be done, Griffin pivoted. His goal became maximizing the return in a Davis deal.

Pelinka reached out around the start of June, after hiring Vogel. He and Griffin began exchanging offers. Winning the lottery made things easier for Griffin. Even without Davis, the Pelicans would still have Williamson, a foundational piece they could build around. Surround him with some good, young talent, and add some future draft picks to the war chest, and the Pelicans could be one of the most well-positioned teams in the league. It helped that the Lakers had also jumped in the draft lottery—they now owned the No. 4 pick, giving them one more asset to dangle in a deal.

Griffin and Pelinka spent a few weeks going back and forth. Before long, they agreed to some basic parameters: In exchange for Davis, the Pelicans could get three of the Lakers' four best young players—Ingram, Ball, Kuzma, and Hart—plus some draft assets.

"The Lakers didn't really push back on anything or negotiate too much," a then–Pelicans executive said. "They just wanted AD."

Griffin knew that both LeBron and the Lakers could be shortsighted. He started pushing Pelinka for more. First, he insisted on not taking back any extra players; because he was short-selling their future, he didn't want to help the Lakers clear cap space to go after a third star. He also told Pelinka that he wanted pick swaps, a simple tool used by NBA front offices to sidestep the "Stepien Rule," which was implemented in the late '80s to prevent teams from trading out of the first round in consecutive years. Named for former Cavaliers owner Ted Stepien, who had crippled the franchise by trading five straight first-round picks, it was supposed to protect teams from themselves.

When Griffin floated the idea of pick swaps, Pelinka said he'd consider it. A few days later, the two spoke again. Griffin then convened his front office in a conference room to provide an update. He told the group that the conversation had taken an odd turn. According to multiple Pelicans basketball operations staffers, Griffin said Pelinka had told him that Jeanie Buss didn't know what pick swaps were. At first, Griffin assumed this was just a bargaining ploy; after all, it was common for GMs to blame their owners for holding up negotiations. But then, Griffin told his group, Pelinka posed a question: If their roles were reversed, how would Griffin go about explaining pick swaps to his boss?

Upon hearing this story, the Pelicans' front office burst into laughter.*

The Lakers, however, weren't worried about minutiae, and they certainly weren't going to let something as seemingly trivial as pick swaps get in the way of their latest star pursuit. Especially Jeanie, who remembered how her father had fawned over Davis during Davis's Kentucky days. This was a franchise built on the backs of star pairings. Magic and Kareem. Kobe and Shaq. LeBron and AD would be next in line. "Ultimately, it was my decision to push the button," Jeanie said years later. On June 15, just two days after the Raptors knocked off the Warriors in the finals, the Lakers and Pelicans agreed to terms. The Pelicans would get Ball, Ingram, Hart, and three first-round picks. They'd also get the right to swap picks in 2023.†

"AD on da way!!" LeBron posted on Instagram that night. "Let's get it bro! Just the beginning.👑 #LakeShow." The deal would become official on July 6, when the league's free-agent moratorium ended.

With the Davis deal done, the Lakers were ready to move on to the next phase of their plan: using their remaining cap space to sign a third star, preferably Kawhi Leonard, an LA native who had just led the Raptors to a title and, after being named the finals MVP, was entering free agency.

Except the Lakers had made a mistake. Had Pelinka insisted that the deal be completed on July 30, he could have drafted the No. 4 pick for New Orleans. Then, once legally allowed to trade that drafted player thirty days later, Pelinka could have used his salary in the Davis deal. Through a series of complex salary cap rules, this would have allowed

---

* The Lakers representative said, "To make it appear that [Jeanie] does not understand basketball and that she needs 'mansplaining' to inform her about pick swaps is false [and] outrageous." The representative added that any "assertion that Pelinka did not understand pick swaps sufficiently to explain them to Jeanie Buss" is "outrageous" and "falsely portrays Pelinka as unknowledgeable about NBA contracts— something that no one has ever claimed about him and is utterly ludicrous to suggest about one of history's most successful basketball agents."

† The Pelicans would use those picks to draft or trade for the following players: Jaxson Hayes, Nickeil Alexander-Walker, Didi Louzada, Herb Jones, and Dyson Daniels. Daniels turned into one of the best defensive players in the NBA. Jones became a premier role player. Louzada washed out of the NBA. Hayes became an end-of-the-bench afterthought. Alexander-Walker turned into a solid reserve.

the Lakers to operate as an "over the cap" team and created $32.5 million in cap space, enough to sign a player to a max contract.* By failing to do so, Pelinka and the Lakers had only $27.7 million in available cap room, a number that dropped to $23.7 million once Davis's $4 million trade kicker—a bonus written into his contract by Klutch—was applied. They'd spent the year preparing to pursue Leonard, even instructing members of their training staff to outline a maintenance plan, and now they wouldn't have the means to do so.

The error was immediately spotted by league insiders and reporters; ESPN highlighted it in its initial report on the trade. To get a third star Pelinka would now need to both find a way to turn the Lakers into an "over the cap" team *and* somehow convince Davis to waive his trade kicker.

Pelinka went to the Pelicans, but they refused to expand the deal. So he began working the phones. Finding a trade partner to offload some additional contracts was the easy part; doing so would just require the Lakers to surrender a pick or two. But the conversations with Paul and his negotiator, Mark Termini, over Davis's kicker were more complicated. Termini wasn't going to let Davis give up $4 million without getting something in return. Over the next couple of weeks, Termini and Paul spent hours on the phone with Jeanie, Pelinka, and Linda Rambis. Pelinka's salary cap expert, Marshall Rader, and Kurt Rambis occasionally hopped on. The Lakers' case was simple: They believed they had a strong shot at signing Leonard, but only if Davis played ball. If he didn't, they pointed out, he'd be hurting LeBron's championship prospects.

Neither Termini nor Paul believed Leonard was interested in joining the Lakers, but, on the off chance they were wrong, they were willing to help clear a path. So they proposed a deal. Davis would waive his trade kicker, but if the Lakers' didn't get Leonard, they'd re-sign Caldwell-Pope. Termini's reasoning was simple. Caldwell-Pope was both a Klutch client and, given his skill set, the perfect player to slot alongside LeBron. The Lakers agreed to the deal and, after being briefed by Termini and Paul, Davis, who was thrilled to be heading to LA and joining a championship contender, was happy to go along. Pelinka then sent a 2022

---

* If these sentences hurt your brain, just know that you're not alone.

second-round pick to the Wizards to persuade them to take on the contracts of reserves Moritz Wagner, Isaac Bonga, and Jemerrio Jones.

In early July, Leonard agreed to a contract with the Clippers, who, at his behest, had also traded for Paul George. The Lakers responded by agreeing to a two-year, $16.6 million deal with Caldwell-Pope (which included an $8.5 million player option for the 2020–21 season) and used their remaining cap space to add a bunch of veterans, like Rondo and McGee. They brought in Danny Green, a wing with two rings coming off a season in which he'd finished second in the league in three-point shooting percentage.

Pelinka might not have put together a Big Three, but, one year after the Lakers had whiffed on nearly every one of their roster decisions, he had surrounded LeBron with a team that made sense. The Lakers had role players who could both shoot and defend. They had veterans. They had a coach with playoff experience. And, in Davis, he had delivered LeBron his Robin. The journey to this point had been rocky. But neither the Lakers nor LeBron had ever been process-oriented. Both were about results, and, despite a year of mishaps, a title was now within grasp.

8

A LION'S PRIDE

Training camp hadn't even begun, yet Laker players had gathered in Las Vegas to get a head start on the season. A few weeks earlier, in their group chat, LeBron had told his teammates that they'd all been brought together to win a championship. In order to achieve that goal, he wrote, he was organizing a run in late September, the week before the team's official camp began.

The entire roster came to Vegas. The Lakers sent some assistant coaches, but it was LeBron's show. He walked around the gym and corrected mistakes. "Don't take it personal, just take it with you," he'd say. He arranged and paid for team dinners. He posted GIFs in the group chat, like a pride of lions walking together through the jungle.

It was a far cry from his approach the previous season, when he seemed disinterested from the start. Part of it was that, with Davis, LeBron knew the Lakers had a championship-caliber roster. But missing the playoffs for the first time in fifteen years had also motivated him. He wasn't going to let himself fall short again, and he wasn't going to take days off. It was why, having committed to spending his summer filming the new *Space Jam* movie, he had a gym built on the Warner Bros. Studios lot. "He'd come onto the set in his workout gear half the time, and whenever he had a few minutes between scenes, he'd be doing some sort of work on the side, like getting a massage," said Malcolm D. Lee, the director of *Space Jam: A New Legacy.* It was why, despite having the opportunity in the spring to disconnect from basketball in a way he hadn't since entering the NBA, LeBron instead spent that time watching every minute of every playoff game, thinking about "what play would I have made in that moment if I was out there."

The good vibes carried over from LeBron's mini-camp into Lakers training camp. It helped that, unlike the previous summer, Pelinka had filled the roster with veterans, bringing back Rondo, Howard, and

McGee while also adding, among others, Danny Green. These were players who'd been around for years. Some were former All-Stars. A few had won rings. None were intimidated by LeBron. They viewed him as a peer.

During training camp, the group came up with LeBron-specific rules, like allowing him to take one play off on defense every game. "But we told him that anything more than that and we'd get on him," Jared Dudley, a veteran forward signed that summer, said. DeMarcus Cousins, a former All-Star coming off multiple injuries who had signed by the Lakers, would mock the stench of the durag LeBron wore every day to practice. Rondo would call out any favorable whistles LeBron received in scrimmages.

I know he's been busting your ass every time down the floor, Rondo once shouted at a staffer after LeBron, having spent the entire run complaining about missed calls, received a phantom whistle on a potential game-winning layup. *But you can't just give the man the game.*

Coming out of camp, everyone within the organization felt great about the team's prospects. The Lakers were slated to begin their preseason in San Francisco on October 5, then head to China for a pair of exhibition games against the Nets. The country, with its millions of basketball-crazed fans, had become one of the NBA's most lucrative markets, and almost every year since 2007, the league had sent a pair of teams on a barnstorming tour. It was a grueling trip, but one many players seemed to enjoy. China was a gold mine, a place where they could land seven-figure endorsement deals and boost shoe sales through local appearances. Few understood this better than LeBron, who'd visited the country at least once in each of the previous fifteen years, usually on trips organized by Nike.

The plan was to depart LAX on Monday, October 7; land in Shanghai on Tuesday; face the Nets the next day in Mercedes-Benz Arena; fly two hours south to Shenzhen; play the Nets again on Saturday; and then head home. A number of ancillary events, like press conferences, receptions with dignitaries, and appearances with the league's social responsibility program, NBA Cares, would be sprinkled in between.

Those plans were derailed when, the week before, Rockets general manager Daryl Morey tweeted an image that expressed support for pro-democracy protests unfolding in Hong Kong. The tweet, seen as being critical of the Chinese government, ignited a firestorm and jeopardized the league's relationship with the country. Both CCTV, China's national television broadcaster, and Tencent, one of its largest broadcasting companies, announced that they would cease showing games. Sponsors pulled their support for the Lakers-Nets exhibitions. Billboards and posters promoting the games were taken down. All media events and meet-and-greets were canceled. Morey's tweet, which was later deleted, and the subsequent reaction, drew headlines in every corner of the media and became fodder for America's publicity-hungry politicians. It also thrust the NBA into a position it had spent years trying to avoid. When it came to China's poor human rights record, the league's strategy had been simple: Stay quiet and steer clear. Thanks to Morey's tweet, that would no longer work. The public had questions, and politicians were taking sides.

And the players had no idea what to do.

Upon arriving in Shanghai, NBA commissioner Adam Silver called a meeting in a ballroom of the Ritz-Carlton, where both teams were staying. He spoke for about ten minutes. He told the players that around two hundred reporters would be arriving at the hotel in a few hours and that he wanted them to answer questions. He said that one of the NBA's core values was freedom of expression and that if the players declined to speak to the media, they'd be opening themselves up to criticism.

LeBron, annoyed, raised his hand. First off, he wanted to know why Morey hadn't been punished; had a player done the same thing, LeBron said, discipline would have been issued. More than that, though, LeBron wanted to know why Silver was putting the onus on the players to answer for Morey, especially if Silver himself wasn't taking questions. After about thirty minutes, Silver and other executives left the room so that the players could discuss the issue among themselves. LeBron led the meeting. Outside, Nets and Lakers executives—and especially Pelinka—made the same case to Silver that LeBron had. Not long after, Silver told the players that they didn't need to speak with reporters.

The Lakers flew home that weekend. For the NBA, the trip had turned into a disaster, but for the Lakers, it would come to represent something else. Seeing how both LeBron and Pelinka had stood up to Silver on their behalf had buoyed the players, and all the cancellations meant more time for bonding at the hotel. The Lakers had overcome adversity and emerged stronger on the other side.

It would become the defining trait of their season.

• • •

The Lakers opened the regular season in Los Angeles with a much-anticipated matchup against the Clippers. Both Davis and Kawhi Leonard were making their official debuts with their new teams (Paul George was sidelined with an injury). The Clippers, officially the home team and therefore in charge of the scoreboard, used the designation as an opportunity to troll their LA rivals. Before the game, messages like "Grit Over Glam," "Squad Over Self," "We Over Me," and "Street Lights Over Spotlights" flashed across the screen. The Lakers played well, but the Clippers, and specifically Leonard, played better, walking off with a 112–102 victory.

After the loss, a reporter suggested to LeBron that the Lakers had failed their first "test" of the season.

"I disagree," LeBron replied. "I disagree on how big of a test it was. It's the first game . . . We're a new group that's coming together. We have a new coaching staff. We have a new system."

The Lakers responded by winning their next four games. The last of those victories came against the Mavericks in overtime, after Vogel had drawn up a play—a crosscourt pass from LeBron into the right corner—setting up Green for a buzzer-beating three at the end of the fourth quarter. The players had already bought into Vogel as their leader, but that basket solidified their belief in him. "That was a big moment for both sides," Kidd, an assistant coach, later told ESPN. "Players learn they can trust the coach, and the coach learns he can trust his players."

Just a few months into his tenure it was apparent that, while Vogel may not have been the Lakers' first choice to coach the team, he was indeed the right one. The way he obsessed over even the smallest details impressed LeBron and the rest of the veterans. He was also a brilliant defensive tactician whose preferred style of defense—stay home on three-point shooters and funnel everything to the giants at the rim—was the perfect match for the Lakers' roster, which now featured multiple elite rim protectors.

But what the players loved most about Vogel was how open he was to feedback. He ran ideas—from schemes to the practice schedule—by LeBron, Davis, and the team's other veterans and didn't mind when LeBron or Rondo interrupted a session to go on a twenty-minute tangent about X's and O's. When the players asked to change some of his defensive terminology to what they'd used in the past—like shouting "ice" when on defense and trying to direct pick-and-rolls down to the sideline because that was what LeBron's teams in Cleveland had always used; Vogel's teams always used "blue"—Vogel happily obliged.

The Lakers won seven straight before losing to the Raptors at home. They followed that up with a 10-game winning streak and then, after a home loss to the Mavericks, another seven in a row. When mid-December rolled around, they were 24–3, tied for the best record in the NBA. They owned the league's third-best defense. LeBron once again looked dominant and spry—he finished second in an early-season MVP straw poll of NBA writers conducted by ESPN—and he and Davis, just a couple of months into their partnership, were thriving alongside each other.

Nurturing that partnership had been a priority of LeBron's. It had started in the offseason, when LeBron challenged Davis in a way few had. Davis had been eager to train with LeBron, but whenever he arrived at the Lakers facility, LeBron would already be done with his morning routine.

One day, Davis pulled him aside.

I thought you said if I came here we'd get to work out together, he said.

We can, LeBron replied. *If you get here at 7:30 instead of 9:30.*

So Davis started doing exactly that. At first, it wasn't easy for him. "You'd look in the weight room early in the morning, and you'd see AD there with a face of, 'I really don't want to be here,'" Troy Daniels, a wing signed in the offseason, said. But Davis kept showing up, and before long had adopted LeBron's routine. They lifted weights together. They shot together. They stretched together. "They were attached at the hip," Dudley said. Davis was quiet by nature but grew more confident and vocal as the days went by. And LeBron, recognizing the role his new costar would need to play if the Lakers were going to make a title run, made it a point to feature Davis once the season began. "If we are not playing through Anthony Davis while he is on the floor, then there's no sense to have him on the floor," he told reporters in September. LeBron still controlled the offense but was running things in a different way; two months into the season he was leading the league in assists, something he'd never done. The approach was paying off. Davis's defense was as dominant as ever, and he was leading the Lakers in scoring.

Meanwhile, most of the veterans Pelinka had signed were fulfilling expectations. "Everyone who came in knew that they were brought in for a specific reason," Green said.

He and Caldwell-Pope provided more shooting and wing defense. Howard and McGee controlled the paint. Avery Bradley, a veteran guard, smothered opposing ballhandlers.

And then there was Jared Dudley, the glue holding the entire operation together.

A thirty-four-year-old forward in his 13th NBA season, Dudley was acutely aware of his limitations. He no longer possessed the legs or speed to command regular minutes for a true championship contender. But he was a savvy veteran respected by his peers and wanted to spend the final years of his career playing for a team where he and his skills would be valued. He wasn't ready to transition into coaching, but Dudley hoped that there was an opportunity for him to play a hybrid role.

After becoming a free agent the previous summer, Dudley called both Paul and LeBron and had his agent reach out to Pelinka. His pitch was simple. "It was basically, 'Hey, let me hold down the locker room,'" Dudley said. "LeBron has to worry about so much stuff. So I told him, 'Let me do all the little stuff.'"

It was the perfect role for Dudley, who had survived in the NBA because he was both one of the league's smartest players and most well liked. "Jared's thing was always, 'I'm going to come in, I'm going to play some defense, hit a three or two, move the ball, and that's it,'" Jason Richardson, who played with Dudley in Charlotte and Phoenix, said. "He wasn't trying to be anything more than that." He was also a great hang. He talked a lot of trash and spoke fast and wasn't much for filtering his thoughts. But, Richardson added, "He knew when it was time for jokes and when it was time to be serious."

The Lakers and Dudley agreed to a deal on the third day of free agency. His impact was evident as soon as training camp began. "Duds came to practice every day like it was Game 7 of the finals," Lionel Hollins, a former NBA player and head coach who had joined Vogel's staff, said. "It set the tone." As promised, he policed the locker room. If a player wasn't spending enough time in the weight room or getting up enough shots on off days, Dudley would say something. If one of the veterans like Howard was being obstinate, Dudley would call them out. If LeBron got annoyed at Rondo or Kuzma for not giving up the ball on a fast break, Dudley would pull them aside. *You gotta give him the ball,* he'd tell them. *You know that.*

"You could shoot a bad shot or mess up sometimes," Dudley said. "But there were nonnegotiables that every player had, and if you messed one of them up, it was my job to say something before the coach even got to them." It didn't matter that he wasn't part of the regular rotation. Because he'd been around so long, his voice carried weight. It was also clear that he was there to help his teammates, not just chastise them. During halftime of games, he'd huddle with teammates to break down matchups and share insights. If a rehabbing player needed help simulating game-like settings, Dudley was willing to come in early or stay late. If the group was tired, Dudley was the one passing the message along to the coaching staff and suggesting a day off.*

"He basically became a liaison between us and the players," said one of Vogel's assistants.

Dudley was always looking for ways to build team camaraderie. In the air, that meant running card games. Booray—best described as a mix of poker, hearts, and spades—was the game of choice, with pots occasionally reaching $50,000 and nearly half the team joining in. "Everyone would be talking trash the whole time," Dudley said. LeBron played, too, though he was known as one of the more conservative players.

On the ground, it meant organizing parties. Dudley wasn't the only one on the team who liked going out. LeBron loved arranging group dinners, often brought teammates to exclusive events to which he'd been invited, and sometimes hosted lavish parties where attendees were required to sign nondisclosure agreements. And Kuzma had become a regular around Hollywood's social scene, too. "I once went to a party with Kuzma where, like, [rapper and actor] Lil Dicky and some other famous people were there," Daniels said. "And the next morning he texts me like, 'Welcome to Kuz World.'" But Dudley was different. His specialty was finding new spots, like a bowling alley on the road or

---

* He also made everyone laugh. A favorite among the group was the way he'd turn to the Lakers bench and shout, "I'm the best verticality guy in the league," whenever he stymied a shot at the rim, a reference to a league rule that allows defenders to make contact with shooters near the basket as long as they keep their entire body vertical. "All the players," one Lakers assistant said, "would crack up."

a hotel in a place like Salt Lake City that was willing to hand over its entire top floor. "And he'd somehow get like a hundred women to show up," a Lakers staffer said.

"At the beginning of the year, everything was all businesslike and tense because it was championship or bust, and everyone was feeling that," Dudley said. "But you can't survive if it's like that all the time. The season is too long."

The team was winning, and the vibes were great. When the Lakers suffered their first losing streak—a four-game swoon toward the end of December—nobody panicked, not even LeBron, who over the course of his career had become known for his mood swings and passive-aggressive reactions to periods of tension. "We'd all heard about that stuff and were waiting for it," Dudley said. "But it never happened." Instead, Daniels said, "[LeBron] went around saying how it's a long season and he was with us to the end. He'd be like, 'All these mother-fuckers talking shit about you, writing about you—they're not in the gym with you putting in this work.'" The Lakers responded to that losing streak by winning nine in a row. As the season progressed, Vogel grew more and more impressed with LeBron's play, IQ, and leadership.

"He's just a fucking machine," he told one coaching friend over mid-season beers.

It was the best the Lakers had looked in nearly a decade. Jeanie, thrilled, extended Pelinka's contract *and* promoted him; he was now the vice president of basketball operations and general manager.

In late January, with Staples Center preparing to host the Grammy Awards, the Lakers boarded a flight for their annual midwinter road trip. Over the course of ten days, they made stops in Houston, Boston, New York—where they faced the Knicks and Nets—and then Philadelphia, where, midway through the third quarter, LeBron passed Kobe for third-most points in NBA history. It was a historic milestone, and a symbolic one, the latest legend to wear a Lakers uniform surpassing perhaps the greatest.

After the game, each star paid tribute to the other. "Seeing him come straight out of high school, he is someone that I used as inspiration," LeBron told reporters. "He helped me before he even knew of me because of what he was able to do." Kobe, meanwhile, congratulated LeBron on Twitter. "Continuing to move the game forward @King-James. Much respect my brother 🐍." Later that night, the pair spoke on the phone. LeBron put the call on speaker so the rest of the team could listen in.

It had taken years for the relationship between the two to reach this point. LeBron, like most basketball-obsessed kids from his generation, grew up idolizing Kobe. The two met a few times while LeBron was in high school, and Kobe was always receptive and genial. On one occasion, he gifted LeBron a pair of his shoes.

But his outlook changed when LeBron entered the league. "You just sensed that Kobe was someone who didn't really want to be fucked with," LeBron once said. Kobe was cold to most players—the competitor in him couldn't fathom the idea of an adversary seeing him with his guard down—but his rejection of LeBron was rooted in something different. In LeBron, Kobe saw a threat. This was the man being hailed as the NBA's future king. "They were pitted against each other for so long, and everyone was always saying that LeBron was going to be better," said a person who worked closely with Kobe. "Kobe heard it all, and it pissed him off."

The way LeBron carried himself bothered him, too. Unlike Kobe, some of LeBron's closest friends were rival stars. Unlike Kobe, LeBron talked a lot about money and off-court goals. Unlike Kobe, LeBron was a pass-first player who was happy to give the ball up in big moments if it meant a teammate getting a cleaner shot. They were both Nike athletes but spent time in different circles. LeBron worked with the executive Lynn Merritt, whom he'd met while in high school. Kobe was close with Nico Harrison, one of Nike's marketing gurus who later became the company's vice president of North American operations.

"Kobe's a[n] asshole," Dwight Howard once said. "[LeBron] want[s] everybody to like him, he want[s] to joke around, laugh, have a good time. I just think they [are] two ends of the spectrum."

It wasn't until the two played alongside each other at the Beijing Olympics in 2008 that the relationship thawed. Kobe was the elder statesman of the group, but LeBron, recognizing that Team USA needed Kobe engaged and involved, took it upon himself to break down his walls.

"I understand Kobe is serious as hell when it comes to work," he later said of his approach, "but he wanna smile, too; he wanna feel accepted, too."

That meant imitating the way Lakers public address announcer Lawrence Tanter would introduce Kobe before games. And mocking the sort of hand signals Kobe would flash during games ("All that means," LeBron would say, "is get the hell out of the way"). And interrupting a group meal so that, when Kobe turned thirty on August 23, every player and staff member could serenade him with a rendition of "Happy Birthday," despite Kobe repeatedly telling the team beforehand not to do anything to mark the occasion.

It also meant occasionally reeling Kobe in. During an exhibition game against Australia, LeBron got annoyed at Kobe's shot selection and, while walking by head coach Mike Krzyzewski, said, "Yo, Coach, you'd better fix that motherfucker." Another time, after showing up to the gym with the rest of the team following a group breakfast and seeing that Kobe had already wrapped up his own individual workout, LeBron pulled Kobe aside.

"He was like, 'We all know what you're about, but if we're trying to get this gold back to the United States, we need to do things together,'" Tayshaun Prince, a fellow member of that year's Olympic Team, said. "Kobe didn't have people talk to him like that. But he saw that LeBron was doing it and recognized his leadership and what he was trying to accomplish."

Team USA went on to win gold that summer. Kobe still wasn't interested in being friends, and LeBron remained scarred from the way Kobe had kept him at arm's length. But the two had gone to battle together and emerged victorious. With that came a lifelong bond.

After retiring in 2016, Kobe kept his distance from the Lakers. He still spoke regularly with Pelinka, but the only game he attended in his first two years away from the team was in December 2017 when the Lakers retired his numbers. He took part in the ceremony and then left early.

LeBron's arrival had brought him out of the shadows. Kobe came to one game during LeBron's first season in LA and twice in 2019. The two always embraced on the sideline. Whenever asked, Kobe denounced Lakers fans who were slow to embrace their team's new star. "Appreciate this guy, celebrate what he's done, because it's truly remarkable," Kobe told the *Los Angeles Times*' Plaschke in January 2020, days before LeBron passed him on the all-time scoring list.

"The two were really starting to build a relationship," a person close to LeBron said.

That night he overtook Kobe, LeBron had inscribed "Mamba 4 Life" and "8/24 KB" on his sneakers in gold marker. "Just to be able to, at this point of my career, to share the same jersey that he wore, be with this historical franchise, and just represent the purple and gold, it's very humbling, and it's dope," he told reporters afterward.

The Lakers lost to the Sixers that night, but they'd won three of their five games on the trip. The next morning, they boarded the team plane at Philadelphia International Airport. Once in the air, some of the guys played cards. Most shut their eyes. The Lakers were 36–10 and headed home. In just a few hours, they'd be stepping out onto the tarmac at LAX, where they'd be greeted with warm weather and sunny skies.

• • •

Davis was watching *Avengers: Endgame* on his iPad when he noticed Howard and Cousins scurrying around a few rows in front of him. He looked up. Howard called him over.

Davis removed his noise-canceling headphones.

Man, Kobe died, Howard said.

The news began making its way around the plane. Players reached for their phones. Davis made his way over to the still-asleep LeBron to share the news.

Man, y'all stop playin'—like, stop playing with me, LeBron said.

He spotted Howard, whose eyes were welling up with tears.

It's true, Howard said.

Jeanie, on the ground in LA, confirmed the news, then informed the team's director of media relations, Alison Bogli, who was on the flight. Bogli told Vogel. Vogel made his way to the front of the plane and told the players.

Some details started making the rounds. A helicopter crash in Calabasas. Kobe was on board. Vanessa was not. Those were the confirmed facts. The rest was unknown. Was anyone else with him? If so, who? Rumors were swirling. Matt Gutman, the chief national correspondent for ABC News, interrupted the network's broadcast of the NFL Pro Bowl to report that all four of Kobe's children had died. Former Lakers forward Rick Fox's name started trending on Twitter.

LeBron gathered the players together. He had no words. All they could do was pray.

"Even though at times we question him and question why he do some of the things that he do, know that [God's] never made a mistake," he later told ESPN when recounting the words he shared. "And just hope that he has his hands on top of Vanessa and the kids at that time, and hope that he continues to watch over all of us."

As the Lakers approached LA, more details were confirmed. Nine people were on board. Kobe, the pilot, and seven passengers. One of them was Kobe's thirteen-year-old daughter, Gianna. They were headed to Kobe's Mamba Sports Academy.

The Lakers landed at around 2 p.m. local time. They were welcomed by foggy skies. The players, shoulders slumped, descended the airstairs and walked onto the tarmac. Most had their sweatshirt hoods pulled over their heads. Jeanie and Pelinka had driven out to Orange County to be with Kobe's family, but other Lakers executives greeted the group. LeBron, wet tissue in hand and sunglasses on, embraced those who knew Kobe best, like Howard, who'd played alongside Kobe in LA; and Davis, who'd grown close to Kobe while playing for Team USA in 2012; and assistant coach Phil Handy, who'd also worked for the Lakers from 2011 to 2013; and Kurt Rambis, who'd known Kobe since he was a teenager.

By the evening, the full story had emerged. Kobe frequently traveled by helicopter to avoid traffic, and just the day before had made the same trip north from his home in Newport Beach to Thousand Oaks, where his academy was based, turning a two-hour drive into a thirty-minute commute. The group was going to a youth basketball game. The helicopter had taken off despite dense fog blanketing the area that had grounded other flights. It had crashed into a hillside and caught fire near a biking trail in Calabasas.* All nine people on board had died, including the pilot, Ara Zobayan. There were three children on board, including Gianna. One, Alyssa Altobelli, was flying with both her parents, John and Keri. Another, Payton Chester, was flying with her mother, Sarah. The group was accompanied by a coach from the academy, Christina Mauser, a mother of three.

The news shook the entire country. "Kobe was a legend on the court

---

* Rick Fox being on board turned out to be an unfounded rumor. Gutman later apologized for his inaccurate report that all four of Kobe's children were on board. ABC News also suspended him.

and just getting started in what would have been just as meaningful a second act," Barack Obama posted on Twitter. "To lose Gianna is even more heartbreaking to us as parents. Michelle and I send love and prayers to Vanessa and the entire Bryant family on an unthinkable day." Taylor Swift wrote, "My heart is in pieces hearing the news of this unimaginable tragedy." Moments of silence were held during that day's NBA games. The Spurs and Raptors opened their game with back-to-back twenty-four-second violations in honor of one of the two jersey numbers Kobe wore. The Atlanta Hawks opened their game with an eight-second backcourt violation in honor of the other. The Grammy Awards, held that night at Staples Center, opened with a moment of silence for Kobe and featured multiple tributes. Thousands of fans gathered outside the arena, filling the plaza with flowers, jerseys, candles, and makeshift memorials.

The NBA postponed the Lakers' next game. Two days after landing, the team gathered at the practice facility. The organization brought in grief counselors. Over a two-hour lunch, players and staff members stood up and shared memories and stories. Robert Lara, a Lakers security official who worked closely with Kobe, spoke. LeBron told a story about how, at the start of the 2008 Beijing Olympics gold medal game, Kobe elected to send a message by knocking Spanish big man Pau Gasol, his Lakers teammate, to the ground.

You're going to have to play with this guy next season, LeBron told the room he recalled thinking.

The group laughed. The group cried. A toast was made in Kobe's honor.

"It helped us out a lot," Dudley recalled. "It helped [us] not move on but to just to get everything out."

On January 31, five days after Kobe's death, the Lakers took the floor for their first game back. Usher sang "Amazing Grace." While Boyz II Men sang the national anthem, cameras showed LeBron, lips pursed, tears streaming down his cheeks.

Soon after, he stepped to center court and took the microphone.

He looked at a small piece of paper on which he'd written a speech.

Then he tossed it away.

"I'm going to go straight from the heart," he said.

He talked about "Laker Nation" and how, over the previous few days, he'd learned that it was "truly a family." He said the night should be about celebrating the player and person Kobe was and the father he had become. He talked about what Kobe meant to him.

"I want to continue, along with my teammates, to continue his legacy not only for this year but for as long as we can play the game of basketball that we love, because that's what Kobe Bryant would want," he said. "So in the words of Kobe Bryant, 'Mamba out.' But in the words of us, 'Not forgotten.' Live on, brother."*

The Lakers fell to the Trail Blazers that night, 127–119. But the season had taken on a new meaning. They were no longer playing for themselves. Nothing mattered more to Kobe than winning, so what better way to honor him and his legacy than bringing title No. 17 back to LA? LeBron even got the words "Mamba 4 Life" tattooed on his thigh.

The group reeled off nine wins in 10 games, and then four in five games, a streak that included victories over the Philadelphia 76ers, Milwaukee Bucks, and Los Angeles Clippers, three of the league's top teams. "After that," recalled Alex Caruso, a third-year wing who had emerged as a key contributor, "we kind of had the realization where if we play how we know we can play, we can get it done."

The Lakers were rolling. They were big and talented and versatile and deep and looked to have destiny on their side.

The only thing that could stop them, it seemed, would be if the games themselves ceased being played.

---

* It's worth bringing up that a few weeks later the Lakers held a memorial service for Kobe, and all indications are that LeBron was not there. No one saw him in the Staples Center during the event, and, when asked by ESPN's McMenamin the following day if he had attended the ceremony, LeBron responded, "I respect your question, for sure. It was [a] very emotional, very emotional day, very tough day for myself, for my family, for everyone involved." In April 2025, Pablo Torre, a podcaster and pundit, reported that he had spoken to eight sources "who are directly familiar with this situation" and that his conclusion was that LeBron had not attended the ceremony. It's also worth pointing out, though, that it's unclear why LeBron did not attend and whether staying home was his decision or something he was asked to do by someone connected to Bryant.

9

BUBBLE BOYS

Even the suggestion offended LeBron. "Play games without the fans?" he asked while standing before a group of reporters. "Nah, that's impossible."

It was March 6, 2020, and, after spending the previous three months spreading from China into Europe, Covid-19 had finally reached the United States. The country's first confirmed case had come seven weeks earlier, but by the time the Lakers took the Staples Center court on this March night, that number had reached the hundreds. Public health officials were stressing the importance of handwashing and social distancing—the latter a term most in the public had never heard—and all indications were that things were about to get worse. Earlier that day, the NBA had sent out a memo instructing teams to begin preparing to play games without fans in the stands, which was the impetus for the question posed to LeBron.

"I ain't playing if I ain't got the fans in the crowd," LeBron added. "That's who I play for. I play for my teammates, and I play for the fans. That's what it's all about. So if I show up to an arena and there ain't no fans in there, I ain't playing. They can do what they want to do."

LeBron wasn't being callous. It was just that, like most Americans, he was in denial. And understandably so. Ignorance was easier than fear.

Four days later, he walked back his comments. "When I was asked the question of would you play without . . . fans, I had no idea that there was actually a conversation going on behind closed doors about the particular virus," LeBron said after a morning practice. A rope marking six feet of distance was placed between him and the small group of reporters present. "Obviously, I would be very disappointed . . . But, at the same time, you've got to listen to the people that's keeping a track on what's going on." Later that night, the Lakers lost by two, but the action on the court felt trivial.

The next day, March 11, the World Health Organization declared the outbreak a global pandemic. That afternoon, NBA team owners met via conference call to discuss how to proceed. Nobody wanted to play games without fans—around 40 percent of the league's revenue came via game-related items like ticket sales and concessions—but the group also understood that, with the way the virus was spreading, there were few realistic options. A public health order prohibiting large indoor gatherings had already been issued in San Francisco, where the Warriors played. By the end of the call, the owners agreed: No fans was the way to go. The plan was for NBA commissioner Silver to announce the news at some point the next day.

Within hours, that plan had gone up in flames. Jazz center Rudy Gobert had tested positive for the virus minutes before a game against the Thunder, making him the first professional athlete in the country to have a confirmed case. Jazz and Thunder officials hopped on a call with the league office. They decided that both teams would leave the court and isolate themselves in their respective locker rooms, where tests would be administered. Fans in Oklahoma City's Chesapeake Energy Arena were told to go home. A little over an hour later, the NBA made official what once seemed unfathomable: Following that night's slate of games, the season would be suspended indefinitely. By the end of the week, nearly every other sports league—along with myriad other businesses, schools, and government organizations—had followed suit.

"Man we cancelling sporting events, school, office work, etc etc. What we really need to cancel is 2020! 🤮," LeBron tweeted a few hours after the league's announcement. "Damn it's been a rough 3 months. God bless and stay safe 🙏."

•   •   •

On March 17, four Nets players tested positive. Worried that their team had been exposed to the virus during their matchup the week before, the Lakers organized a conference call. Players were told to self-quarantine for fourteen days.

LeBron spent the stretch holed up in his Brentwood mansion, looking for ways to pass the time. He used his home gym but largely fell into a routine similar to millions of others across the country. He binge-watched shows like *Tiger King*. He played Uno with his kids. He posted videos of his family on TikTok and drank lots of wine. He scrolled through social media and got stuck on emotion-triggering videos. "DAMN, I really miss sports!!!!! 😭," he wrote in a quote-tweet of a video from Major League Baseball's official account, a two-and-a-half-minute reel of kids reacting to acts of kindness from MLB players and fellow fans.

The NBA's initial plan was to reevaluate the situation in mid-April, thirty days after the initial suspension of play, but with the virus surging throughout March and killing hundreds of Americans every day, there was nothing much to assess. All the league could do—all anyone could do—was wait and hope.

In the meantime, LeBron and the rest of the league's players were learning the meaning of the term "force majeure." French for "force of nature," the phrase is a provision inserted into most commercial contracts that allows a party to withhold or end its obligations under certain sets of circumstances, like war, terrorism, and natural disasters. They are often described as "acts of God," events that alter the landscape upon which the original deal had been agreed, and a global pandemic certainly qualified. On conference calls, union leaders informed players that, with the season on hold, teams could soon begin withholding a percentage of salaries. Not only that, but if the season were to be canceled, the league would have the right to invoke force majeure and rip up the collective bargaining agreement.

Things remained in a state of limbo throughout most of April. But by early May, return-to-play scenarios began circulating. Players started hearing about a so-called bubble—though the league office preferred terms like "campus" and "bubble-like environment"—a single location where teams would both live and play and where individuals would be allowed to enter only following a quarantine. Covid tests would be administered daily, and families would be left behind. It wouldn't make up for the lack of fans at games, but it would allow the NBA to fulfill its media contracts, which represented the majority of its revenue.

After learning about the potential financial ramifications of a canceled season, most players wanted the season to resume. But the bubble concept—especially the idea of being under constant surveillance in an enclosed space—left many uncomfortable. Some also doubted the NBA's ability to keep them protected from the virus.

"There was some consternation," Michele Roberts, executive director of the NBPA, said.

To answer players' questions, Silver and Roberts hosted a conference call. Over the course of an hour, Silver outlined where the league stood financially and what its options were going forward. "The CBA was not built for extended pandemics," he said. He answered questions about return-to-play scenarios and how the league planned to keep players safe. Four days later, on May 12, the union started polling players' interest in resuming. The majority said that they were in favor of doing so.

Most crucially, the league's most important player was on board. "I don't think I would be able to have any closure if we don't have the opportunity to finish this season," LeBron told reporters on a Zoom call in early April. A few weeks later, he was even blunter on Twitter. "Saw some reports about execs and agents wanting to cancel season??? That's absolutely not true. Nobody I know saying anything like that. As soon as it's safe we would like to finish our season. I'm ready and our team is ready. Nobody should be canceling anything." This was welcome news in the league office.

"We all knew that the only way a return-to-play format would work was if he was in," a league office executive said.

With a restart being discussed, some players began fantasizing about an extended stay in Vegas. "Of course that's what they wanted," Roberts said. "But we shut that down." The league zeroed in on Walt Disney World in Orlando. It had hotels and restaurants and, thanks to the ESPN Wide World of Sports Complex, basketball courts, too. Also, the company had a preexisting relationship with the NBA; its CEO, Bob Iger, was close to both Silver and NBPA president Chris Paul. Talks advanced fast. On May 26, the NBA sent a statement to reporters confirming that it was engaging in "exploratory conversations" with Disney about using its campus.

Covid might have thrown the country into chaos, but a few months into the pandemic, it had become a form of chaos that the league believed it could work around.

What neither the NBA nor anyone else knew was that another form of chaos, one bubbling beneath the surface and rooted in America's original sin, was about to move to the forefront of the country's consciousness.

•   •   •

In October 2008, LeBron strolled onto a stage inside Cleveland's Quicken Loans Arena. It was his home turf, a building in which he'd played over 400 games, and yet on this night he was doing something he'd never done before.

"You know who I'm voting for," he declared to the sold-out crowd. "I'm voting for Obama."

He'd come out that night at the behest of Jay-Z, who, as a part of voter registration drive, was performing a series of free concerts in battleground states. Just a few months earlier, LeBron had told an interviewer, "You want to keep athletics and politics separate," but the prospect of a Black man occupying the Oval Office and the vision that Barack Obama was pitching for the country had convinced him to reverse that stance. It appeared to be a watershed moment in American culture. Here was the heir to Michael Jordan—famous for his refusal to wade into politics—endorsing a presidential candidate, and doing so at just twenty-three years old. It felt like the dawn of a new age.

LeBron spent the next eight years dipping his toe into those waters, but he remained reticent to fully jump in. His next major political statement came in February 2012, when a Black teenager named Trayvon Martin was shot to death in Sanford, Florida, by a neighborhood watch volunteer who deemed him "suspicious" for wearing a hoodie. A month later, LeBron posed for a photo in a hoodie—but alongside his Heat teammates instead of by himself.

Two years later, when in Brooklyn for a game just days after a grand jury had declined to indict the NYPD officer who killed a Black Staten Island man named Eric Garner by placing him in a chokehold, LeBron had appeared reluctant to join his teammates in wearing "I Can't Breathe" warm-up shirts. When reporters had asked LeBron before the game whether he would be joining his teammates' gesture, he replied, "It's a possibility." Asked what would determine if he did, LeBron replied, "Y'all stop asking." When ESPN's Jeremy Schaap said he didn't understand, LeBron said, "Me either," and ended the interview. He did wear the shirt, but his hesitation did not go unnoticed.

One year after that, LeBron took heat for dodging questions after a grand jury did not indict the Cleveland police officers who fatally shot a twelve-year-old Black boy named Tamir Rice. "I haven't really been on top of this issue," LeBron told reporters. "So it's hard for me to comment." The stance angered both activists and Rice's family. "I think it's quite sad that LeBron hasn't spoken out about my son," his mother, Samaria Rice, told the website NewsOne in January 2016. "I'm not asking him to sit out a game. I know his kids got to eat too, but you can at least put on a shirt or something."

Donald Trump's political ascent during the 2016 presidential race seemed to change LeBron's approach. He endorsed Hillary Clinton, both in print and by appearing at a few of her Ohio campaign rallies, and he wasn't shy about hiding his contempt for Trump after the election, either. When Trump tweeted in December 2017 that he was rescinding the White House's invitation to Stephen Curry and the Warriors to honor their NBA title from the previous season, LeBron tweeted, "U bum, @StephenCurry30 already said he ain't going! So therefore ain't no invite. Going to White House was a great honor until you showed up!" The tweet was liked by over a million users, including Kobe Bryant and New Yorker editor David Remnick.

But there were still times when LeBron appeared unsure of how to balance the concerns of his business empire with his ambitions of activism. One day he'd talk about how much he looked up to former athletes turned civil rights heroes like Muhammad Ali and Jim Brown; the next he'd take issue with Daryl Morey's support of pro-democracy protests in Hong Kong. "So many people could have been harmed not only financially, physically, emotionally, spiritually," LeBron, sounding very much like a spokesperson for a shoe company with business interests in China, told reporters after Morey's tweet. "So just be careful what we tweet and say and we do, even though, yes, we do have freedom of speech, but there can be a lot of negative that comes with that, too."

His reluctance was understandable. Anytime he spoke out on social issues, he became a target of the right-wing media ecosystem, with the attacks vicious and often not even coded. "Keep the political comments to yourselves," Fox News anchor Laura Ingraham declared during a February 2018 prime-time broadcast in which she took repeated shots at LeBron's intelligence. She punctuated the segment by saying, "Shut up and dribble." But the more LeBron wavered, the more he opened himself up to criticism from all political corners; following his condemnation of Morey, Deadspin, a liberal sports and culture website, accused LeBron of "licking the boot," while Barstool Sports, a right-leaning operation, printed T-shirts featuring an image of LeBron donning a Chinese military uniform.

As the calendar flipped to 2020, and with another presidential election around the corner, LeBron felt that activism itch again. He started talking to Maverick Carter and Adam Mendelsohn, his communications advisor and strategist, about ways to get involved. Strolling out onto a few stages and offering public endorsements wasn't enough. He wanted to do more, and the most effective way to do so, he felt, would be by doing what he and his group had always done when it came to matters off the court: Bring in experts and let them lead the way.

In early March, Carter and Mendelsohn met with Addisu Demissie, a political consultant and strategist who had run numerous successful Democratic campaigns. The conversation was a mix of a job interview and brainstorming session. Carter and Mendelsohn said that LeBron wasn't looking to just cut a few ads. He wanted to do something substantive, they told him, particularly around fighting voter suppression in Black communities.

"I realized that they were dead set on the issues that have been the passions of mine my entire career," Demissie later recalled. "Voting, racial justice, and the intersection of the two. They really wanted to get their hands dirty and do the real work."

The meeting ended with Carter and Mendelsohn telling Demissie they'd be in touch.

One month later, the pandemic hit, halting their plans.

Everything changed on May 25. That night, just after 8 p.m., a Black man named George Floyd was arrested in Minneapolis after a convenience store clerk called 911 to report that Floyd had used a counterfeit $20 bill to purchase cigarettes. Two Minneapolis police officers responded to the scene. By 8:12, Floyd was in cuffs. Five minutes later, two more officers arrived. At 8:19, Floyd was thrust to the ground. All four officers surrounded him. One held his torso. Another held his legs. Another, a veteran cop named Derek Chauvin, plunged his knee into Floyd's neck.

"I can't breathe," Floyd said.

"Please," he pleaded.

"Mama," he cried.

Chauvin held the position for more than nine minutes. An ambulance arrived at 8:27 p.m. Floyd had no pulse. A little over an hour later, at the Hennepin County Medical Center, he was pronounced dead.

Bystanders recorded the incident. The footage went viral, sparking a wave of mass protests. The demonstrations started in Minneapolis but soon spread throughout American cities. Many were staged by Black Lives Matter, a movement formed after Trayvon Martin's death, and even those not officially associated with the organization adopted its slogan. Dozens of NBA players marched. Floyd's death put America's history of racial injustice—from policing practices to housing discrimination—under the microscope, replacing Covid-19 at the forefront of the public's mind.

The day after Floyd's murder, LeBron started sharing his thoughts on social media.

One day it was an Instagram post showing a split screen of Chauvin kneeling on Floyd's neck alongside former San Francisco 49ers quarterback Colin Kaepernick kneeling during the national anthem. "Do you understand NOW!!??!!??" LeBron wrote as his caption. "Or is it still blurred to you? 👀 #StayWoke👁️."

Another day he tweeted a photo of himself wearing a shirt featuring the words "I can't breathe."

Another day it was a question to his Twitter followers: "Why Doesn't America Love US!!!!!???? TOO."

LeBron was frustrated and furious and eager to enter the ring. "What are we doing?" he asked Carter and Mendelsohn. Within a week of Floyd's death, they reached back out to Demissie, who brought in fellow Democratic Party veteran Michael Tyler. The mandate was to take all the energy surging through the country and, using LeBron's platform, channel it into a form of activism around the 2020 election. Not long after, the group was on a Zoom call with Michigan Secretary of State Jocelyn Benson, who had served with Carter on the board of a nonprofit organization funded by Stephen Ross, the owner of the Miami Dolphins and a Michigan native. Benson was impressed with what LeBron's group was pitching—"It was clear he was hiring serious people and that this wasn't just going to be performative," she recalled—and helped them formulate a game plan. The group knew it wanted to emphasize voting, but it also wanted to get more granular and specific. Like fighting misinformation aimed at disenfranchising

Black voters, helping set up polling places and early-voting stations, and recruiting poll workers. By June 10, the organization, named More Than a Vote, was up and running.

"We want you to go out and vote, but we're also going to give you the tutorial," LeBron told *The New York Times* in an interview that day. "We're going to give you the background of how to vote and what they're trying to do, the other side, to stop you from voting."

• • •

Even with a pandemic raging and people protesting in the streets, LeBron made sure to maintain his focus on the game that had given him his platform. "Keep the main thing the main thing" had long been a favorite phrase of his, and after a twenty-two-team format was approved on June 4 and a season restart date of July 30 was announced, LeBron got to work. He was in shape and ready to go, but he needed to make sure his teammates were as well.

The problem was that LA remained in lockdown. "It was like *I Am Legend,*" Dudley said. All gyms and schools were closed, and per NBA rules, players weren't allowed to work out in team facilities. In fact, they weren't supposed to be working out as a team at all. So LeBron had to get creative and keep his efforts quiet. He enlisted Phil Handy, a Lakers assistant coach, to go searching for a gym. Handy worked his connections and found two: One was at Sierra Canyon School, which LeBron's son Bronny attended. The other was YULA, a Jewish high school in LA that was happy to unlock its doors in exchange for some signed jerseys.

Starting around June, the players met four days a week for a few hours a day. Players were given locations and directions. "It was like, 'Hide in the back over here, don't park your cars here, don't put them too close to each other,'" Dudley said. Davis didn't participate. Neither did Avery Bradley or Dwight Howard—both were unsure if they'd take part in the restart—but almost every other member of the team did. Some showed up in masks. LeBron ran the sessions. They'd talk basketball but also discuss everything taking place outside the gym. There'd be serious talks but also jokes.

Be careful when you drive home because of the police, LeBron once said. *Except Kuz,* he added. *You're light-skinned. You're good.*

The players were getting in shape and eager for the games to begin.

But as that date to report approached, some of their peers started to question the decision to restart the season. On the second Friday night in June, nearly a hundred players participated in a conference call in which they voiced their concerns. The charge was led by Kyrie Irving, a vice president in the union, who urged the group to reconsider.

"I don't support going into Orlando," he said during the ninety-minute call. "I'm not with the systematic racism and the bullshit." He added, "Something smells a little fishy. Whether we want to admit it or not, we are targeted as Black men every day we wake up." Irving's overarching concerns were shared by many. "Once we start playing basketball again, the news will turn from systemic racism to who did what in the game last night," one player told ESPN's Wojnarowski. "It's a crucial time for us to be able to play and blend that and impact what's happening in our communities. We are asking ourselves, 'Where and how can we make the biggest impact?' Mental health is part of the discussion too, and how we handle all of that in a bubble."

For a moment, it looked like the NBA's plans could be in jeopardy. Three days later, Roberts and Paul hosted another conference call, outlining again the financial implications of not playing, but also how a restart would give players an even bigger megaphone than the ones many were carrying in the streets. Most got on board.

They also recognized it wasn't their decision to make.

"Hoopers say what y'all want. If @KingJames said he hooping. We all hooping," Clippers guard Patrick Beverley tweeted a few days after that Irving-led call. "Not Personal only BUSINESS."

Beverley had a point. And to LeBron, who recognized that his team had a legitimate shot at a title, the decision was easy.

"[It] never crossed my mind that we did not need to play," he'd later say.

•   •   •

On the morning of July 9, Lakers players woke up, gathered their things, hugged their families goodbye, and met on the tarmac at LAX. They came in masks and all packed enough stuff to last them three months, the length of time they'd be staying if they reached the finals.

"Shit felt like I'm headed to do a bid man!" LeBron wrote on Twitter.

It was dark when they arrived in Orlando, and a bus took them from the airport to the Coronado Springs Resort, where they were staying. Covid tests were administered to every member of the traveling party—a swab of the nose, a swab of the throat—before everyone was sent to their rooms, where they'd remain for a forty-eight-hour quarantine period. Each player was greeted with a gift bag featuring all sorts of toys and treats. A Bluetooth keyboard and speaker. An Amazon Fire Stick and NBA-branded masks. Hand and phone sanitizer. Various snacks, like chocolate-covered popcorn and Doritos and wafers and Skittles and Hostess Cupcakes. Also, three books: W. E. B. Du Bois's *The Souls of Black Folk,* Kelly Lytle Hernández's *City of Inmates,* and *The Autobiography of Malcolm X.* That night, the players opened their room doors and, while standing in their entryways, made a group toast over glasses of red wine to celebrate Dudley's thirty-fifth birthday.

Two days later, with the quarantine period over, practices began. Suites were turned into training rooms, and courts were constructed on ballroom floors. Mornings started with testing. Practices were during the day. Beyond that, it was on the players to find ways to fill the rest of the time. Some players golfed. Some fished. Some hung at the pool, where they'd toss footballs and zip down the waterslide. LeBron biked.

"It felt like we brought the best players in the world to a three-month basketball camp," said former NBA coach Stan Van Gundy, who was in the bubble for TNT's broadcast of the games.[*]

LeBron was given the best room—and, because of his presence, the Lakers were given the best hotel—so at night, players congregated in his suite. They'd play *Madden* while drinking from one of the fifty or so bottles of wine LeBron had stashed in his room.

The rest of the time was passed by engaging in another national Covid-era pastime: "Man, I ordered so much shit," said veteran forward Markieff Morris, whom the Lakers added to the team in February. Dozens of packages arrived every day: a whiteboard to keep track of *Madden* records and schedules; a set of golf clubs for Kuzma, who had decided to pick up the sport; a fridge for Green; some sage for Howard,

---

[*] The players weren't the only ones who picked up hobbies. The referees played pickleball, and a bunch of coaches used a path on the campus for regular jogs and walks. Clothing, apparently, was optional. "[Milwaukee Bucks head coach] Mike Budenholzer would always do laps around [a path], and he would always not wear his shirt, and he's just walking around," ESPN's Wojnarowski once recalled.

which he lit in the hallway to encourage good vibes (it set off the hotel fire alarm); a mattress for J. R. Smith, whom the Lakers had added to the roster for the restart; a blow-up cold tub for Morris, which he set up in his shower. Within a few weeks, the hotel hallway was overflowing with discarded boxes and plastic wrap.

Some teams struggled adjusting to the atmosphere. Not the Lakers, though. LeBron wouldn't allow it. "I'm here for one goal, and one goal only, that's to win a championship," he told reporters during his first press conference after arriving at the bubble. He made sure practices were serious and film sessions were tedious.

Yet at the same time, LeBron also maintained an eye on everything going on with the Black Lives Matter movement outside the bubble. He believed there was an opportunity at hand, and he wanted to take advantage. He knew that with parts of the country still shut down, and with the protests still headline news, all eyes would be on the NBA, be it for a momentary escape from hardship, a cure for boredom, or a desire to see how the league's predominantly Black workforce would respond to the moment. It was why the players had pushed for the words "Black Lives Matter" to be printed in prominent locations on all the courts and to replace the names on the backs of their jerseys with social justice messages, like "Equality," "I Can't Breathe," "Vote," "Group Economics," and "Education Reform."

Like many of his peers, LeBron used his press conferences to speak out on social and political issues. He repeatedly called for justice for Breonna Taylor, a twenty-six-year-old Black emergency medical technician who was shot and killed in March by Louisville police officers who were executing a no-knock warrant at her home. He paid tribute to congressman and civil rights icon John Lewis after his death in July. But that wasn't enough. He wanted results, not just rhetoric, and building out More Than a Vote's infrastructure became a priority. LeBron had Mendelsohn, his advisor, speak daily with Demissie and Tyler. He also recruited other athletes, with the group focusing on stars from teams in battleground states like Trae Young from the Atlanta Hawks and Ben Simmons from the Philadelphia 76ers. On July 15, more than a dozen athletes and celebrities convened over Zoom with LeBron, Carter, and the More Than a Vote staff. LeBron opened the meeting.

"He shared why he felt More Than a Vote needed to exist and how frustrated he was that we even have to be fighting for people to have the right to vote in the country," said Jonae Wartel, a veteran Democratic strategist brought in to bolster the group. "The message was, 'We can't just sit on the sidelines. We have to use our platforms.'" LeBron then handed things over to Carter, who shared his thoughts before letting the professionals outline More Than a Vote's plan.

A few weeks later, as "The Star-Spangled Banner" blared before their first official games in the bubble, the Lakers and Clippers knelt at mid-court alongside each other, arms locked. "Black Lives Matter" warm-up shirts covered their uniforms. The Lakers won, 103–101, thanks to a go-ahead layup from LeBron in the final minute, but after the victory, what reporters wanted to know most was how it had felt to be kneeling alongside his peers.

"I hope we made Kap proud," LeBron said, adding, "If you go back and go look at any of his postgame interviews when he was talking about why he was kneeling, it had absolutely nothing to do about the flag, it had absolutely nothing to do about the soldiers, the men and women that keep our land free. He explained that and the ears were closed. People never listened. They refused to listen and I did."

•   •   •

Everything about the atmosphere was strange. On the court, with no fans in the building, "all you heard," LeBron said, "was sneakers and basketball. There was literally nothing. It was straight dead silence." Off the court, the experience quickly morphed from exciting to draining. Players missed their homes, their families, their routines. There were only so many dishes to try at the restaurants, only so many ways that an Amazon delivery could improve a hotel room.

"There's nowhere to go, there's no way to release anything," Howard said. "Any feeling that you might have, it's just like we're stuck." He added that it was "very difficult, seeing the same walls every day." Paul George would later say that while in the bubble he dealt with a bout of depression.

"Just being locked in here," he'd say. "I just wasn't there."

After the victory over the Clippers, the Lakers' offense fell off a cliff. They clinched the top seed in the Western Conference with a win over the Jazz but dropped four of their final five seeding games. Their struggles stood out. The play in the bubble was some of the most crisp and explosive that the league had ever seen—overall shooting percentages had spiked, a trend players attributed to the lack of travel and nightlife* and the clean shooting backdrops—and yet here were the Lakers, a championship contender, finishing the seeding round with the second-worst offense of all the bubble teams. They were also down two of their top guards; Rondo broke his thumb in early July, and Avery Bradley, whose son had a history of respiratory illness, had elected not to join the team.

Just one month into the bubble, LeBron seemed worn down. During press conferences, he often sounded despondent.

"This is a totally different season, a totally different, drastic situation for all of us, including myself," he told reporters after a loss.

Heading into the playoffs, the Lakers looked to be in trouble, especially after drawing Portland in the first round. The Blazers had won six of their eight seeding games, and their star point guard, Damian Lillard, was playing the best basketball of anyone in the bubble (37.6 points and 9.6 assists per game during the seeding games). Watching Lillard drain 25 of 27 shots from just inside halfcourt during warm-ups before Game 1, all Pelinka could think was, *Is this really your typical first-round opponent as a No. 1 seed?* Pelinka's fear proved to be well founded. Lillard dropped 34 points on the Lakers that night, leading Portland to a 100–93 win. Afterward, during TNT's postgame show, Charles Barkley, who had picked the Blazers to win the series, brought out a broom and started sweeping the floor, his way of announcing that he was doubling down and predicting that Portland would do so without losing a single game.

Yet despite the loss, the Lakers remained confident. They knew they'd failed to execute Vogel's game plan—big men were told to pressure Lillard when he came off screens—and the next day discussed those mistakes in a film session. They'd also connected on just five of their 32 attempts from deep, an improbable number even for a struggling group.

In Game 2, they fixed both issues, drilling 14 threes and holding Lillard to 18 points en route to a 111–88 win. Lillard caught fire again in Game 3 (34 points), but thanks to MVP-level performances from

---

* Or, as Jared Dudley put it, "No distraction, no females, people weren't going to clubs, no drinking."

both LeBron (38 points, 12 rebounds, 8 assists) and Davis (29 points, 11 rebounds, 8 assists), the Lakers were able to hold on for a 116–108 win. They then ran the Blazers off the floor in Game 4, 135–115, once again keeping Lillard in check (11 points). He'd also exited the game with a knee injury, which forced him to leave the bubble, effectively ending the Blazers' season.

Before the playoffs, the Lakers had put a board against a wall in their hotel hallway with sixteen boxes, one for each win they'd need to become champions. Three of those boxes now had an "X" drawn above. The team that had drubbed opponents throughout the fall and winter was back. On the afternoon of August 26, the Lakers' players lay down for their pregame naps assuming that, in a few hours, they'd be on the court in their uniforms, leading the Lakers into the playoffs' second round.

•   •   •

LeBron woke up around 4 p.m. to receive some pregame treatment from his trainer, Mike Mancias. Sitting on a couch in his hotel room, he flipped on the TV, looking for that afternoon's Magic-Bucks playoff battle.

The game wasn't on.

Confused, LeBron reached for his phone and saw that the Bucks were refusing to come out of their locker room.

"No one knew what was going on," LeBron recalled. At least not until 4:19 p.m., when Bucks guard George Hill told ESPN's Marc Spears that his team would not be playing that night's game.

"We're tired of the killings and the injustice," Hill told Spears.

Two days earlier, another American Black man had been shot by police. This time, the incident had taken place in Kenosha, Wisconsin, a city about forty miles south of Milwaukee. The details of this shooting mirrored so many of the others. A 911 call. Police responding to the scene. A back-and-forth. Drawn guns. Shots fired.

In this case, the victim was a twenty-nine-year-old man named Jacob Blake. He was shot seven times in the back. The incident was recorded by bystanders and shared on social media, where it went viral, pouring oil on the open flames spreading across the country. Blake survived, but it didn't change the facts of what had transpired. Protests erupted in Kenosha, where a state of emergency was declared.

In the bubble, players appeared broken by the news. Many had only agreed to participate in the restart thinking their platform could affect change, yet here was another Black man being shot by police. It felt like they'd been played.

"If we're going to sit here and talk about making a change, then at some point we're going to have to put our nuts on the line," said Raptors guard Fred VanVleet.* "What are we willing to give up? Do we actually give a fuck about what's going on or is it just cool to wear Black Lives Matter on the backdrop or wear a T-shirt?" Multiple players told reporters that a boycott was being discussed. During his press conference the day after the Blake shooting, Hill seemed particularly shaken. "We shouldn't have even come to this damn place, to be honest," he told reporters. "I just think coming here just took all the focal points off what the issues are."

The next morning, over a breakfast of bacon and tangerine juice, Hill informed the Bucks' coaching staff that he didn't feel comfortable playing that afternoon. His teammate Sterling Brown, who in 2018 was involved in an incident with Milwaukee police that ended with his being thrown to the ground and tased (the officers were later disciplined and Brown received $750,000 from the City of Milwaukee in a settlement), later said he wouldn't play either. Upon returning to the locker room after his pregame warm-ups and seeing that Hill and Brown would not be suiting up, Bucks star Giannis Antetokounmpo joined them in refusing to play. Soon after, the team made a choice: They would not participate in their playoff game.

Back in his hotel room, LeBron worked the phones. He spoke to NBPA president Chris Paul, who was in the bubble with the Thunder, and with Rockets star Russell Westbrook. Their two teams were scheduled to face off later that evening.

There's no way we can go out on the floor, LeBron told them.

Paul and Westbrook agreed.

The three were annoyed, not just because they felt blindsided but because it seemed like the Bucks had acted without mapping out any sort of plan. Were they done for good, or just for one game? Were there specific things they wanted, or were they just interested in making a

* It's worth noting that VanVleet's stepfather, who helped raise him, was a police officer in Rockford, Illinois.

point? It didn't seem as if they had any answers, meaning it now fell on LeBron and Paul to map out the next steps and draw up a way out of what they felt was a no-win situation. They could back the Bucks, who seemed to be leaning toward going home, but doing so would cost both themselves and the league hundreds of millions of dollars and likely trigger an ugly labor war. They could remain in the bubble, but they'd be accused of selling out. LeBron was particularly annoyed. He wasn't someone who made drastic decisions without first thinking everything through. It wasn't how he operated.

"When it hits in your backyard, you feel a little bit more," LeBron later recalled. "But we're an army, and we're going off to battle [and] we say we're in solidarity and someone in the front decides to go before we can say 'charge,' now we're all caught off guard."

A little after 5 p.m., the NBA, in conjunction with the union, announced that it was postponing all three of that day's games. Around that same time, Paul, Westbrook, and Miami Heat forward Andre Iguodala, a union vice president, huddled with Roberts and NBPA senior counsel Ron Klempner.

We've got to get everybody together, Paul said.

At 8 p.m., more than two hundred players, along with numerous coaches, filed into a cavernous hotel ballroom. Teams sat together. The Lakers found a spot in the back. Paul had asked Klempner to address the group and outline the financial impact of not finishing the playoffs. Klempner explained that if the players left, they would likely lose 30 percent of their salaries for the *next* season and the league would also be within its right to tear up the current collective bargaining agreement, forcing the union to negotiate a new deal under the far less favorable economic conditions created by the pandemic.

"And the response was basically, 'Who gives a shit?'" recalled a person in attendance.

The eyes of the country were now on the NBA. The strike led all newscasts. Legendary athletes like Bill Russell and prominent politicians like Barack Obama and Alexandria Ocasio-Cortez had tweeted their support. Other professional sports unions had announced that they'd be sitting out, too.

At this point, there was just one question on the players' minds: Would they accomplish more by staying or leaving?

Paul and Iguodala led the meeting. Multiple players stood and spoke.

"It was the most incredible thing I've ever experienced," Roberts said years later. "It was democracy in action." Several players confronted Hill and the Bucks, asking why they had taken action without consulting the group, LeBron chief among them. *You should have given us a heads-up,* he said. Antetokounmpo defended his team. Celtics star Jaylen Brown, an outspoken and politically inclined member of the NBPA executive committee, also took their side.

You have nothing to apologize for, he told them. He shared that he too felt demoralized.

We thought we'd come here and make some changes, he said. *But it's just going to keep happening.*

LeBron said they should push for more concessions from the league and its owners. Iguodala talked about the importance of voting and how the best way to institute change was through political action. The union, he said, had data on how many of its members voted, and the numbers were low. Westbrook and Heat veteran Udonis Haslem both said the group needed to consider the younger players and those who hadn't already banked millions of dollars.

At one point, the referees barged in. *We're with you guys,* they said, *no matter what you decide.*

Clippers coach Doc Rivers and Rockets assistant John Lucas—both former players—urged the group to remain in the bubble.

Your talent is your power, Rivers told them.

What's your real motivation for wanting to go home? Lucas asked.

Are you going home to work, or are you going home to be on the front lines? added Brown.

There was yelling. There was laughing. Rivers led the coaches out of the room so that the players could come to a decision among themselves. The teams broke into circles. In a few minutes, they'd take a group vote. Union reps were told to tally up those who were in and those who were out.

The group reconvened. "Everybody was giving their opinions, but nobody was listening," recalled NBA guard Austin Rivers, who was there with the Rockets. "We were all just waiting to see if LeBron was gonna play or not." As the votes were being relayed, Haslem grabbed the mic and looked at LeBron.

Hey, yo, bro, what we doing? he asked, according to Rivers. Haslem was just saying what everyone was thinking—that it didn't matter what the rest of them wanted to do; it was LeBron who had the power and LeBron who, in the end, would be making the call.

LeBron didn't like being challenged. Especially considering how the walkout had occurred without anyone first consulting him. He and Haslem went back and forth before LeBron decided he'd had enough.

We're out, he said. He stood and stormed out of the ballroom. "We all sort of looked at each other and were like, 'I guess we're leaving, too,' " Lakers forward Devontae Cacok said. Everyone followed except Howard. The Clippers did, too.

"We sat there and talked for two, three, four hours, and there was still no plan," LeBron explained a few months later. "When you're dealing with a group [with] a lot of emotions, a lot of ego, a lot of guys that's passionate about themselves and what they believe in, then it's hard to figure out a plan at that very moment. So it was best for me to step up." Part of it, he recalled, was that he was emotional himself, and didn't want to make any rash decisions. "I was ready to walk away," he said. "So I needed a moment to digest the whole situation."

It looked like the season was over. "I thought it was 70–30, us not playing," Dudley recalled. When news of LeBron's walkout reached Vogel, he was stunned.

Not long after, at around midnight, LeBron, Paul, Iguodala, Westbrook, and Carmelo Anthony—who was in the bubble with the Blazers—huddled again. Searching for guidance, they got Obama on the phone. His advice was simple: The league had billions of dollars on the line and needed the playoffs to continue. This gave the players leverage. Use it, Obama said, to address two or three specific issues. Nothing would be solved overnight, he added, but the group now had an opportunity to lay the groundwork for meaningful change.

The union scheduled a follow-up meeting with team representatives for 11 a.m. the next morning. Everyone showed up on time except the Lakers. "Guys were grumbling," Roberts said. "They were wondering if they were coming." Word got back that the team was working through some final issues, but that LeBron and others were on their way. Upon their arrival, Paul and Iguodala announced that a consensus had been reached.

We're gonna restart, they said.

Everyone in the room looked at the Lakers. *LeBron, are you playing or not?* one player said.

We're playing, he replied.

A call with the league and a group of owners was scheduled for 4 p.m. Not even twenty-four hours had passed since the Bucks had refused to come out of their locker room, and now the players had only four more to come up with a list of demands. There was so much they wanted to address—no-knock warrants and police chokeholds and body cams and dash cams and racial profiling and qualified immunity and education and racial discrimination—but they knew they had to be smart. They were in the spotlight now, and in the crosshairs of the country's political right wing, and they knew that those they were trying to take power from were going to fight back.

"I think that the NBA players are very fortunate that they have the financial position where they're able to take a night off from work without having to have the consequences to themselves financially," Jared Kushner, President Trump's son-in-law and senior advisor, had told CNBC earlier that day.

In the end, the players landed on three items, all building off what LeBron had started with his own organization in June. They wanted more in-game advertisements urging viewers to vote. They wanted owners to convert team arenas into polling places for the 2020 election. And they wanted to establish what they later referred to as a "social justice coalition," which would be a partnership between players, owners, coaches, and the league that would focus on various issues ranging from advocating for police and criminal justice reform to fighting voting-related misinformation.

By 4 p.m., they were ready.

Roberts led the conference with the owners. In detail, she laid out the demands.

We all believe it's important that NBA owners play a significant role, she said.

The call for more in-game advertisements was simple, and the owners signed on. Turning arenas into polling places was self-explanatory and, for teams that owned their own buildings, an easy request to grant.

The social justice coalition was more complicated, so Roberts outlined what it was and exactly what it entailed. In short, the players wanted an ally in their fight. That meant voter registration drives. That meant working with elected officials. That meant lobbying for legislation to address the ways racial bias impacts the criminal justice system.

The league and owners were on board.

This will be part of a long tradition of athletes fighting for change, Silver said.

This is a great start, Blazers owner Jody Allen said.

We support the players, Rockets owner Tilman Fertitta said. He added that, as someone who'd made his fortune in hospitality and gambling, *Nobody uses lobbyists more than me. If you want to know how to get something done in Congress, I know how to do it.*

We're here in support, Raptors owner and Board of Governors chairman Larry Tanenbaum said.

We got your word? LeBron asked.

He was told that they did.

The next day, the league and union announced that, after a three-day layoff, they'd agreed to resume the playoffs the following day. The joint statement also outlined the commitments that the players had extracted from the owners. The day after that, the Lakers announced that Staples Center would serve as a polling place for the 2020 election. Later that night, LeBron led the Lakers to a 131–122 win over the Blazers, giving Jeanie the first playoff series win of her ownership tenure. The Lakers were moving on, and, after spending the previous few days bolstering his off-court legacy, LeBron, who finished the series averaging a triple-double (27.4 points, 10.2 rebounds, and 10.2 assists per game), was one step closer to bolstering his on-court one, too.

•   •   •

A few weeks earlier, the NBA had announced that once the playoffs got down to eight teams, the bubble would open up to players' families and friends. Each team was given an additional seventeen guest rooms. The only stipulation, outlined in a memo, was that guests had to have "longstanding" relationships with the players. Those who knew "the player only through social media or an intermediary" were not allowed.

Of course, that didn't stop players, reeling from weeks of isolation alongside mostly men, from trying to sneak in women they'd recently met online. "They'd try saying that these Instagram models were actually longtime friends," one league executive said. The cap on available rooms also occasionally created tension. The Rockets, for example, sent home an executive who had just completed a seven-day quarantine period because Westbrook insisted that one of the team's extra hotel rooms be given to his massage therapist.

But walking around the bubble after the guests had arrived, league executives couldn't help but notice a vibe shift. It wasn't just the sounds of children filling the hallways, and sometimes the practice gyms, too. It was the smiles they'd see stretching across the faces of players.

"It's the longest time I've ever been away from my family," Markieff Morris told reporters at the time. "I've missed them a lot. I missed my daughter a whole lot. I missed my wife a whole lot. I'm just happy to have them here to come see a game and spend some time with me."

The Lakers drew the Rockets in the second round, who had surged during the second half of the season after benching their big men and rolling out a starting lineup of wings and guards. The goal was simple: Spread the floor for James Harden, who had led the league in scoring during the regular season, and Westbrook, a former MVP. It was a tough matchup for the Lakers, who, by starting McGee alongside Davis, were one of the few NBA teams still playing two big men at the same time, and in Game 1, the Rockets' speed and spread offense gave the Lakers fits. Harden scored 36 points, leading Houston to a 112–97 win.

"It's like in the early 2000s, when the St. Louis Rams were the Greatest Show on Turf," LeBron said after the loss. "People would always say how they'd scout them, and scout them, and scout them. Until they got on the field, and they'd see Isaac Bruce and Torry Holt. Marshall Faulk, and Az[-Zahir] Hakim, and all those guys. And they were like, 'We need to play them again.' Because there's no way you can simulate that speed. Getting out on the floor and having a Game 1 will give you a good feel for it."

The Lakers did get a good feel and, thanks to another dominant performance from LeBron, were able to even the series in Game 2 with a 117–109 win. But in the first half of Game 3, the Rockets once again took control of the pace, racking up 64 points. Despite the Lakers trailing by only three entering the break, Vogel knew that if the second half was played at that same pace, his group would be toast. Going away from the big lineups that had been a season-long strength, he benched Howard and replaced McGee with the more agile Morris, who had scored 16 points in Game 2. The smaller and faster lineups slowed the Rockets' attack. The Lakers were in prime position to take control of the series. All they needed was someone to step up and lead the way.

• • •

There was no one in the NBA quite like Rajon Rondo.

He was such a film junkie that he'd study games at night while out with teammates at clubs. "He'd come in with his iPad and just set it up in a booth," Troy Daniels said. He hated losing so much that during shooting games with teammates he'd often cheat to try giving himself an edge. "He'd do things like change the rules or how many points were needed to win," Green said. He was such a gambling nut that, when he was with the Pelicans in 2018 and learned that the team would have to spend an hour in the locker room before a game due to an arena leak, the first thing he did was wonder out loud which teammates owed him money and then announce, "Fuck it, bring out the cards."

The ride with Rondo wasn't always smooth. There was a reason that, prior to joining the Lakers, he'd played on five teams in four years. He was moody and stubborn and "always trying to prove that he was the smartest person in the room," one of his former coaches said. He developed a reputation for chasing assists and caring more about racking up steals than sticking to defensive game plans. Once, while with the Celtics during the 2011 playoffs and in the midst of being criticized by head coach Doc Rivers during a film session, he fired a bottle of Vitamin Water toward the front of the room, shattering a video screen.

But there were also reasons why teams kept bringing him in. One was that he was considered one of the sharpest players in the league. "You were fucking annoying, because you knew every single play, you would call out the coverage, you knew every hand signal," NBA veteran and future Lakers coach JJ Redick told him in a 2023 podcast interview. Another was that he had become one of the league's most eager leaders, a veteran who, when it came to camaraderie, went above and beyond. He led individual film sessions with younger players, who were thrilled to receive tutoring from a four-time All-Star with a championship ring. He handed out homemade chocolate chip cookies on team flights. After reading about a study showing that teammates on winning teams were more likely to physically touch each other during games, he began making a point of handing out as many high-fives and back-pats as possible. All of which made him perfect for these Lakers. All the roles LeBron didn't want, Rondo relished taking on.

Rondo had fractured his thumb shortly after arriving in the bubble, an injury that required surgery and sidelined him for all the seeding and the entirety of the first round. He rejoined the Lakers for the start of the Rockets series, and his impact was immediately felt. "He's a leader," LeBron told reporters after Game 1. "And for us to have him back in the postseason, it's a key for our team." Rondo had also developed a reputation over the years for upping his game in the postseason. In 2010, his then-teammate Kendrick Perkins had started calling him "Playoff Rondo" after Rondo had carved up LeBron's Cavaliers in a series, and now it was time for Playoff Rondo to make his first Lakers appearance.

With the team trailing the Rockets by one in the fourth quarter, Rondo took over. He hit LeBron in the paint for an easy layup. He buried a pair of spot-up threes. He picked Harden's pocket and took the ball all the way for two more points. He set up Caruso for a three. It was a 13–2 run, giving the Lakers a 10-point lead. Rondo finished the game with 21 points and nine assists, leading the Lakers to a 112–102 win.

"Playoff Rondo is real," Davis told reporters after the victory.

The Lakers pummeled the Rockets on the boards in Game 4, held Harden to 2-for-11, and won 110–100. Two nights later, they closed the deal with a 119–96 win, earning their first conference finals trip since 2010, the year they had last won a ring.

•   •   •

Next up were the Clippers. Or that was at least what LeBron and the Lakers assumed. This was *the* matchup, the heavyweight battle the NBA world wanted, the two top teams in the West facing off, Kawhi Leonard and Paul George taking on Anthony Davis and LeBron. And, after jumping out to a 3–1 series lead over the Denver Nuggets in the second round, an LA conference finals face-off felt inevitable.

"I just did not see them losing," LeBron said.

But the bubble had worn the Clippers down. "It was a huge fucking disaster for us," a member of their front office said. "You saw the difference between teams who were led by our guys, and one led by someone with the will of LeBron." The Clippers blew a double-digit lead in Game 5, and then again in Game 6, and then again in Game 7. Late in the fourth quarter, when it became clear that the Lakers would be facing Denver and not their in-city rivals, LeBron FaceTimed his friend and former teammate Richard Jefferson, who was in the bubble with ESPN, to share his shock.

"I couldn't believe it," LeBron later recalled.

The Nuggets were led by budding superstar Nikola Jokić, a 6-foot-11, nearly 300-pound beast with soft hands, a dazzling array of post moves, and an uncanny ability to create space. He also happened to be one of the greatest passers the game had ever seen. "Big, strong, powerful, mobile, skilled, intelligent, creative, collaborative. Empty the thesaurus," was how Hall of Famer Bill Walton described Jokić in an interview with *GQ* that summer. Jokić was flanked by Jamal Murray, a streaky but electric scorer who'd caught fire in the bubble.

With Jokić on the floor, Vogel went back to his big lineup. The switch worked, and the Lakers took Game 1, 126–114.

Game 2 was close throughout. The Lakers were careless with the ball but made up for it by thumping the Nuggets on the glass. With just over three minutes remaining, they led by eight.

Jokić, however, wasn't ready to fold. He reeled off nine straight points, and then, after a Lakers bucket, backed Davis into the paint and tossed a baby hook shot into the hoop. With 20.8 seconds left in the game, the Nuggets led by one.

The Lakers called a timeout.

Davis was furious.

It's all right, Davis recalled Rondo telling him. *He scored on you. Now you go get it back.*

Vogel drew up a play to get the smaller Murray isolated on LeBron. LeBron drove, kicked the ball out to Caldwell-Pope, who swung it to a wide-open Caruso at the top of the arc.

He missed short.

The ball caromed off the front rim and bounced off multiple hands. Green grabbed it near the left corner and turned to shoot.

Murray swatted the shot out of bounds.

Two-point-one seconds remained. The Lakers had no more timeouts.

Vogel, standing near halfcourt, called out a play. He then turned and saw Rondo next to him.

Different passer? Rondo asked.

Vogel subbed Rondo into the game.

The setup was simple. "It was a 'wing it' play," Green recalled. Rondo would inbound the ball on the left baseline. LeBron stood at the left elbow. Davis stood at the right elbow. Green was positioned to the right of Davis, on the wing. Caldwell-Pope set up in the right corner.

The official handed Rondo the ball. The Nuggets, looking to block Rondo's passing lanes, stationed Jokić in front of him; he waved his arms high and wide and jumped up and down.

Green cut to the hoop but was covered.

So was Caldwell-Pope.

Rondo had two options remaining. Hit Davis curling toward the perimeter, or loft the ball into LeBron, just outside the paint.

He made eye contact with LeBron but, behind him, spotted Davis running open toward the three-point line. Instead of trailing him, and despite there being no screen, Nuggets center Mason Plumlee had switched onto LeBron and pointed for Jerami Grant, who was guarding LeBron, to jump out on Davis.

Because there was no screen, Grant never left LeBron's side.

Rondo bounced a pass under Jokić's outstretched arms and into Davis's hands. Jokić, recognizing the breakdown, turned and sprinted toward Davis. Before Jokić could reach him, Davis rose up. The ball splashed through the net as the final buzzer sounded, giving the Lakers a 105–103 win.

"Kobe!" Davis shouted as he sprinted toward his teammates and the Lakers' bench. The tribute continued later in the locker room. "That was Mamba right there," Vogel announced to the team. "Mamba mentality."

"It's for sure the biggest shot of my career," Davis later told reporters. Two years earlier, Davis had put his reputation on the line. After he'd demanded a trade out of New Orleans, some fans and members of the media began viewing him as a poster boy for everything wrong with the NBA. Here, they said, was yet another superstar quitting on a small-market team so that he could play under the bright lights in a bigger market. The criticism was loud and unrelenting. But now, with this shot in this moment, Davis believed he had his vindication.

"When I left [New Orleans]," he told reporters that night, "I just wanted to be able to compete for a championship, and I know that moments like this come with it."

Davis wasn't just along for the ride, either. He'd averaged 30 points and nine rebounds in the first round, and 25 points and 12 rebounds per game against the Rockets, and he'd dropped 37 points on the Nuggets in Game 1, and gone for 31 points in Game 2, all while shooting better than he ever had from the perimeter and playing the best individual defense of anyone in the bubble. It was a dominant stretch, one that changed the way many people viewed him.

When Davis had first arrived in LA, his reputation preceded him. "We know he's soft," one Lakers coach had said during a preseason meeting. The coach received no pushback, either; this, after all, was an opinion shared by many in the public and across the NBA. Everyone knew Davis was a great player, but he was also viewed as one of those big men who didn't like physical play, the sort of player who didn't know how to deal with the regular aches and pains that pop up over the course of a season, so much so that, when he first arrived, the Lakers coaching staff, out of fear that he'd get nicked up and then take time off, informed staffers to keep it light with him during drills and warm-ups.

"I watched him a lot in New Orleans where he would get these little nagging injuries and he would be out games, multiple games," LeBron said. "He would get the shoulder, or he would get the ankle, and he would sit out."

Davis's first year with the Lakers stood as his counter to that narrative. He missed just nine games during the regular season and, despite dealing with various foot injuries that he and the team were keeping under wraps, had to that point suited up for every playoff game. His toughness left a mark with his teammates. They saw how swollen his foot was, and the grotesque collage of black and blue that had spread across it, and all the treatment he received—often while playing *Madden* in LeBron's hotel suite—so that he could suit up.

"AD, he knows how special he is. If he don't, I'll be the first one to tell him how special he is," LeBron said after Game 2. "And he wanted to be here. I'm happy he wanted to be here because if he didn't we wouldn't have had a moment like we had tonight."

The Nuggets came back to steal Game 3, but the Lakers held on in Game 4 for a 114–108 win. They ended the series two nights later with a 117–107 victory.

"One thing about dogs, we finish our motherfucking food," McGee had shouted during the Lakers' pregame huddle. "Let's go out here, kill these motherfuckers, and go to the motherfucking finals!"

They did, and now they were.

•   •   •

The Lakers were just one win away from a title, and the tension inside the room was palpable. It wasn't nerves filling the room. It was anger.

"We were upset that we had to keep playing," Dudley said.

They had stepped onto the court the previous night confident that it'd be their last time doing so that season, donning their special-edition "Black Mamba" jerseys in which, to that point, they had gone 4–0.* It's not that they didn't respect their opponent, the Heat; it was that, after four games of battle, they felt like they had figured them out. They'd punished Miami on the offensive glass, and their wings had drilled a bunch of threes. Davis had continued to play the best basketball of his career. LeBron, angry after learning that he'd finished second to Antetokounmpo in that season's MVP voting, was playing like a man eager to reclaim his crown.

The Lakers knew the Heat—who were loaded with long-range snipers and led by four-time All-Star Jimmy Butler and coached by Erik Spoelstra, one of the most revered minds in the NBA—were talented and tough. And they weren't about to take lightly a team that, despite entering the playoffs as a No. 5 seed, had made the finals by ripping off 12 wins in 15 games.

What they were, though, was confident in their abilities and the adjustments they'd made throughout the series.

The biggest one had come after Game 3. Butler had spent that entire night targeting the Lakers' weaker and smaller defenders, getting to his favorite spots, and using the unusual amount of strength packed into his 6-foot-7, 230-pound frame to create space for feathery pull-up jumpers. He finished with 40 points, 13 assists, and 11 rebounds, handing the Lakers their first loss of the finals with a 115–104 win. After the game, Davis had told the coaching staff that he wanted to guard Butler, and after waking up at 3:30 a.m. the next morning to review film, Vogel agreed. The move worked. The Lakers limited Butler to 22 points in Game 4, and, with Davis controlling him on his own, were able to stay home on the Heat's shooters and walk off with a 102–96 win.

"I love what we did tonight," LeBron told reporters after the game.

---

* They also ended all huddles during the bubble with a chant of "One, two, three, Mamba!"

He was confident and came out in Game 5 like a man intent on ending the series. He repeatedly rumbled to the rim and sank long-range bombs and midway through the fourth quarter led the Lakers on a 14–3 run, giving them a three-point lead with just 5:28 remaining. The NBA had confetti cannons on the sidelines, loaded and ready to launch. But Butler had come out with a plan of his own, which was to be everywhere and do everything. He racked up 35 points and 13 assists and 11 rebounds and five steals and played all but 48 seconds of the game, enough to overcome LeBron's 40 points and give the Heat a 111–108 win to keep their season alive.

"Jimmy Effin' Butler" was how Spoelstra summarized the performance after the game. The night's most memorable moment had come when ESPN's cameras captured Butler, following a foul-drawing drive to the rim in the game's final minute, slumped over a video board and gasping for air.

The Lakers felt like they had let one slip away. Not only had they allowed Butler to impose his will, but Green had also misfired on a wide-open three on the final possession, one that would have sent the game to overtime. Later that night, Green and his fiancée received death threats from Lakers fans on social media. To top it off, Davis had aggravated his foot injury.

The next day, the Lakers filed into the hotel conference room for their morning film session. Vogel's film reviews were always exhaustive and intense, but they knew this would be different. Kidd, who usually led the discussion about offense, took the first half hour. Then it was Vogel's turn. Earlier that morning, Kidd had suggested replacing Howard in the starting lineup with Alex Caruso, and, after mulling it over, Vogel informed the team that he was making the change. He wanted more athleticism on the court and to smother the Heat's shooters. Starting Caruso, the team's top perimeter defender, made sense.

Vogel went over the new plan for guarding Butler. The Lakers would be more aggressive in their pick-and-roll defense and Davis would cease switching onto the screener when picks were set for Butler. The goal was to stop letting Butler dictate matchups. Meanwhile, Caldwell-Pope would remain glued to Duncan Robinson, who had knocked down seven threes the previous game, and Caruso would wreak havoc all over the floor.

Do all that, Vogel said, and the Lakers would be in good shape.

But LeBron didn't want to leave his championship chances in anyone else's hands. He knew that no one was more equipped to handle Butler than him, and that if the Lakers could just contain Butler for one more game, he'd be leaving the bubble with his fourth ring.

Coach, all due respect, he shouted out about midway through Vogel's presentation, *fuck that, I got him.*

Rondo also had a thought.

We're picking him up full-court, he said. *I'm tired of this man feeling comfortable. He's the only one that can make plays. So we're going to wear him all the way down.*

Vogel signed off on both ideas. The Lakers spent the rest of their film session and that day's practice implementing the scheme.

"It was the most intense film session and practice I ever had," Dudley said years later.

The Lakers came out the next night eager and engaged. The game plan was followed to a tee. LeBron stuck to Butler, even when the Heat set screens, and pushed the pace whenever he had the ball. Green hounded Butler in the backcourt. Caldwell-Pope didn't leave Robinson's side. Caruso flew around the court. The defense was suffocating, and, in the second quarter, thanks to another electric stretch from Rondo and Caldwell-Pope finding his outside stroke, they were able to blow the game open.

The Lakers entered the locker room at halftime leading 64–36. The lead ballooned to 82–46 late in the third quarter. The Heat kept fighting and outscored the Lakers by 16 points in the fourth quarter, but by then the celebration was already on.

With less than one minute on the clock, ESPN caught LeBron wrapping his arms around Davis's neck, like a big brother embracing a younger sibling. An expression of pure joy had spread across LeBron's face. For the first time since arriving in the bubble, he looked happy. After the final buzzer, he and his teammates leapt into each other's arms. J. R. Smith shed his shirt. Davis sat by himself off to the side, face buried in a towel. Confetti rained down as the league pumped in artificial cheers. LeBron went teammate to teammate, offering hugs and daps.

The Louis Vuitton travel case carrying the Larry O'Brien Trophy was wheeled onto the floor. As Adam Silver took the mic to congratulate the team, LeBron found Jeanie, who'd only recently arrived in the bubble and who hadn't been allowed to mix with her team until now, and wrapped his arms around her.

"We accomplished what we set out to do," he told her.

Soaking in the moment, Jeanie closed her eyes and smiled. She nodded.

"Thank you," she said.

After Silver was done, Jeanie stepped to the mic. She thanked Pelinka. She thanked Vogel. She thanked the coaching staff. She thanked the training staff. She thanked the employees back in Los Angeles. She told the players she was proud of them "on and off the court."

"You have written your own inspiring chapter in the great Laker history," she said.

She took a moment to recognize Kobe and Gianna Bryant.

"Let this trophy serve as a reminder of when we come together, believe in each other, incredible things can happen," she said.

She told Lakers fans that she looked forward to celebrating with them "when it's safe."

Silver announced, to the surprise of no one, that LeBron had won Finals MVP.* It was his fourth time winning the award, moving him past Magic, Tim Duncan, and Shaq for second all-time.

"I told Jeanie when I came here that I was going to put this franchise back in a position where it belongs," he said after accepting the award. "Her late, great father did it for so many years and she just took it on after that and for me to be part of such a historical franchise is an unbelievable feeling."

He paused and rubbed his brow. Standing there after the three months he'd just endured, confetti raining down, had stirred something within him. For just one moment, the joy turned to indignation.

"We just want our respect," he continued. "Rob wants his respect"—Pelinka could be seen in the background of the live shot, nodding—"Coach Vogel wants his respect, our organization wants their respect, Laker Nation want their respect."

LeBron knew all the history, he'd heard all the noise. That Jeanie had to save the team from her brothers, that Pelinka was in over his head

---

* Davis finished the finals averaging 25 points, 10.7 rebounds, and 3.2 assists per game while shooting 57.1 percent from the field.

and there only because he was close with Kobe, that Tyronn Lue should have been coaching the team and not Vogel, that the organization was a clown show, nothing like the one made famous by Dr. Buss.

Some of the criticism, LeBron recognized, was valid. Or at least maybe it was before this title run. Now, though? Not only had Pelinka pulled off the Davis deal, but he'd also nailed his other signings, giving the Lakers a roster with the skills and versatility to roll through the playoffs. And not only had Vogel jelled with his veterans—so much so that he received no pushback during the playoffs after yanking some from the rotation—but he'd also transformed the Lakers into an elite defense and spent the playoffs proving to be as good on the fly as any of his peers. And not only had LeBron averaged nearly a triple-double in the finals (30 points, 12 rebounds, and nine assists per game while shooting 59 percent), but he'd done so in unprecedented circumstances. At the same time, he'd followed in the footsteps of some of his idols, not just using his voice to call for social and political change but also using his resources to effect change on the ground; earlier that month, More Than a Vote had announced that it had signed up ten thousand volunteer poll workers. Standing there, in a mostly empty gym but with millions of people watching on TV, he paused one more time. And then:

"I want my damn respect, too."

Some players laughed. Others cheered.

"King James!" Pelinka shouted while clapping. "King James!"

Jeanie nodded.

Two years earlier, she and LeBron had come together because each had something the other needed.

Two years into their partnership, they'd both gotten what they wanted.

What neither knew, standing there amid all the confetti, was that this partnership had just reached its peak.

10

SEVENTY-ONE DAYS

Trophy ceremony complete, the Lakers moved the celebration to the locker room, where they were greeted by bottles of champagne. "Goggles! I need some goggles!" LeBron shouted. "You're not about to spray me and burn my fucking eyes." A four-time champion, he knew the dangers that awaited. He also knew that, this time around, the party would be different. He and his teammates weren't simply celebrating a title. They were also celebrating that, after spending ninety-six days in the bubble, they were finally heading home.

"I'm free out of this bitch," Danny Green shouted as he sprinted down the hallway. "I'm fucking free!"

The music inside the locker room was turned all the way up. J. R. Smith took out his phone and began broadcasting on Instagram Live. LeBron doused a group of reporters outside the locker room and then headed down a hallway. After finding a spot he liked, he splayed himself out on the carpeted floor and, in full view of the media, hit the call button on FaceTime.

"Mama, Mama!" he shouted between puffs of a cigar.

"I love you. I love you, you are the reason why I'm able to even do this, Mom," he told Gloria James. "You don't understand—sixteen years old, you bring a little-ass, big-headed-ass boy into the world? C'mon. C'mon, Mom."

"God is good," Gloria said.

"God is good. God is great," LeBron said. "I hope I continue to make you proud, Mom."

LeBron and his teammates spent the next hour-plus making the media rounds. A little after midnight, they staggered onto the team bus and headed back to the hotel. Smith continued streaming on Instagram.

"QC!" he shouted, after noticing that one of his teammates, Quinn Cook, was writing in the comments.

"Gotta walk back after I win a fucking ring," Cook wrote. "Wtf."

"Yo, we left QC, bro," Smith, clearly a few glasses in, said out loud.

"Come backkkk," Cook added.

Back at the hotel, Pelinka filled out the sixteenth and final "X" on the board in the hallway. Davis told teammates to start referring to him as "Champ." Everyone met up at Three Bridges Bar & Grill. Family and friends joined, many of whom Lakers players and staff hadn't seen in months. On his way to the celebration, Pelinka spotted his ten-year-old daughter. "She came running down [the dock] like a scene out of a movie, and it felt like it was slow-motion to me," he recalled. "When she grabbed my neck, I felt like she wasn't gonna let go. She had tears in her eyes."

The players passed around bottles of Ace of Spades and 1942 Dom Pérignon as the music blared. Assistant coach Mike Penberthy handed out cigars. The party went past 4 a.m. "If we were in LA at the time and not in the bubble, it would have been a hundred times better," Markieff Morris said. "Ain't too much you can do in the damn bubble, but we enjoyed each other, did the best we could."

Later that morning, the Lakers boarded a plane headed back to LA. "You ever see the movie *Shawshank Redemption*?" Dudley asked an interviewer later that month. "I've never been to prison. I'm not saying it was like prison, but it felt like you were isolated from the world, and so to get out, man, and to be a champion and have a trophy, no better feeling I've ever had."

•   •   •

The title celebrations were barely complete and Pelinka was already concerned.

The pandemic and subsequent suspension of games had thrown the league's calendar in flux, and now that the bubble was done, the NBA was looking to get things back on track. It needed to, for financial reasons. Covid had already cost the league hundreds of millions of dollars. In order to prevent a further loss of between $500 million and $1 billion in revenue, the NBA was looking to start the season before

Christmas. Doing so would ensure that Disney had games to air on Christmas Day—one of the most valuable TV days of the year—and prevent the finals from overlapping with the Olympics in July, which would hurt ratings.

By the first week of November, the NBA and the NBPA had settled on a start date of December 22. That meant that the Lakers' offseason would last just seventy-one days, the shortest for any team in league history. As if that wasn't enough, the league would now be squeezing a 72-game season into five months, as opposed to the typical six it used to play 82. This would be a difficult task for any veteran roster, but especially so for one like the Lakers, not even three months removed from a grueling playoff slog.

Pelinka didn't think his championship roster, as constructed, could make it through such a season. He believed his group needed younger bodies and more playmakers. The former would boost the Lakers' odds of staying healthy, the latter would ease LeBron's regular-season load and help ensure that, come playoff time, he still had his legs.

Pelinka spent the weeks after the finals canvassing the league for options. "It's easy to fall into complacency when you win a title and just say, 'Hey, let's just run it back,'" he later told reporters. "But my school of thought is always, 'Let's find a way we can become even better. Every offseason, let's get better.' We never want to just settle." In mid-November, a few days before the draft, he made his first move, acquiring Dennis Schröder from the Thunder for Green and a first-round pick. Schröder, a twenty-seven-year-old point guard, was exactly the sort of player Pelinka was looking for, a talented, off-the-dribble shot creator with a decent shooting stroke who, the Lakers thought, could both run the offense when LeBron sat and also play alongside him.

After the draft, Pelinka continued tinkering. He pried twenty-six-year-old power forward Montrezl Harrell, a skilled young scorer and the reigning Sixth Man of the Year, away from the Clippers with a two-year, $20 million deal. He also signed former Defensive Player of the Year and three-time All-Star Marc Gasol, who had played a key role in the Raptors' 2019 title run, and brought back Caldwell-Pope on a three-year, $40 million deal. The moves were widely praised.

"This team should be considered favorites to repeat," ESPN's Zach Lowe, a prominent and widely respected NBA analyst, wrote in an offseason column. He listed the Lakers as one of his free-agency "winners."

The praise for Pelinka's offseason wasn't just coming from outside the building, either. "We absolutely can [repeat]," LeBron said in a podcast interview in early December. He lauded Gasol's defensive skills and "IQ." He complimented Schröder's disposition on the court. "He's Dennis the Menace," LeBron said. "What he brings to the game, the tenacity, he's a dog." He described Harrell as someone "who's gonna help our bench, which we struggled with this past year." LeBron was so thrilled that he felt comfortable agreeing to a two-year, $85 million extension before training camp, yet another break from his previous one-plus-one deals and the sort of multi-year commitment he never gave the Cavaliers during his second stint. The contract meant that, barring a trade, he'd be in a Lakers uniform through the end of the 2022–23 season. One day later it was reported that Davis had also agreed to a new contract with the Lakers, this one a five-year, $190 million deal, the maximum amount allowed.

In the span of two days, Pelinka had locked up two of the league's top players. Forget defending champions. The Lakers now looked like a budding dynasty.

• • •

After free agency, agents and executives around the league began playing a game with media members. *Go look at the Lakers' roster,* they'd say. *Count up how many Klutch guys they have.*

LeBron, Davis, and Caldwell-Pope had been there for a few years. And Talen Horton-Tucker, whom the Lakers drafted 46th overall in 2019, was a Klutch client, too. But Harrell was also with Rich Paul, meaning Klutch now had five players on the roster, four of whom were slated to get major minutes. "The whole league would joke about it," Horton-Tucker said. "Things like calling us the 'Klutch Mafia,' and stuff like that." Paul wasn't the first agent to have multiple players on one roster. What made this different, though, is that the relationship between the two entities had morphed into something closer to a partnership.

"It's an agency town, and the Lakers became an agency team," a rival NBA executive said.

The evolution had started in July 2019, after Paul sold a chunk of his business to the Hollywood powerhouse United Talent Agency. That a shop like UTA was interested in Klutch was a testament to his success and a sign of just how far Paul had come. But joining UTA changed Klutch's business. Paul was now part of a new, different, and larger world. He was still hustling—colleagues often laughed at how few hours had passed between his first call to them in the morning and his final call to them the night before—but his priorities were different. He'd proven his critics wrong, and that meant he no longer had to fight the same sort of battles. His days of taking contract negotiations or team decisions personally were over. "It's a business, and I always tell my guys it's a business," he'd say. As the years had gone by, he'd also begun embracing his role as a mentor, someone who, by showing his clients all the things he'd learned through the years, could pave the way for others from similar backgrounds, whether they were athletes or just kids from Black neighborhoods trying to break into the business. He'd preach to clients the importance of diversifying portfolios and connect them to different departments within UTA. He shared his email address with young professionals looking for guidance. He even took on the NCAA in 2019 after it instituted a rule requiring agents to have a bachelor's degree in order to work with prospects. The change was viewed by many as a shot at Paul (and was casually referred to by many as the "Rich Paul Rule") and a method for barring others like him from breaking into the business.

"Requiring a four-year degree accomplishes only one thing—systematically excluding those who come from a world where college is unrealistic," Paul wrote in an op-ed for *The Athletic*. Six hours after his piece was published, the NCAA announced that it had amended the rule to remove the degree requirement.

Going to UTA without Mark Termini, whose contract with Klutch had expired, also changed things.* In Klutch's early years, Termini's relentlessness perfectly complemented Paul's congenial attitude. "Termini could be the fucking assassin, and Rich never had to damage his relationship with the teams," one former general manager said. Termini fought for every provision and every dollar, insisted on contracts being

---

* Termini would sue Paul and Klutch in June 2024 for breach of contract, claiming that he was owed more than $4.9 million, plus interest, for services he performed. The two sides later settled for an undisclosed amount.

front-loaded, and on multiple occasions used the Eric Bledsoe play-book to get Klutch clients paid; Cavaliers role players Tristan Thompson and J. R. Smith had both received significant raises after sitting out the beginning of training camps.

But by this point Paul had succeeded in everything he'd set out to do. He'd both built a narrative about himself—Termini's name was almost never mentioned in the press—and put together a championship team in LA for two of his top clients. Now he was ready for the next phase of his professional life. "I'm an entrepreneur," he'd often tell people, "not just an agent," and over the next few years he'd make a point of flexing those muscles. He'd become the face of a lifestyle brand (New Balance's Klutch Athletics) and write a *New York Times* bestselling memoir. He'd also get engaged to the pop star Adele.

The goals had changed, and Klutch's days of holding feet to the fire on every contract negotiation were over. Caldwell-Pope, for example, received a bump in salary when he re-signed during the 2020 offseason, but the third year of his deal was only partially guaranteed. His contract didn't contain any form of a player option or trade kicker either, player-friendly clauses that Klutch had often demanded in the past. And if Paul was more interested in a partnership, the Lakers, for the time being, were more than happy to play along. After all, if there was one thing Jeanie had learned from her father, it was the importance of catering to stars. Not that someone like Pelinka, whose entire career was built on his ability to make clients feel special and secure, needed much prodding. During an interview with the *Los Angeles Times* after winning the 2020 title, Jeanie even went out of her way to compliment Klutch COO Fara Leff: "She's bright, and she brings an energy and ideas and creativity."

The strategy appeared to pay off. While speaking with *The New Yorker* for a May 2021 profile, Paul referred to the Lakers as "us."

"This sounded like a strangely partisan observation for an agent with clients across the NBA," the writer, Isaac Chotiner, wrote. He said he raised this point to Paul.

"C'mon," Paul replied. "I've got six guys on the team."[*]

---

[*] That April, the Lakers had signed guard Ben McLemore, another Klutch client.

• • •

Opening night of the 2020–21 season had arrived, and the atmosphere might have been stranger than the bubble's. The stands in Staples Center were empty, the coaches wore masks on the sidelines, and Adam Silver, on hand to present players with their 2020 title rings, couldn't go near any of the individuals he was congratulating.

"These are obviously highly unusual times," Silver said during the ceremony. He then turned things over to Jeanie.

"I'm gonna take a second to speak directly to Lakers fans," she said. "We miss you so much, the team misses you, but someday soon we'll be together, and when we are together we have something special to celebrate."

The Lakers fell to the Clippers that night, but a week later ripped off four straight wins. Then came a five-game winning streak. Then a seven-game one. On the morning of February 14, they woke up in Denver with a 21–6 record, second best in the NBA. Everything seemed to be clicking. The returning players showed no rust; the new ones fit in seamlessly. The defense was ranked No. 1. LeBron was coasting a bit but still controlling things. Davis's jumper was off, but he was still dominant on both ends of the floor. Schröder was producing offense in a way no Lakers point guard had the season before. Harrell was providing offense off the bench. Caldwell-Pope and Caruso were both shooting lights out while locking down opposing wings.

"Everything was going smoothly," Harrell said.

The Lakers faced the Nuggets that night. With just over two minutes remaining in the first half, Davis attacked Nikola Jokić from the left wing. Jokić bumped him. Davis stumbled. A foul was called, but Davis grimaced while strolling to the free throw line. After he buried both shots, the Lakers chose to take an intentional foul and subbed Davis out. He hobbled to the locker room. He'd aggravated a minor Achilles injury that he'd suffered the previous week. After the game Davis underwent an MRI. The good news was that there was no rupture. The bad news was that he would be out indefinitely.

The Lakers held on the next night for a win in Minnesota but, with Davis out, dropped six out of their next eight. A month later, Hawks forward Solomon Hill crashed into LeBron's right ankle while diving for a loose ball. LeBron left the game soon after—knocking over a chair on his way to the locker room—and wound up missing more than a month. With their two best players out of the lineup, some cracks that had been forming beneath the surface began revealing themselves. Pelinka's offseason moves had boosted the team's talent, but all that wheeling and dealing had come at a cost.

"Everybody with the title team just bought into their roles," said Markieff Morris, whom the Lakers brought back on a one-year deal. "Nobody took anything personally. We were all there to win. It was different the next year. Some guys were in contract years; people just weren't as happy."

Schröder, despite putting up strong numbers, irritated teammates with his shoot-first approach. He was also just a few months away from free agency and asking for more money than the Lakers were offering. The two sides were so far apart that the team had included him in proposals leading up to the March 25 trade deadline.

Schröder wasn't the only new addition struggling to find his footing. Gasol shot well from deep, but he turned thirty-six in January and couldn't handle big minutes. Harrell was fine as a backup but, as an undersized big man who couldn't protect the rim or keep up with wings on the perimeter, was too poor a defender to be much more.

Pelinka tried addressing his problems at center in late March by signing Andre Drummond, an affable former client of his who was one of the best rebounders in the league. But to secure him, the Lakers had to promise Drummond that he'd be the starting center, which angered Gasol. "It's a hard pill to swallow," Gasol told reporters a few games after the signing. It was a stark contrast to the previous season and how McGee, Howard, and others had handled the way their roles were altered and swapped throughout the playoffs. The move poisoned the locker room. Drummond, who was, somehow, even slower than Gasol on defense, failed to make a difference on the court, either. After arriving in LA he averaged just 11.9 points per game, nearly six fewer than his output with the Cavaliers earlier that season.

"A lot of the new guys didn't fit how we wanted to play," assistant coach Lionel Hollins said.

Making matters even worse was that the Lakers had to deal with Schröder, Caruso, and Gasol all missing extended periods due to the NBA's "health and safety" protocols (the fancy, HIPAA-compliant term used by the league to protect the privacy of players who had tested positive for or been exposed to Covid). And they'd wiped out a part of their home-court advantage by barring fans from Staples Center for nearly the entire season due to the pandemic. The Lakers weren't the only team dealing with Covid-related absences, playing in empty arenas, or worn down by the condensed offseason, but they were the only one trying to do so while defending a title.

Davis didn't return to the court until April 22. LeBron returned April 30 for two games but, after feeling soreness, sat out the next six. The Lakers went 12–15 in the games without him and plummeted into seventh in the Western Conference standings. Their punishment was a matchup with Stephen Curry and the Warriors in the play-in tournament, a new format introduced by the NBA that season. The winner would advance into the playoffs and face the second-seeded Phoenix Suns, with the loser relegated to one final win-or-go-home contest.

The game was tight throughout. Then, with one minute left and the shot clock running out, LeBron buried a jumper from deep behind the three-point line, giving the Lakers a 103–100 lead and win. They fell to the Suns in the opening game of the first round but bounced back by taking Games 2 and 3. It was evident that LeBron's ankle was hampering him—he attempted just four foul shots in those two games—but Davis stepped up, scoring 34 points in each win. Somehow, despite all the new faces and all the growing pains and all the injuries, the Lakers were now just two wins away from advancing in the playoffs.

Game 4 was tight early. Then, with under a minute left in the first half, Davis crumpled to the ground after cutting to the hoop. This time it was his groin. He left the court and did not return. The Lakers fell 100–92. Davis remained sidelined for Game 5. The Lakers lost again. Davis tried playing in Game 6 but, after trying to block a shot early in the first quarter, came up hobbling and asked out. The Lakers fell behind by 29 before losing 113–100, ending their season.

"The one thing that bothers me more than anything is we never really got an opportunity to see our full team at full strength," LeBron told reporters after the loss. Sitting there in his press conference, he showed no signs of anger, no flashes of frustration. He talked about his ankle injury. He commended the Suns. He made a joke about the new *Space Jam* movie, which was set to premiere the following month. He looked loose and relaxed, and while he wasn't happy to go home, he did seem relieved.

"From the moment we entered the bubble to now, today, it's been draining," he said. "Mentally, physically, spiritually, emotionally draining."

The bubble had affected everyone who participated, but the teams that advanced furthest had seemed to be impacted most. Three of the previous season's conference finalists—the Lakers, Celtics, and Heat—had failed to advance out of the playoffs' first round. The Lakers had fallen short in their bid to repeat, but they'd also been dealt as bad a hand as any defending champion in league history.

"Either because of injury or Covid or something going on with our ball club this year, we could never fully get into a rhythm and never really see the full potential of what we could be capable of," LeBron said. LeBron and Davis were locked up on long-term deals. So were some of the team's top role players. The core of the team that had jumped out to a 21–6 start remained. All LeBron and Pelinka had to do were remain patient and tweak things around the edges. A few small moves here, and they figured they'd be back in title contention.

· · ·

LeBron might have sounded at ease. But behind the scenes, he was far from it.

Within a month, he made clear that he was not actually interested in seeing what the previous season's roster could do under more normal circumstances. What he wanted was another star, and he wasn't going to wait for Pelinka to figure out a way to get one.

The calls and texts started going out around July, about a month before the start of free agency. LeBron, Davis, and Dudley—who'd become the duo's consigliere—huddled in LeBron's house and pored over the league's rosters. They were looking for insurance. LeBron was thirty-six years old. Davis had a history of injuries and had missed 36 games the previous season. They needed a better version of Schröder, someone who could ease the burden on them both and carry the load if one of them went down.

The trio landed on a few names. DeMar DeRozan, a four-time All-Star wing who, despite being thirty-one years old, was coming off one of the best seasons of his career and was entering free agency. Damian Lillard, one of the league's top point guards, who was flashing signs of frustration with how the Blazers' front office was building the team. Bradley Beal, who'd finished the previous season second in scoring and was stuck on a Wizards team seemingly going nowhere.

Beal and Lillard became the primary targets. Each of them met with LeBron at his house. "It was basically engaging my interest in LA, trying to see how the system could fit together and how we could all potentially fit together," Beal said. He was intrigued. So was Lillard. But the Lakers didn't have enough assets to pry either away from their respective teams.

Next, LeBron turned his attention to DeRozan.

"I wanna see you win one," he texted DeRozan during the 2021 finals.

"Let's figure out a way to make it happen," DeRozan replied.

A few weeks later, the two were having lunch on the patio in LeBron's backyard, discussing strategy and how a partnership could work. Using a napkin, they drew up plays and schemes. They reviewed the roster and discussed what sort of players would fit best alongside the two of them and Davis. Growing up in Compton, California, DeRozan had always dreamed about wearing a Lakers uniform. When he left LeBron's house that afternoon, he believed he was just a few weeks away from the dream coming true.

"The next episode of my career was set," he recalled.

But despite operating as if he was GM of the Lakers, LeBron was not the one with the power to make those calls. That job belonged to Pelinka, and while he, too, was eager to shake up the roster, he knew that adding DeRozan was more complicated than LeBron seemed to believe. The Lakers didn't have the cap space to give DeRozan the sort of contract he was looking for, not with Davis and LeBron inked to long-term deals. DeRozan's agent gave no indication that his client was willing to sign for a discount, and Pelinka was unable to make headway on a deal with the Spurs. DeRozan was crossed off the list, joining Lillard and Beal. With the draft and the start of free agency rapidly approaching, Pelinka and LeBron were running out of time and options. If they indeed wanted another star, they'd have to look elsewhere.

•   •   •

Like DeRozan, Russell Westbrook grew up in Southern California, dreaming of playing for the Lakers. He was the sort of kid who cut middle school classes so that he could attend Lakers championship parades and who, when it came time to pick a college, chose UCLA so that he could stay close to home. Westbrook was drafted fourth overall by the Thunder in 2008, and in Oklahoma City he became one of the top players in the league, a fierce competitor with a relentless motor whose speed and athleticism stood out even when surrounded by some of the fastest and most athletic men in the world. But while he loved his time there, he always hoped to, at some point, end up back in LA.

In the summer of 2019, he thought he'd found his path. Kawhi Leonard, a fellow Southern California native, was about to become a free agent, and coming off a season in which he'd led the Raptors to the title and been named Finals MVP, he'd enter the market with all sorts of leverage. The Clippers and Lakers were two of his top suitors; this, Westbrook thought, was his chance. He called up Leonard and told him to tell the LA teams that if they wanted him, they would have to trade for Westbrook, too. Given that he was an eight-time All-Star and former MVP just one year removed from becoming the first NBA player since 1962 to average a triple-double in a season, Westbrook didn't think including himself in a package would be hard to sell.

Leonard listened to Westbrook's pitch—then formulated a plan of his own. He'd use Westbrook's playbook, only instead, he'd pair up with a different All-Star: Paul George, Westbrook's Thunder teammate. Leonard called George. He told him that Westbrook was angling to leave but that he had a way for George to get out first. A son of Southern California who had no interest in being stranded in Oklahoma City, George went to Thunder general manager Sam Presti and asked for a trade. Presti hadn't planned on breaking up his team, but he recognized that, after three straight first-round playoff exits, the Thunder's current core had likely hit its ceiling. He also understood that he was being presented with a unique opportunity, one he'd likely never have again. If the Clippers wanted to add the two stars, they needed to go through him. From the perspective of a negotiator, he couldn't ask for more leverage.

Within a few days, the Thunder and Clippers had agreed to a deal. The Clippers, after signing Leonard, got George. In return, the Thunder received five first-round picks, the right to swap first-round picks in 2023 and 2025, one aging rotation player in Danilo Gallinari, and Shai Gilgeous-Alexander, a talented second-year guard.[*]

Westbrook's plan had backfired. Instead of heading back to LA he was now marooned in Oklahoma City on a rebuilding team. He told his agent Thad Foucher to get him out. A week after the George trade, the Thunder sent Westbrook to the Rockets for Chris Paul and multiple first-round picks.

Westbrook was thrilled. He and Harden, both West Coast guys, had played together a decade earlier in Oklahoma City and remained close. But once the season started, problems arose. Westbrook wasn't used to sharing the ball or playing off another star. He and Harden clashed, and after the season, Westbrook once again asked Foucher to find him a new home.

This time around, there was no market. Westbrook's numbers remained impressive, but his stint in Houston, where he'd spent chunks of the season pouting, complaining, and showing no interest in adjusting his game, combined with his bloated contract, scared potential suitors away. The only team interested was the Wizards, and only because they had their own aging star signed to a lucrative, long-term deal in John Wall, who, due to a series of injuries, hadn't appeared in a game since December 2018. Westbrook, on the other hand, was coming off a Third-Team All-NBA season, and the Wizards figured a backcourt featuring him and Beal, a fellow All-Star, would have some punch. In December 2020, a few weeks before the start of the season, the two teams agreed to a deal.

Westbrook thrived with the Wizards. "He was tremendous with us," then–Wizards general manager Tommy Sheppard said. It helped that they were led by Scott Brooks, who had coached him in Oklahoma City, but he'd also arrived at training camp with a different attitude than what he'd brought to Houston.

This is Brad's team, he declared during one preseason practice, refer-

---

[*] The package of picks made this a great deal for the Thunder from Day One, but Gilgeous-Alexander becoming a 30-points-per-game scorer within two seasons of the trade and an MVP candidate by 2023 transformed this haul into one of the greatest of all time.

ring to Beal. *Our job is to help him.* Westbrook took it upon himself to be a leader for the team's younger players, many of whom grew up looking up to him. He would tell them to put away their phones in the locker room. He would drape his arm around rookies after mistakes during practices. He would encourage teammates to keep launching when they'd gone cold.

You're playing hard as shit, he told Wizards third-year forward Isaac Bonga during one game in which Bonga struggled from the field. *If you're open, you keep shooting. I got confidence in you.*

Westbrook enjoyed his time with the Wizards, and the Wizards enjoyed their time with him. He put up his typical gaudy numbers—he led the league in assists and once again averaged a triple-double—and helped lead Washington to the playoffs. The Wizards were eliminated in the first round, but management felt no urge to shake things up.

Then LeBron and Davis came calling with a pitch too good for Westbrook to turn down: an opportunity to suit up for a team with a legitimate title shot and, even better, a chance to return home.

"LeBron always wants to bring in ball-dominant guys who are really good one-on-one players," said a member of the Cavaliers' front office during LeBron's time with the team. "Even if it was clear to the rest of us that they wouldn't be good fits next to him."

The two future Hall of Famers talked about how they'd fit together. Westbrook insisted he was ready to sacrifice individual numbers, that at this point in his career all that mattered was winning, that the prospect of living in LA and having friends and family attending games was exciting, that he didn't care how many points he scored. Both parties thought the conversations went well. Westbrook then called up Foucher, told him that LeBron and Davis wanted him in LA, and, for the third time in three years, asked his agent to orchestrate a trade.

Foucher's first call was to Pelinka, whom he'd worked with years earlier at SFX. Pelinka didn't respond, but soon after, Linda Rambis did. She told Foucher that, for the time being, she'd be his contact. (The Lakers representative described this as a "lie," saying, "Rambis did not even know who Thad Foucher was at the time.")

Pelinka loved the idea of adding Westbrook. Throughout the previous spring, he'd told his front office that he, too, believed the Lakers needed another star playmaker. He repeatedly brought up the Big

Three of Kevin Durant, Kyrie Irving, and James Harden that the Nets had assembled, asking, *How do we beat them?* Pelinka wasn't the only one in the building interested in the Wizards star, either. That summer, Tim Harris, the Lakers' president of business operations, reached out to Corey Gaines, a former Wizards assistant coach he was friendly with, to get his thoughts on Westbrook.

"He wanted to know what was the best way to handle him as a coach," Gaines recalled.

At the same time, Pelinka was working on a contingency plan. The Kings were offering sharpshooter Buddy Hield for a package centered around Kuzma. Hield wasn't a star, but he'd likely fit nicely around LeBron and Davis, and he'd cost less than Westbrook to acquire. Pelinka told the Kings they had a deal. All the Lakers needed was for Harrell to pick his player option; they needed Harrell's contract to make the salary math work. Pelinka told members of both his front office and the Kings that, if Harrell opted in, the deal would be done.

On July 29, just a few hours before the draft, Rich Paul, Harrell's agent, informed the Lakers that his client was exercising his second-year option. The Kings drafted up a press release. At 5:02 p.m. ET, ESPN's Wojnarowski tweeted, "With Harrell opt-in, Lakers are able to move toward completing a deal to acquire Kings guard Buddy Hield for forward Kyle Kuzma and Harrell, sources tell ESPN." Kuzma began preparing to move to Sacramento. "That shit was done," he later recalled.

All that was left was for Pelinka to get on the phone and finalize the deal.

But that morning, Pelinka had received a call from Sheppard, who'd received a call from Westbrook, who'd heard about the Lakers' impending trade. Westbrook knew that if their deal went through with the Kings, the Lakers would no longer be able to acquire him. He told the Wizards that he wasn't demanding to be moved, but if there were any way for them to figure out a way to get him to LA, he'd be incredibly appreciative. Sheppard put Westbrook on the phone with Wizards governor Ted Leonsis. After hearing Westbrook out, Leonsis instructed Sheppard to reach out to Pelinka and see what could be done. Westbrook, meanwhile, had also spoken with LeBron, who told Pelinka that

---

* The three stars wound up playing just 16 games together in less than two seasons.

he preferred Westbrook over Hield. "We thought it'd be a good trade," Dudley, who'd helped advise LeBron and Davis, said years later. Pelinka agreed. He and the Wizards began negotiating and were still doing so when Wojnarowski reported that the Lakers were on the verge of getting Hield.[*]

For the Lakers and Wizards, the basic parameters of a Westbrook deal were straightforward. To make the salaries match, the Lakers would send Kuzma, Caldwell-Pope, and Harrell. The only sticking point was draft compensation. The Wizards wanted the Lakers to include their first-round pick (No. 22 overall). Pelinka refused to budge, but, knowing that LeBron was leaning on Pelinka, the Wizards held firm. Within a few hours, Pelinka relented, and the two teams agreed to terms.

Westbrook hadn't been one of LeBron's or Pelinka's top targets, but after all the work put in over the previous month, both were happy with where they'd landed. "When an opportunity like that comes, you're thoughtful, you analyze it, you look at the pros and cons, and you make a decision," Pelinka would tell reporters before training camp. "That's what leaders are tasked to do." He wasn't the only one taking a victory lap. "It was exciting helping put this team together this summer," LeBron said that same day. "Understanding what I felt and we all felt was going to make us a title-contending team."

The trade became official on August 6.

A few weeks later, it was time for Westbrook to complete the final step of his initiation. All new Lakers players were brought to Jeanie's office. There, they were shown all the championship trophies the Lakers had won under the stewardship of the Buss family, which Jeanie had arranged in chronological order atop a desk overlooking the practice court.

---

* The Lakers representative disputed this chain of events. "The fact that ESPN reporter Adrian Wojnarowski had been given a bad tip is irrelevant to the true facts—and this is just another biased attempt to falsely portray Pelinka as incompetent, dishonest, or both," the representative said. "Whomever the source is, this is, at best, Monday morning quarterbacking, seemingly ever willing to blame Pelinka if things don't work out and personally taking credit if things do." When notified of the Lakers' response, Wojnarowski, who left ESPN in September 2024 to become the general manager of the men's basketball program at St. Bonaventure University, said, "Even in my retirement, I stand by that reporting."

"I'm so happy that you're here," Jeanie said as she welcomed in Westbrook and Pelinka, past the copper bust of Dr. Buss.

"My dad bought the team in 1979, and his first year of owning the team was Magic's rookie year, and they won a championship that first year," she said. "And his goal in buying the Lakers was to someday surpass the Boston Celtics. So we're now tied with 17 titles."

"We know what we need to do then," Westbrook said.

They all smiled.

11

RUSS BEING RUSS

The players found seats inside the film room. It was late September, the first official day of their new season, and they'd gathered for what, under Pelinka, had become an annual tradition.

"Welcome to the Lake Show," Pelinka announced. He then explained the reason for the meeting. "What we do every year in training camp is, we have a theme. We put it on a training camp T-shirt, and our theme for this year is 'mindset.'" The word, printed in white cursive with a picture of the Larry O'Brien Trophy in place of the "I," was projected onto a screen in the front of the room.

Pelinka gazed out at all the players seated before him. LeBron, Davis, and Westbrook sat in the front row. Dwight Howard and Rajon Rondo, two expats returned home, sat beside them. Former All-Stars DeAndre Jordan and Carmelo Anthony, both signed in the summer, were there, too.

"You could say this room has the greatest basketball talent assembled on a team in recent history," Pelinka declared. "You could say that."

He paused.

"But without the proper mindset as a team," he added, "that amounts to jack shit."

•   •   •

The Lakers opened their season a month later at home against the Warriors. The atmosphere inside Staples Center, full for the first time since the pandemic, was electric.

"Let's get ready to rumble!" Howard bellowed into a microphone before the game. "We want to welcome all you guys back. We missed you guys."

Players could feel the energy in the building as fans filed into their seats. The crowd erupted into a roar during Westbrook's pregame introductions, and again when Anthony—finally in Lakers purple and gold after spurning them in free agency nearly a decade earlier—subbed in midway through the first quarter, and again when Westbrook recorded his first basket as a Laker. The game was close throughout. Then, late in the fourth quarter, the Warriors pulled away, knocking off the Lakers 121–114.

LeBron (34 points) and Davis (33 points) had both played well. Westbrook had not. He'd misfired on nine of his 13 shots and turned the ball over four times. He finished with just eight points and, for the first time in more than a year, didn't attempt a single free throw. The most telling moment, though, came after the game, when he sauntered into the media room with a scowl on his face and proceeded to spend his two minutes at the podium downplaying the experience of suiting up for the team he'd rooted for as a kid. He was asked five questions. He answered them with a total of sixty-four words, barely looking up from his phone.

"How do you strike that balance, in terms of doing the things that you've done throughout your career versus trying to find the right ways to play off of guys like LeBron James and Anthony Davis?" the *Los Angeles Times'* Dan Woike asked.

"I just gotta figure it out," Westbrook replied. "It's that simple."

Westbrook being testy with the media was nothing new. It was his style, whether discussing a poor playoff performance or scholarships donated by his foundation. It was one thing, though, to mope during a midseason losing streak. It was another to look miserable after just one game.

Three nights later, the Lakers were back on the Staples Center floor for a matchup with the Suns. Late in the first half, TV cameras caught Davis and Howard shoving each other during a huddle on the bench over a pick-and-roll coverage gone wrong. The two insisted after the game—a 115–105 loss—that it was nothing more than a momentary flare-up, and that there were no lingering issues. Not everyone agreed.

"In my 42 years of being associated with the Lakers organization, I've never seen something like that smh," Magic Johnson tweeted afterward.

The Lakers bounced back two nights later with an impressive win over the Grizzlies. They followed up that victory by going 11–10 over the next six weeks. LeBron, despite missing 10 games with a strained abdominal, looked great. Davis was anchoring a defense that, despite all the roster changes, was hovering around the top 10. Anthony, despite being thirty-seven years old, was providing nice scoring off the bench. Westbrook often flirted with triple-doubles.

To the outside world, it looked like the team had figured things out. The coaching staff, however, had a different view.

"It didn't matter that we won a few games," one of Vogel's assistants said. "With everything we were seeing, it was already, like, 'Oh shit. We're fucked.'"

•　　•　　•

By late December, the Lakers' season was careening out of control. Davis had gone down with a knee injury eight days earlier and Covid had once again ravaged the roster. Entering their Christmas showdown with the Nets, the Lakers had lost four in a row. That evening, under their building's new name, Crypto.com Arena,* the Lakers fell behind by 17 points before losing 122–115 to a Brooklyn team missing both Kyrie Irving and Kevin Durant. "We literally haven't had an opportunity to log in anything," LeBron told reporters after the loss, which dropped the Lakers to 16–18. "We have no chemistry with any lineup for the simple fact that we literally haven't logged enough minutes." During one stretch, he had shared the floor with two players—Darren Collison and Stanley Johnson—whom the Lakers had signed the previous day.

The biggest problem, though, was Westbrook, who, despite his decent box scores, had become an anchor dragging the entire team down.

He'd entered the season pledging a willingness to evolve, first in private conversations with Davis and LeBron and then in public comments. "There's many different ways you can impact the game without having the ball in your hands," he told reporters during his introductory press conference. But his viewpoint seemed to change once the games began. He insisted that teammates pass him the ball after defen-

---

* AEG, which owns the building, sold the naming rights to the soon-to-be-beleaguered cryptocurrency platform for a twenty-year deal worth a reported $700 million.

sive rebounds, despite the roster being stacked with strong ballhandlers capable of triggering fast breaks. *I'm the point guard, give me that shit,* he told Vogel during one early-season practice. When he had the ball, he was reckless and careless, committing turnovers at one of the highest rates in the league. He missed so many dunks that he had a specialist examine his hands. He'd charge ahead one-on-five over and over again, like a runaway train ramming into a brick wall, even after pledging during film sessions to stop.

"Every game," an assistant coach said, "we'd be on the bench saying to each other, 'We just talked about this, and he's right back to doing the same crazy shit.'"

And then there were his shooting struggles.

Westbrook's jumper had never been his strength, but when he was younger, his once-in-a-generation combination of athleticism and explosion rendered that weakness moot. This version of Westbrook, though, was in his early thirties and was no longer the best athlete on every court. His shooting had also regressed over the years, a defect Vogel had exposed in the playoffs two seasons earlier when the Lakers had slowed down the Rockets' high-octane attack by ignoring Westbrook outside the paint,* a strategy that other teams now employed. For the Lakers, the tactic was creating issues, especially with Davis's jumper mysteriously deserting him, further cramping the Lakers' spacing (after shooting 38 percent on threes during the 2020 playoff run, he was now connecting on fewer than 20 percent of his looks).

Entering the season, the Lakers' plan was to go back to playing another big man alongside Davis, like they had for the majority of their 2020 title run. It was why Pelinka brought back Howard and signed Jordan, a former first-team All-NBA center. The idea thrilled Davis, who, dating back to his time in New Orleans, never liked playing center and was never shy about sharing it.

But there was a reason most of the league had gone away from playing two big men. Anytime Howard or Jordan—who were both about five years past their primes—shared the floor with Westbrook and

---

* "The Lakers should have known better than anyone how opponents would end up guarding him and what that could do to your offense," said an NBA executive who was in the bubble.

Davis, the Lakers' offensive spacing disappeared and they became easy to defend. Six games into the season, Vogel scrapped the dual-big line-ups and replaced Jordan in the starting unit with Avery Bradley, a guard the Lakers brought back that offseason.

Removing the second big opened up the floor for the Lakers' offense. But it also presented Vogel with a new set of problems.

In building the roster, Pelinka had failed to give Vogel any two-way players other than Davis and LeBron. The Lakers had score-first, -second, and -third wings like Anthony and Malik Monk, a former lottery pick signed in the offseason to a one-year deal. And they had strong defenders like Horton-Tucker and Stanley Johnson, neither of whom could shoot. Vogel could either go with two big men and sac-rifice spacing on offense or roll with the smaller group and watch his defense get torched. But there was no pathway for building a lineup that could excel at both ends. Pelinka had tried addressing this in the offseason by signing Trevor Ariza, who was once considered one of the league's top 3-and-D wings. But Ariza was also thirty-six years old and coming off a season in which he had played just 30 games. In October, he suffered an ankle injury, which sidelined him until December.

•　　　•　　　•

Of all the offseason moves, the decision to let Alex Caruso walk in free agency had confounded the coaching staff the most.

Caruso was the ultimate Lakers success story. He was an undrafted guard out of Texas A&M whom the Lakers—specifically their devel-opmental league coaching staff and scouts—had fallen in love with during a 2017 showcase in Chicago. They signed him to a "two-way" deal—meaning he'd split his time between the NBA and the South Bay Lakers—and then watched as he grew into a brilliant and tena-cious 6-foot-5 lockdown defender who boasted enough offensive skills to keep opposing defenses honest. Lakers coaches marveled at how on defense he'd often predict which plays LeBron preferred to stay home and then make his rotation for him, or on offense how he seemed to know precisely when to make an off-ball cut not to receive the ball him-self but to trigger a shift that would benefit a teammate. In other words: He had become the perfect running mate to slot alongside stars. Caruso and LeBron complemented each other so well that the pairing became, statistically, one of the most effective of LeBron's career.[*]

"Caruso was so smart at reading offenses and so good at covering the entire floor that he'd make up for the times when LeBron would be staying put," one of Vogel's assistants said.

Caruso had wanted to remain in LA. But as a player who went undrafted and then spent parts of his first three professional seasons in the G League, his priority entering free agency was financial security.

"I need to get as much money [as I can]," he'd later say of his approach. "Like, this is real life."

After the playoffs, Caruso and his agent, Greg Lawrence, received no signals from Pelinka. That, they knew, wasn't a good sign. On August 2, the first night of free agency, Caruso set up shop in the office of his parents' College Station, Texas, home. When the clock hit 5 p.m.—3 p.m. in LA—opening the market, Pelinka called Lawrence.

The Lakers, he said, were offering three years for $21 million, with only the first two seasons guaranteed.

Lawrence rejected the deal. That number, he told Pelinka, wasn't even in the ballpark of what he and Caruso could receive on the open market. Pelinka told him that he wasn't authorized to offer more. Lawrence told Pelinka that Caruso very much wanted to stay with the Lakers and would possibly be open to working out some sort of compromise. Pelinka held firm.

Soon after, the Bulls came to Lawrence with four years and $37 million, $30 million of which was guaranteed.

Lawrence took the offer back to Pelinka.

Pelinka refused to budge.

Still, Caruso was eager to return to LA. He told his family that if the Lakers gave him two years and a guaranteed $20 million, he'd accept.

Lawrence proposed the deal.

Pelinka again declined. The original offer, he said, was as high as he could go.

---

[*] We'll get nerdy for a second. In the 2019–20 season, when the Lakers played LeBron and Caruso together, they outscored opponents by 18.6 points per 100 possessions. Not only was that the No. 1 pairing in the league that season by that measure, it was also LeBron's most effective partnership since the NBA started tracking lineup data in 2007.

"So I said, 'Okay, if that's what it comes to, I'm ready to go to Chicago and start the next chapter,'" Caruso recalled.

Pelinka had conducted the negotiations on his own. Both Joey Buss and Nick Mazzella, the team's longtime scout and G League general manager and Caruso's biggest backers within the organization, were shocked when they heard the news. Annoyed, too. Pelinka then gave Horton-Tucker—a Klutch client—a three-year, $31 million extension and signed Kendrick Nunn, a third-year guard from the Heat whom he'd grown enamored with while watching him with Miami during the 2020 finals, to a two-year, $10 million deal. The decision to let a beloved homegrown talent walk infuriated Lakers fans. And they only became angrier after hearing Pelinka's and the team's explanations.

"He had choices, and he chose another team," Pelinka told reporters before training camp. "We pursued him and wanted to keep him. Alex moved on." The Lakers also leaked that one reason they didn't re-sign him was due to the impact it would have had on their luxury tax bill—even though the combined contracts for Horton-Tucker and Nunn exceeded Caruso's asking price by about $6 million.

In November, with the Lakers a middling 6–5, Caruso shared his side of things. "Essentially we got that offer [from the Bulls], went back to LA, asked if they could do the same, they said no, asked for something else that was a little bit less, they said no," he said during an appearance on JJ Redick's podcast. Redick told Caruso he was going to guess what number the Lakers had offered and told Caruso to blink once if his guess was too high and twice if it was too low.

"Two for $15 [million]," Redick said. "That was their initial offer." Caruso blinked once.*

A video of the exchange went viral. Lakers fans were enraged. Here was a player whose odds-defying journey they'd tracked over multiple years, whom they'd seen grow from an anonymous minor leaguer into a starter in a title-clinching game, who played the game the right way and a fun way and, as a cherry on top, was an ideal fit with the team's stars. This was exactly the type of player a team should have been eager to lock up.

---

* The guaranteed part is the reason the number confirmed here by Caruso is different. Only the first two years of the Lakers' three-year, $21 million offer were fully guaranteed.

Five days after Redick's podcast was published, the Lakers faced Caruso for the first time. The Bulls won, 121–103. Caruso took just one shot in 34 minutes but grabbed six rebounds and dished out five assists. The Bulls outscored the Lakers by 28 points when he was on the court. Before the game, Vogel had called Caruso one of his "favorite players" to ever coach. Later, a reporter asked him why.

"How do you not love a guy that plays as hard as Alex does?" Vogel replied.

•   •   •

It was the middle of January, and the Lakers had lost three out of four. On this night, they were hosting the Pacers. Before the game, Vogel and his staff had emphasized the need to force Indiana wing Caris LeVert to his left anytime he caught the ball. And yet there was Westbrook, in the middle of the fourth quarter and having just reentered the game, allowing LeVert to drive to his right and convert an easy layup to give the Pacers a six-point lead. For the Lakers' coaches, the blown coverage was the final straw. With 3:52 remaining, Vogel pulled the former MVP. Westbrook spent the rest of the game—a 111–104 loss—watching from the sidelines. Instead of waiting for the final buzzer alongside his teammates, he retreated to the locker room during a stoppage with 8.3 seconds left.

During his postgame press conference, a reporter asked Vogel what had gone into the decision.

"Playing the guys that I thought were going to win the game," the usually congenial Vogel replied.

The move, in the eyes of many, had been long overdue. And from an X's-and-O's standpoint, Vogel didn't disagree. He was against the Westbrook trade from the beginning. *It's going to get me fired,* he told his staff after the deal. But to him, the decision to bench Westbrook was more complicated than that. Vogel's job was to win a championship, not just individual games, and the only chance the Lakers had to do that, in his view, was if Westbrook found his groove. Given how sensitive Westbrook had become, Vogel worried that benching him would be a blow he'd be unable to overcome. He'd seen the way Westbrook had reacted to the struggles, how he'd spent the season's first three months brooding and sulking and blaming everyone but himself. "My job changes every night, honestly," Westbrook told reporters in early January. "Sometimes I'm in the dunker spot* a lot of the game. Sometimes I have the ball in my hands, sometimes I don't. Sometimes I'm the screener. Sometimes I'm cutting." Vogel, though, had now reached his breaking point. The team was running out of time. He was, too.

The day before the Pacers loss, *The Athletic* reported that Vogel was "being evaluated on a game-to-game basis and remains at risk of being fired soon." Given that the Lakers had declined to give Vogel a new contract following his championship run, tacking on just a single season—taking him through the 2022–23 season—the news wasn't surprising. But it remained jarring to see a coach less than two seasons removed from a championship fighting for his job.

Most of that pressure was being applied by Kurt Rambis, who had become one of the most influential voices within the organization. Considering that his career record in four seasons as a head coach was 65–164, many on Vogel's staff and around the league found this newfound power laughable. Even Phil Jackson, one of Rambis's lone boosters in the NBA, had passed over him in 2016. Rambis at the time was coming off a half-season as the Knicks' interim head coach when his most noteworthy moment was "liking" a pornographic tweet. The Knicks claimed that Rambis's Twitter account was hacked,† but the next day Jackson taped the back page of the *New York Post* to the glass above the steam table in the kitchen. When staffers came in to get their breakfast they were greeted by Rambis's picture and the words "PORN LOSER" in big, bold print. Jackson sat there the whole time laughing. That offseason, he hired Jeff Hornacek as his head coach.

Now with the Lakers, where he had the backing of the owner and his wife in a position of power, it was Rambis who was showing up a coaching colleague. Early in the season, he was a frequent presence in Vogel's meetings. At one point, he had told Vogel and his staff that they could be out of jobs if things didn't turn around. ("Kurt Rambis always supportively *encouraged* Frank Vogel and he never threatened Vogel with being fired," a Lakers representative said. "Which, of course, would

---

* The dunker spot is the area along the baseline just outside the lane. The idea being a player can catch the ball in that area and dunk it easily.
† They doubled down on the "hacked" defense and claimed that they were reaching out to Twitter to investigate.

not have been Kurt Rambis's message to convey, anyway.") In December, while Vogel was sidelined with Covid, Rambis and Pelinka tried convincing lead assistant David Fizdale to remove Westbrook from the starting lineup. Fizdale refused, Vogel returned, and, with a four-game winning streak around the new year, the Lakers climbed to 21–19. But they followed that up with a pair of losses—including a 125–116 defeat to the Kings in which Sacramento's game operations crew played a clip from Foreigner's 1977 song "Cold as Ice" every time Westbrook, who went 2-for-14, missed a shot. The Lakers responded by losing in Denver to the Nuggets by 37 points. Two days later, back in LA, Rambis, for the first time that season, attended the coaches' pregame meeting in person. There, he pushed for Vogel to go back to lineups with the thirty-six-year-old Howard or the thirty-three-year-old Jordan playing alongside another big man, despite those pairings being ineffective all season. Vogel stuck with his typical rotations, and the Lakers won, but two days later he came around to Rambis's point of view and made a move.

Westbrook reacted exactly as Vogel had expected.

"You never know when you're coming in, you never know when you're coming out," he told reporters in early February after another late-game benching. Vogel had now lost Westbrook, and the change had also failed to make a difference on the court. The Lakers lost six of their next 10 games, including a 131–116 drubbing at the hands of the defending champion Bucks, a loss that dropped them to 26–29 and seemed to break the locker room. Asked after the game what it told him about the state of the team, LeBron said, "It tells me we ain't on their level, I mean, I could have told you that before the game." With less than forty-eight hours until the trade deadline, another reporter asked LeBron if he believed the current roster could reach that level.

"Um, no," he replied.

Later that night, Bill Oram, a well-sourced Lakers beat writer for *The Athletic,* published a piece reporting that "sources have indicated that the Lakers no longer believe they can win at a high level with Westbrook alongside James and Davis." Oram added, "Whether it is by Thursday's deadline or in the summer, the Lakers know they need to find their way out of the Russell Westbrook business."

Doing so, however, would prove to be easier said than done.

• • •

The trade deadline came and went, and the Lakers' roster remained the same. There was no way to significantly upgrade the team without trading Westbrook, and there was no way for the Lakers to trade Westbrook without including their 2027 first-round pick, the one first-round pick they were allowed to deal.* There was interest around the league in those assets—who wouldn't want to short an aging Lakers roster?—but the Lakers' key decision-makers decided they weren't going to throw good money after bad. The Westbrook deal, they felt, had rendered the season a sunk cost. The best thing the team could do was take its lumps and then use the offseason to reset. The NBA also had a rule prohibiting teams from trading away first-round picks more than seven years into the future. Waiting until the offseason, therefore, would give the Lakers an additional first-round pick (2029) to dangle in a trade, which would allow them to go hunting for a bigger fish.

"You can't force another team to present yourself with a deal that is going to make your team be better. That's up to them," Pelinka told reporters after the deadline. "And throughout this process we had different things we looked at and, like I've done in the past, had conversations with LeBron and Anthony about it, and I would say there's alignment here. And that's all that matters."

Once again, Pelinka had misrepresented the facts on the ground. LeBron was not aligned with this approach, and less than a week later, he decided to clarify his thoughts.

He started by quote-tweeting a picture of Los Angeles Rams general manager Les Snead celebrating his team's 2022 Super Bowl victory while wearing a T-shirt with the words "fuck them picks" on it, a tribute to the multiple trades he'd made in which he'd swapped draft capital for players. "LEGEND!" LeBron wrote. "My type of guy!" Then, while in Cleveland a few days later for All-Star weekend, LeBron used a media session to praise Thunder general manager Sam Presti. "The MVP over there is Sam Presti. He's the MVP," he said. That same day, *The Athletic*'s Jason Lloyd asked if it was possible that LeBron could once again return to his hometown Cavs.

---

* Because of the aforementioned "Stepien Rule," which prohibited teams from trading first-round picks in consecutive years.

"The door's not closed on that," LeBron replied. He then commended Cavaliers general manager Koby Altman and his front office. "Those guys have done an unbelievable job drafting and making trades," he said.

Even those not well versed in the inner workings of the NBA could pick up on the subtext. This wasn't the first time LeBron was annoyed with the Lakers, either. In the summer of 2021, for example, they'd ignored his wishes and declined to bring back Jared Dudley. But the situation had never been this dire. A meeting was called for the Tuesday after All-Star weekend at the Lakers' El Segundo offices. There, Paul, Pelinka, and Jeanie spent two hours talking things out. The parties all vowed to work together and keep the lines of communication open. But the bond between Klutch and the Lakers appeared to be broken.

On February 23, with the Lakers still on break, *The Athletic*'s Oram published another piece outlining these fissures. "One source close to the Lakers likened [the situation] to the early days of war." The report went viral, sending both sides into damage control mode. "We have a great partnership with the Lakers," Paul told *The Athletic*'s Sam Amick two days after Oram's report.

That night, the Lakers returned to the floor for the first time since the All-Star break. They lost to the Clippers, 105–102, falling to 27–32 on the year. After the game, it was time for LeBron to clarify where he stood on, well, everything.

"The question I have," Oram asked, "is what is your level of confidence that the Lakers' front office can put championship-contending rosters around you for as long as you're here?"

"Very confident," LeBron said. "I mean, they've done it. They've shown me that. I mean, ever since I got here, the front office—Jeanie, Linda, Kurt, and everybody—has welcomed me with open arms and has given me an opportunity to play for a historical franchise and welcome my family in."

That LeBron had singled out the Rambii—as some fans and league insiders had begun referring to Kurt and Linda—and not Pelinka stood out.

"I don't understand how some of my comments over the weekend was taken to a whole different area of, 'Could I see myself retiring as a Cavalier?'" LeBron continued. "I never said I would see myself playing in a Cavaliers uniform."

Meaning that before retiring he could see himself maybe, possibly, signing a ceremonial contract with his hometown team, but that there was no reason for Lakers fans to worry about his bolting in free agency.

"You guys take some of my words and just twist them to different places where they shouldn't go. If I comment or compliment a GM in OKC, I really believe that he's done a phenomenal job. And you guys spin that to me saying that Rob [Pelinka] is not doing a great job. Or if I say the GM of the Rams, I loved his fucking T-shirt, and I believe the same way. I don't care about picks. I care about winning championships. How is that directed at Rob and the Lakers franchise? Rob has done the same thing. When we went and got AD, he didn't care about picks as well, obviously.

"It's so weird that you guys can take . . . not you guys, whoever started this whole thing."

LeBron looked around the room.

"I mean, Bill doesn't like the Lakers anyway," he said, referencing Oram's recent article. "So it's always gonna be a negative any time Bill says anything about the Lakers, it's gonna be negative, so I hope no one in Lakers faithful listen to Bill Oram, I hope not. He hasn't said one great thing about the Lakers in so long."[*]

A big smile stretched across LeBron's face.

Another reporter asked, "Is this a team that you see yourself playing with beyond your contract?"

"This is a franchise I see myself being with," LeBron said. "I'm here . . . I see myself being with the purple and gold as long as I can play."

Next, LeBron was asked about the meeting earlier that week between Paul and Lakers management.

---

[*] LeBron's comments led to Oram receiving so many online threats toward him and his family that Lakers security offered to come by his house and present some home security tips. Oram would later write than when he mentioned these security concerns to LeBron a few days later, LeBron initially brushed them off. "Well," Oram recalled LeBron saying, "better buy a gun." Following their private conversation, LeBron did offer a semi-apology on Twitter. "@Billoram and I had a candid conversation after the game tonight and I know he has a job to do," he wrote. "I know what he wrote wasn't truthful cause it never came from me. But I get it, SOURCES run this game. Nevertheless #LakerNation let him be cause he ain't a bad guy."

"Why did you think that was important?" the reporter asked.

"I mean, I heard it just like you guys heard it. You guys saw the report, I saw the report," LeBron said. But, he added, "I think a lot of people are, to be honest, just jealous of the relationship that Rich has with the front office and with this team and the relationship that I have that I've grown over the last four years."

Next, Dan Woike of the *Los Angeles Times* asked, "How does that responsibility of pushing the right buttons—does that make the winning and losing harder?"

"First of all, I don't push the buttons," LeBron said. "They ask for my opinion, and I voice my opinion and what I believe, but I don't press any buttons. That's what our front office is for, that's what our leadership group is for, I don't press no buttons. So we can just state that right now."

That said, LeBron did have a stat he wanted to share. "Between me, AD, and Russ on the floor at the same time, I think it's less than 15 games this season,"* he said. "And that's the biggest disappointment so far, that us three, because we all wanted to see this work and we just haven't been on the floor."

LeBron's message was clear. Anyone with an issue with the Westbrook trade should take it up with the team. But also, it was too early to judge the Westbrook trade. But at the same time, if you did want to judge the Westbrook trade, just know that he had nothing to do with it. But also, he and the Lakers had an incredible relationship. But just to be clear again, he wasn't the one who had decided to make that trade. Oh, and anyone who criticized the Lakers, even if it was someone as well sourced as Oram, was either ill-informed or, more likely, jealous.

Two nights later, the Lakers welcomed the 24–36 Pelicans to Crypto .com Arena for a nationally televised game. The score remained tight in the first half, but coming out of the locker room, the Pelicans ran the Lakers off the floor. After the game, a 123–95 loss, videos from inside the arena circulated online. There was Ariza calling a fan sitting behind the bench a "bitch." There was Westbrook telling a different fan behind the bench to go home. There was LeBron telling a courtside fan to "shut yo ass up."

---

* At that point, it was 17.

And there was Jeanie, leaving her seat with 5:27 left in the third quarter and never returning.

. . .

The losses just kept coming and coming. In April, the Lakers were eliminated from postseason contention. LeBron had now missed the playoffs twice in four seasons since joining the team. Before coming to LA, he'd missed the playoffs just twice in his fifteen-year career.

There were valid reasons for the failures. Davis had missed more than half the season. LeBron missed nearly a third. The two of them and Westbrook had shared the floor in only 21 games. Nunn missed the entire season with a knee injury. The Lakers used a franchise record 41 different starting lineups, a seemingly impossible mark.

But these were also problems the Lakers should have anticipated. Davis had been injury-riddled his entire career, LeBron was not young anymore, and while the two of them might have barely played with Westbrook, the Lakers were outscored by 34 points in the 393 minutes the trio had shared the floor. The disastrous season was a result of bad decisions, not bad luck, and with the season reaching its conclusion, Lakers fans were furious at everyone involved. In a poll conducted by the popular Lakers fan site Silver Screen & Roll, only 29 percent of respondents said they believed that Jeanie's ownership group could lead the Lakers back to title contention, and that came just a few weeks after the *Los Angeles Times'* Plaschke, the city's most prominent sports columnist, wrote a piece imploring the Lakers to trade LeBron.

Someone needed to take the fall.

The Lakers traveled to Denver for their final game of the season. With LeBron, Davis, and Westbrook all out, and behind a triple-double (31 points, 16 rebounds, 10 assists) from undrafted rookie Austin Reaves, they erased a nine-point deficit in the final minute of the game and then held on in overtime for a 146–141 win, giving them a 33–49 record. It was a nice end to a disappointing season, but one that was short-lived.

"Frank Vogel has coached his final game for the Lakers, a decision that's expected to be shared with him as soon as [tomorrow]," ESPN's Wojnarowski tweeted moments after the final buzzer.

Vogel was sitting with his coaches in a private area of the locker room when the news broke. His phone buzzed. He looked at it and slammed the device down.

Woj just tweeted that I don't have a fucking job anymore, he told his staff.

He had now joined Caruso, Caldwell-Pope, Kuzma, and Dudley as key members of the 2020 title group who, less than two years later, were no longer with the team. LeBron and Davis remained, and as long as they did, the Lakers would have a shot. But that all-important banner No. 18 that Jeanie had entered the season dreaming about seemed further away than it had in years.

"I'm growing impatient just because we had the fourth-highest payroll in the league, when you spend that kind of money on the luxury tax, you expect to go deep into the playoffs," she said in a sit-down interview with Plaschke that May. "So, yeah, it was gut-wrenching for me to go out on a limb like that and not get the results that we were looking for. I'm not happy, I'm not satisfied."

- 12 -

THE PURSUIT OF HAPPINESS

It was the spring of 2022, and the Lakers, once again, were facing a pivotal offseason. They needed to hire a new head coach. They needed to solve the Westbrook situation. They needed to repair the relationship with Klutch, which, despite the Band-Aid that was the post-deadline summit the previous winter, remained strained.

Most of all, they needed to salvage their partnership with LeBron, which, to some, was increasingly looking like a disappointment. "When you actually look at the last twelve years and the amount of draft picks they used just to get LeBron and Davis, we're talking about a decade of assets that they gave up basically for this one bubble season title, that, by the way, their fans didn't even get to enjoy," Bill Simmons said on a March 2022 podcast. Some fans and media members began arguing that having come during a shortened season and in a controlled environment, the 2020 championship was deserving of an asterisk.

"They won the title, I feel like it was all worth it, but it's weird to say, like, you basically have had one good season out of the last ten and the next five are looking probably not awesome," Simmons added during that podcast. "So, was it worth it?"

Jeanie recognized that with LeBron and Davis getting older and the team running low on assets, the next few months might be her last chance to flip the narrative. To help ensure that the franchise got things right, she did what the Lakers often did in times of need: reach into the past. For her, that meant once again speaking to Phil Jackson about basketball matters.

"He's somebody that knows this environment and knows the challenges I have and wants to see the Lakers successful," she had told Plaschke during her interview in May. "So he's somebody I know doesn't have any other agenda than for the Lakers to be successful, so he's somebody that I can lean on."

Lakers fans weren't thrilled. Jackson was a legend, but he was also coming off a disastrous tenure running the Knicks (they went 90–171 in his three-plus seasons as president of basketball operations). That he wasn't the only former Laker great whom Jeanie was consulting only added to the sense of dysfunction, as word had recently spread that Magic Johnson was back in the fold. "To me, he's still working with us," Jeanie told *The Athletic* in February 2022.* And all this was in addition to the roles that Kurt and Linda Rambis were playing. Three years earlier, a *Los Angeles Times* headline had read, "Who's Making Decisions for the Lakers? It's Complicated," and the picture had only grown murkier ever since.

But the truth was that while there were a handful of people from whom Jeanie sought advice, Pelinka remained the one driving basketball decisions, and, just like in his agent days, he operated as an island. Aside from salary cap matters—for which he relied on the expertise of his top cap staffer, Marshall Rader—he did most of the job himself. Unlike his peers, he almost never outsourced trade calls, and, when preparing for the draft, he kept most of his scouting opinions to himself. ("Although Pelinka does his own private draft work to contemplate potential draft decisions," the Lakers representative said, "many NBA executives and scouts do the same.") Pelinka was so independent that he sometimes asked agents if they could send him clips of their draft prospects.

"The Lakers are the only team where, if I need to reach them for something and Rob's on a flight, I wouldn't even know who else to call," a rival GM said.

Despite the team's recent struggles, Jeanie still believed in Pelinka. More importantly, she trusted him. Having him and Linda Rambis by her side made her feel safe, and she became even more comfortable delegating. In the spring of 2022, Jeanie extended Pelinka's contract, taking him through the end of the 2025–26 season. "I wanted to make sure that the new coach that we hired knew that there would be this

---

* The rest of that quote: "In terms of an official capacity, in the NBA, you have to be very clear as to who can negotiate on your behalf and who can't. So he doesn't have that official designation. But in terms of his support, his wisdom, his insight, I freely call on him as needed."

support," Jeanie said in an October 2022 interview, "that there would be this long-term opportunity to build success and that it wouldn't be about who's on the hot seat next."

Pelinka's first offseason task was finding a replacement for Vogel. With the help of Rambis and Jackson, he compiled a list of around a dozen targets. Preliminary discussions took place over Zoom—with Pelinka, Kurt Rambis, and Joey and Jesse Buss leading the interviews—and by mid-May, the Lakers had zeroed in on Darvin Ham, a down-to-earth, widely respected former player with more than a decade of experience as an assistant.

Ham grew up in the hard-nosed industrial city of Saginaw, Michigan. He was raised on the east side, an area hit hard by the crack cocaine epidemic and besieged by violence. Friends of his were murdered, and when he was fourteen, he spent eleven days in the hospital after getting hit in the face by a stray bullet while out getting pizza. The shot, which pierced his cheek and landed in his neck, nearly killed him.

Ham never wanted that life. "I had great parents, man, and I wanted something better for myself," he'd later say. He fell in love with football and, after a growth spurt late in high school, joined the basketball team. His jumper was crooked, but as an avid weight lifter, he was bigger and stronger than most of his peers. He earned a scholarship to a Colorado community college, and then to Texas Tech, and then caught on with the Nuggets in 1996 after going undrafted. He bounced around the professional ranks before taking a job as an assistant with the D-League's Albuquerque Thunderbirds. In 2011, the Lakers hired him as an assistant; Mike Brown, their new head coach, was a video coordinator with the Nuggets when Ham was in Denver. Two years later, Ham joined the staff of new Hawks head coach Mike Budenholzer. He remained there for five seasons and then followed Budenholzer to Milwaukee, where they won the 2021 title.

Ham played an essential role on Budenholzer's teams. He knew the game and, because of his time in the league, knew how the NBA worked. That background, combined with his size—he was 6-foot-7 and built like a brick house—and baritone voice, enabled him to challenge players in ways many coaches could not. "He was basically an enforcer as an assistant coach," a colleague of Ham's said. "He bought into everything Bud was doing and made sure everyone in the building did as well."

Ham wasn't a shouter. His approach was more nuanced. He'd put his hand on players' shoulders and pull them aside, though he was willing to confront serious issues head-on. While with the Hawks, Budenholzer had repeatedly asked a veteran player to stop drinking hard liquor on team flights, only to be ignored. *I got it,* Ham told Budenzoler one night after landing. Early the next morning, he knocked on the player's hotel room door.

Is everything okay? the player asked.

Coach told you to stop fucking drinking on the plane, Ham told him. *That means there's no fucking drinking on the plane.*

The player never drank hard liquor on the plane again.

Ham's tough love wasn't reserved for players. He hated the way Budenholzer would lose his temper with officials, and sometimes during halftime he instructed the rest of the staff to wait outside the coaches' room while he had a private moment with his boss. This willingness to call out those with more power extended up to Bucks star Giannis Antetokounmpo as well. "He didn't have a problem getting fired up at him during practice," said a Bucks colleague. "But the key was always his perspective. Winning was everything on the floor, but he made clear that he believed the things off the floor mattered, too."

Numerous teams had talked to Ham over the years about their head-coaching vacancies, but this was his first time being considered a top candidate and the Lakers weren't the only team expressing interest. The Hornets had also reached out. Looking for advice, Ham called up one of his former coaches, the Hall of Famer Larry Brown. "He asked me what I thought," Brown said, "and I told him to tell me his thoughts first. And when he did, they all seemed to point him in the direction of Charlotte. So I said, 'Well, I think you answered your own question.'" There were so many reasons to be wary of the Lakers. The Westbrook problem, the lack of shooting, the fact that Pelinka had fired two coaches in just four years. Then Ham flew out to LA to interview in person. There, he pitched a vision built around three words: "competitiveness," "togetherness," and "accountability." The Lakers loved what they heard and said they were willing to accept some of his demands, like not allowing Kurt Rambis into coaches' meetings. Ham, figuring he couldn't turn down a chance to lead one of the NBA's crown jewels, took the job.

The news broke on May 27.

"So damn EXCITED!!!!!!!!" LeBron wrote on Twitter the day after news of Ham's hiring was broken. "Congrats and welcome Coach DHam!! 👏 👏 👏 👏 👏 #LakeShow💜 💛."

The next day, Ham FaceTimed Julian Taylor, a close friend.

They looked at each other and burst out laughing.

Can you believe it? Taylor said. *You're the head coach of the Los Angeles Lakers!*

•　　•　　•

LeBron strolled into Las Vegas's Thomas & Mack Center, flanked by his security team. His arrival sent a jolt through the arena. Fans held up their cell phones. Photographers flocked toward him. Players, coaches, and executives congregating around the court came over to say hello. It was early July, and tip-off for the Lakers' summer league squad's first game was just a few minutes away.

An official escorted LeBron to a seat on the baseline. Throughout the game's first half, new teammates like Thomas Bryant and Juan Toscano-Anderson paid their respects. So did Ham, Pelinka, and Kurt Rambis. In the second half, Talen Horton-Tucker swung by.

Seated across the court, on the opposite end of the floor, was Westbrook.

He saw LeBron enter the gym before the game.

He didn't budge.

The first quarter came and went.

He never crossed halfcourt.

The second quarter reached its final minutes.

Westbrook rose from his seat and exited through a tunnel, never returning.

The scene became the talk of the night. Side-by-side images contrasting how LeBron and Westbrook had interacted at summer league the previous year—they'd entered the building together and sat next to each other—made the rounds on social media. The noninteraction was red meat for talking heads. It also sparked concerns within the team's new coaching staff.

"We knew that we'd have to bring Westbrook off the bench eventually because things weren't a good fit," a Lakers coach said. "But seeing that play out that night it was like, 'Oh, these motherfuckers aren't even talking to each other.'"

The impetus appeared to be the recent rumors involving Kyrie Irving. LeBron's former costar was entering the final season of his contract with the Nets, a $36.9 million player option, and wanted an extension. The Nets, however, were unwilling to hand over tens of millions of guaranteed dollars to a player who, since arriving in Brooklyn, had missed chunks of games for, among other things, a refusal to get a Covid vaccine and promoting an antisemitic film on social media. Recognizing he had no future in Brooklyn, Irving asked for a trade. The news had leaked in late June, with multiple outlets reporting that the Lakers were one of Irving's preferred destinations and that LeBron wanted a reunion.

Negotiations between the Lakers and Nets went nowhere. Pelinka never showed any real interest in Irving. And even if he had, the Nets had no desire to take Westbrook back. Irving picked up his option and remained in Brooklyn,* but by then the damage was done. Because of the NBA's salary-matching rules, the only way for the Lakers to acquire Irving would have been by dealing Westbrook. Westbrook knew this, and he knew that LeBron did as well. Meaning that no matter what LeBron said in public, the reality was clear: He was pushing for the Lakers to ship Westbrook out.

The Lakers opened their season in mid-October with a 123–109 loss to the Warriors. Two nights later, in their home opener, Westbrook misfired on all 11 of his shots, and the Lakers fell to the Clippers, 103–97. Asked during his postgame press conference how he thought he played, Westbrook replied, "Solid. Played hard. That's all you can ask for." Three days later, on a Sunday afternoon, the Lakers were back on their home floor to take on the Blazers. This time their first win of the season was within their grasp.

With just 36 seconds remaining and clinging to a one-point lead,

---

* "Normal people keep the world going, but those who dare to be different lead us into tomorrow," was what he told NBA reporter Shams Charania when sharing the news. "I've made my decision to opt in. See you in the fall." How exactly signing on to earn $36.9 million for a season of playing basketball made him a person leading society "into tomorrow" was unclear.

Westbrook brought the ball up the court. Instead of draining the clock, he dribbled directly into a 15-footer on the right wing. The shot ricocheted off the rim. Watching from the perimeter, both Davis and LeBron turned their palms toward the sky, putting their indignation on full display. The Lakers ended up losing 106–104, falling to 0–3.

After the game, one reporter asked LeBron about the team's late-game "shot selection." Another wanted to know, "basketball philosophy-wise," how LeBron preferred to manage the clock late in games.

"I feel like this is an interview of trying to set me up to say something. I can tell that you guys are in the whole 'Russell Westbrook category' right now," LeBron said. Later he added, "You guys can write about Russ and all the things you want to try to talk about Russ, but I'm not up here to do that. I won't do it. I've said it over and over. That's not who I am."

Westbrook wasn't buying it. To him, this was just the latest example of LeBron saying one thing but doing another. "People are saying, 'Let Russ be Russ,'" he had told reporters the previous December. "I think nobody understands what that means. I think people just say it." It was a clear shot at LeBron, and one Westbrook doubled down on after the season when asked about LeBron's repeated use of the phrase.

"That wasn't true," Westbrook told reporters. "So let's be honest."

Westbrook knew LeBron's reputation. He'd seen all the examples of LeBron seemingly misrepresenting himself. There was the time LeBron claimed that *The Godfather* was his favorite movie but then failed to recall a single line when asked during a press conference to name one. There was the time he carried *The Autobiography of Malcolm X* into a media session but stumbled when asked to name his biggest takeaway. There was the time during an interview when he claimed that, the night Kobe scored 81 points, he'd predicted beforehand that he'd go for 70, a clip so widely mocked that it became a popular meme. LeBron's reputation for bending the truth was so widespread that he even got teased while appearing in would-be safe spaces.

"They say you be cappin',"* Jacksonville Jaguars cornerback Jalen Ramsey told him during a November 2022 episode of *The Shop,* a talk show produced by LeBron and Maverick Carter's media company.

---

* I guess I need to add a definition here for the boomers: "cap" means "lie." I'll also confess that the first time I heard the phrase, I had to look it up.

This, in Westbrook's view, was who LeBron was. And he was done putting up with it.

Two days after losing to the Blazers, the Lakers were back at their facility for a practice. Pelinka informed the players a special guest would be coming through. He'd created a program called the Genius Series, where he'd bring in luminaries from various fields—Dwayne "The Rock" Johnson, Kendrick Lamar, Elon Musk—to address the team. For this day, he'd secured an A-lister: Will Smith, just six months removed from slapping Chris Rock during the 94th Academy Awards.

The team gathered in the film room to review the Blazers game. Ham was tough on the group, highlighting all sorts of mistakes that had led to the 0–3 start. When the session concluded, Pelinka came by. He'd already shown Smith the practice court—they shot free throws together—and Jeanie's office. Now, he told the players, Smith was on his way to them.

When Pelinka and Ham left to fetch him, LeBron, seated in a middle row, stood up.

Y'all got this, he said.

He stormed out a back door.

Shit, man, Davis said.

He stood and followed LeBron out.

Stunned, the rest of the players sat there, looking at each other, unsure what to do.

"We're like, 'Yo, what the fuck is going on?' " one recalled.

Westbrook rose next.

So, we all leaving? he asked.

Nah, Russ, said Patrick Beverley, a brash veteran point guard the Lakers acquired over the summer. *We gotta stay.*

Westbrook didn't understand. *What do you mean?* he asked.

Them two guys can do whatever the fuck they want, Beverley said. *They won a championship.*

As the two went back and forth, it became clear to the other players in the room what Westbrook was thinking: As a nine-time All-Star, and former MVP, and future Hall of Famer, why would there be a difference between him and them?

Pelinka came back in.

We ready? he asked

We ain't ready, Beverley said. *We need five minutes.*

Pelinka left.

Minutes later, Ham reentered and sat silently at the front of the room as Westbrook and Beverley continued arguing. He then stood up and exited through the same door LeBron and Davis had used. Soon after, he returned with both stars. Next, Ham went to get Pelinka and Smith. When they all returned, Smith was greeted with smiles and daps.

Smith talked to the players about his new movie, *Emancipation*. He talked about overcoming adversity. He cracked some jokes at the team's expense. Then he opened the floor for questions.

LeBron was first. He had a question, he said. Smith answered. Then LeBron had another question. And another after that and another after that and another after that. On and on he went, stretching what was supposed to be a thirty-minute session into nearly an hour.

"The same guy who was trying to leave is now quoting back movie lines and going through the guy's whole life story," one attendee recalled thinking. Seated in the third row, picking at a bowl of fruit, Westbrook watched in disbelief, shaking his head and rolling his eyes every time LeBron spoke.

I hate that fake shit, Westbrook said to a teammate afterward, as the Lakers gathered for a team photo. *I just can't do it.*

The next afternoon, the Lakers posted the picture on social media. Standing among Lakers players, coaches, and Pelinka was Smith, holding up a custom jersey. There, standing a few feet to Smith's right, was Westbrook, his face twisted into a scowl.

•   •   •

Even before taking the job, Ham knew that the only chance he had at orchestrating a turnaround was if he figured out a way to move Westbrook to the bench. But he had to make sure not to alienate Westbrook while doing so. He figured his best chance was to build a relationship first and then pitch the change. And he figured the best way to do that was through public flattery.

"Don't get it messed up. Russell is one of the best players our league has ever seen," Ham had said during his introductory press conference in July. "He still has a ton left in that tank."

He then waited until the end of the preseason to make his move. Before the team's final preseason game, Ham pulled Westbrook aside and told him that he was going to experiment with bringing him off the bench. Doing so, he said, was best for everyone, Westbrook included. It meant he'd have the ball in his hands and would no longer have to worry about fitting in.

"He totally looked me in my eye and said, 'Yeah, Coach, whatever you need me to do,'" Ham later told reporters.

Westbrook entered the game midway through the first quarter. Five minutes in, he strained his left hamstring.

The following week, he blamed the injury on Ham's decision.

"I've been doing the same thing for fourteen years straight. Honestly, I didn't even know what to do pregame," he said. "Being honest, I was trying to figure out how to stay warm and loose . . . The way I play the game, it's fast-paced, quick, stop-and-go. And I just happened to, when I subbed in, I felt something."

Ham slotted Westbrook back into the starting lineup for the season opener. The Lakers then lost their first four games of the season, allowing Ham to move Westbrook back to the bench. Two games later, at home against the Nuggets, Westbrook recorded 18 points, eight rebounds, and eight assists in his new role, helping lead the Lakers to a 121–110 win, their first of the year. He even received a standing ovation after checking back into the game late in the fourth quarter.

"Tonight, we needed to prove something to ourselves," Ham told reporters afterward. "Not to the world. Not to the media. We had to prove it to ourselves, and I felt great about how we responded."

The Lakers won their next game, too, a 120–117 victory in overtime over the Pelicans.

It looked like a turning point.

It was not.

The Lakers matched wins with losses over the next two months, and in late December they arrived in Miami with a 14–20 record, the third-worst record in the conference. It felt like déjà vu. Once again, Davis was watching games from the sideline due to a foot injury he sustained a few weeks earlier; once again, the Lakers were bad on both sides of the ball; once again, they were hovering around the bottom of the Western Conference standings.

And, once again, LeBron was losing patience.

That night, after another loss, a reporter asked LeBron about his mindset with his thirty-eighth birthday two days away.

"I think about that, I don't want to finish my career playing at this level from a team aspect," he said as part of his response. Later he added, "I'm a winner, and I want to win. And I want to win and give myself a chance to win and still compete for championships."

The Lakers bounced back, winning five in a row, but that only seemed to trigger LeBron even more. In early January, following a two-point victory in Sacramento, he did an interview with *The Athletic's* Sam Amick.

"You're thirty-eight, and you're doing things that have never been done," Amick told him. "And the idea that a team would hold on to some picks and wait for next year—"

"Well, if you guys know, then you guys know," LeBron said, cutting him off. "You guys know. I don't need to talk about it. You guys know." While walking away after the interview, he turned toward Amick and shouted, "Y'all know what the fuck should be happening. I don't need to talk."

Unlike his goading of his teams' front offices in years past, there was nothing passive or ambiguous about these statements. LeBron knew the Lakers had options. The Pacers, for example, were reportedly offering a package featuring sharpshooting guard Buddy Hield and starting center Myles Turner. Neither was a needle-mover, but since he was still performing at an All-NBA level, LeBron didn't think he needed another star. In his eyes, all he needed was for the Lakers to give him a little help, which they could do simply by attaching either or both of their available first-round picks (2027 and 2029) to Westbrook's salary in a deal. After that, he'd take care of the rest.

Pelinka was reticent. He wasn't interested in singles and doubles. He was saving the picks for a home run, for a trade that could both bolster the current roster and help set the Lakers up for life after LeBron.

"I think the calculus for the Lakers is to win a championship or not," he told reporters in late January. "There's no in-between or incremental growth. So as we analyze opportunities, we have to do it through that lens . . . The completely unwise thing to do would be to shoot a bullet early and then not have it later when you have a better championship move you can make." In previous years, the threat of his expiring contract would have given LeBron leverage. But after he signed an extension in August, one that tied him to the Lakers for at least one more full

season, Jeanie and Pelinka no longer had to capitulate to his demands.*
"He gets this, 'Oh, he's controlling the team,' right? And the reality of
it is, that's not true," Rich Paul would later say. "But for him it probably
becomes very, very frustrating to be positioned as you have the control
without actually having the control."

Recognizing his lack of leverage, LeBron continued using the only
tool left at his disposal: media pressure. On February 3, less than a
week before the trade deadline, news broke that Irving had requested a
trade from the Nets. Not long after, LeBron tweeted "👀👑." The next
night, following a 131–126 loss to the Pelicans, ESPN's Dave McMenamin, citing Pelinka's previous statement that the Lakers would "part
with any assets" if it pushed them into championship contention, asked
LeBron if Irving was "the type of player who could help your team get
to the finish line."

"That's a Rob question. You got to see him when y'all get back to
LA," he said. "I've told y'all a couple weeks, I don't speak for our front
office." But, he added, "Obviously, that's a . . . what's the word you use?
A 'duh' question when you talk about a player like that."

Neither Pelinka nor the Nets had changed their stance. Pelinka
seemed to still not want Irving and the Nets still had no interest in taking back Westbrook. Two days later, they dealt Irving to the Mavericks.

"I can't sit here and say I'm not disappointed on not being able to
land such a talent," LeBron told ESPN. "Someone that I had great
chemistry with, and know I got great chemistry with on the floor,
that can help you win championships." He claimed that his focus had
"shifted back to where it should be, and that's this club now and what
we have in the locker room." But no one was buying it, and the Lakers
had just two days to find a solution.

First, though, it was time for the two parties to come together for a
rare night of celebration.

•   •   •

This was what both sides had envisioned when they joined forces back
in the summer of 2018. The plan was for each party to elevate the other,

---

* The extension was for two years and $97.1 million. The second year a player
option.

for LeBron to give the Lakers moments to celebrate and the Lakers to dress them up in a way only they could. But then came the pandemic, and various injuries to Davis and LeBron, and a series of team-building mistakes.

Five years into their partnership, LeBron and the Lakers had yet to share an iconic achievement together, in LA, in front of Lakers fans.

After this night, that would no longer be the case.

LeBron sauntered into Crypto.com Arena a few hours before tip-off, 35 points shy of Kareem Abdul-Jabbar's all-time scoring mark. *Tonight's the night,* he told teammates as he changed out of his shiny black suit and into his gear for the game against the Thunder. It had been a rough couple of seasons for him and the team, but for one evening, all the drama would be relegated to the background. For thirty-nine years, Abdul-Jabbar had held the title of the game's most prolific scorer. Soon, that title would belong to LeBron. He might never match Michael Jordan's six rings, but Jordan would never have this.

Before tip-off, the arena buzzed with excitement. Jay-Z, Denzel Washington, and LL Cool J were among the celebrities in the building. Magic Johnson, James Worthy, and, of course, Kareem showed up to witness history, too. A pair of courtside seats went for $24,000 a pop on the secondary market.

Looking to honor his pregame promise, LeBron came out firing. He scored eight points in the first quarter and 12 in the second. He entered halftime needing 15 to tie Kareem, 16 to surpass him. Coming out of the locker room, he drilled two free throws, and then buried a spot-up three, and then an off-the-dribble three in transition, and then hit a layup on a fast break, and then he converted another layup, this one off a backdoor cut.

With just over a minute left in the third quarter, the Lakers forced a miss. LeBron sprinted from one end of the court to the other, his thirty-eight-year-old legs outrunning all five Thunder players, and laid the ball in.

Two points to go.

The arena broke into a frenzy.

Kareem smiled and clapped.

One minute later, with just 18 seconds remaining in the quarter, Westbrook tossed the ball to LeBron on the right elbow.

He turned and faced the hoop.

Everyone in the building stood.

LeBron took three dribbles to his left.

He rose up over Thunder forward Kenrich Williams.[*]

He lofted the ball into the air.

"There it is!" bellowed TNT's Brian Anderson on the game broadcast as LeBron notched points 38,387 and 38,388. "LeBron stands alone."

The game was stopped to acknowledge the moment. LeBron threw his arms toward the sky and jogged to the other end of the court, where his family was seated. He didn't dance or strut or unveil a choreographed celebration. There was no Jordanesque pose or Kobe-like scowl. He took a deep breath and put his hands on his knees. A true smile—the sort he only rarely flashed in public, one radiating a pure, boyhood-type joy—stretched across his face.

As the crowd chanted "M-V-P," LeBron waved his mom, wife, two sons, and daughter onto the court. He and Rich Paul embraced. A highlight video played on the jumbotron. Abdul-Jabbar and Adam Silver walked to center court.

"LeBron, you are the NBA's all-time scoring leader," Silver said.

LeBron squinted to hold back his tears.

"I just want to say thank you to the Laker faithful. You guys are one of a kind," LeBron said to the crowd. He thanked his wife and daughter and sons and friends and family and mom and "everybody that's ever been a part of this run with me the last twenty years." He thanked the NBA and Silver but also "the late, great David Stern," Silver's predecessor. It was as humbled as he'd ever come off in public. He seemed to be at a loss for words.

"I thank you guys so much for allowing me to be a part of something I've always dreamed about," he said.

He ended his speech the way he ended so many of his speeches: "So, fuck, man. Thank you, guys."

Tears welled in his eyes as he made the rounds to various luminaries.

"Ladies and gentlemen," Lakers public address announcer Lawrence

---

[*] Forget the scoring record, though. My favorite part about this play was the blissfully unaware Lakers center Thomas Bryant cutting to the hoop, parking under the rim, and calling for the ball as LeBron went to work. Just incredible stuff. I urge you to go watch.

Tanter said, "at this time, join us in celebrating LeBron James." Unlike the night when he had passed Michael Jordan on the all-time scoring list, they did just that.

In the lead-up to the moment, some members of the coaching staff had expressed frustration to each other and to friends across the league that LeBron's record chase was overshadowing everything. And it was. But for Jeanie, that was a feature, not a bug. And in a slog of a season, it was nice to have something worth celebrating.

• • •

LeBron might have won the night, but, fittingly, the Lakers lost the game. Part of it was that LeBron, visibly gassed after the ceremony, took just two shots in the fourth quarter, hitting only one.

But the seeds of the loss were planted earlier. The defense was non-existent from the start, and late in the second quarter Westbrook had shown up Ham by lingering on the court after being subbed out. He then got into an argument with assistant coach Phil Handy on the sidelines. As the Lakers entered the locker room at halftime, trailing 76–66, Ham told an assistant coach that he was about to lace into the team, and especially Westbrook, and that they should have a security member stationed outside the door just in case things went south. Ham did, and Westbrook shouted back, and the exchange grew so heated and loud that their voices could be heard in the hallway.

The Lakers returned to the court and, after ceding the night to LeBron, lost 133–130.

If it wasn't clear beforehand, it was now: Westbrook had to go.

"There was just so much heat on him from the beginning of the season," Troy Brown Jr., a wing the Lakers had signed in the offseason, said. "Everyone was scapegoating him, and you could just see it getting to him. We spent the whole season trying to get him, LeBron, and AD on the same page, and it just didn't work."

The next day, Pelinka found a taker. As part of a three-team deal involving Utah and Minnesota, the Lakers sent the Jazz a package built around Westbrook and their 2027 first-round pick. In return, they got sharpshooting guard Malik Beasley, defensive stalwart Jarred Vander-bilt, and, perhaps most notably, D'Angelo Russell, their former lottery pick who was averaging 17.9 points and 6.2 assists for the Timberwolves and shooting an impressive 39 percent from deep.* These moves had come in addition to a deal with the Wizards in late January, in which Pelinka had traded Kendrick Nunn and three second-round picks for Rui Hachimura, a talented 2019 lottery pick who'd put up decent numbers in Washington but had never popped.

In the span of a few weeks, Pelinka had turned over nearly half the roster. Six players had gone out, six players had come in. The Lakers had gotten younger and better. They'd added shooting and playmaking.

The most interesting part, though, was what these moves suggested about the Lakers' future. All six players traded away were on expiring contracts. Had the Lakers held on to them, they could have entered the offseason with enough cap space to possibly pursue a star. But instead of waiting to roll the dice in the summer, Pelinka, using a strategy he billed as "pre-agency"—a term Jeanie found clever—figured the Lakers would be better off trading for players who they hoped would stick around.

"We very intentionally planned these moves to provide optionality in July," he told reporters after the deadline. "You could really start to see a young core crystalizing that gives us optionality for the future, but also gives us an improved team now to finish our last 26 games with this season."

Over the next two months, the Lakers looked like a different team. Davis, after spending January and February playing so passively that Lakers coaches noticed LeBron growing frustrated during games, upped his scoring and defensive activity. With him healthy and spry, and with the long and bouncy Vanderbilt by his side, the Lakers defended at a top-five rate. D'Angelo Russell played some of the most efficient basketball of his career, and his shooting and playmaking both opened the floor and lightened LeBron's load. No one grumbled over minutes or

---

* Funny story: A few months earlier, before a Timberwolves-Heat game, I had asked Russell if he was open to doing an interview about his time with the Lakers for this book. I told him there was no rush, and that my only aim with the book was to make sure it was accurate and properly captured all the various perspectives, and that I could send all the details to the team's PR staff. I had a whole speech ready. His response? "I got nothing good to say about them, I don't care about them. Let's just do it now." That was December 26, 2022. Less than two months later, he was a Laker again.

roles. The influx of young players added a burst of energy and lifted the mood around the team; during LeBron's postgame scrums, reporters were often forced to shout out their questions over a symphony of goat noises emanating from his teammates.[*]

And then there was the continued emergence of Austin Reaves, who, nearly two years after going undrafted, had taken over Westbrook's role with the Lakers and done more with it than the future Hall of Famer ever had.

A Kobe fan growing up, Reaves always dreamed of playing for the Lakers. He skipped parties and school dances so that he could chase that dream, but as a skinny white kid who grew up on a farm in Newark, Arkansas (population as of the 2020 census: 1,880), he wasn't a prospect who jumped out to college recruiters. Wichita State, however, was intrigued, and gave Reaves a scholarship. In two years with the Shockers, he developed into a knockdown shooter. He then transferred to Oklahoma for a bigger role. There, he developed into one of the top pick-and-roll players in college basketball.

In March 2021, Reaves decided to forgo his final year of college eligibility and enter the NBA draft. With most analysts pegging him as a mid-to-late second-round pick, he and his agents, Aaron Reilly and Reggie Berry, decided to take fate into their own hands. They told any team that inquired about taking him in the second round to do so only if they were offering a guaranteed deal. If not, they weren't interested; they'd rather Reaves go undrafted and then take their chances on the two-way market. It was a bold strategy, especially coming from a prospect of Reaves's stature and a pair of young and inexperienced agents.

At first, Reaves was unsure. The dream was to be drafted—why would he turn that down? But Reilly and Berry were thinking bigger. "It was all about playing the long game," Reaves recalled.

The day before the draft, Pelinka called Reilly. The Lakers scouting department—which for years had excelled at finding NBA talent outside the lottery—liked Reaves, and Pelinka wanted to offer him a two-year deal. That night, Reaves, his agents, and his brother joined his father at his cabin. Sitting around a fire, they talked it all out. Reilly and Berry believed the Lakers would be the best fit for Reaves. They thought he boasted both the mindset and skill set to thrive alongside

---

[*] As in: LeBron is the GOAT, greatest of all time.

LeBron, and they liked that the roster was full of aging vets, meaning at some point Reaves would likely get a chance.

Reilly drafted a text to send to Pelinka. He wrote that they were ready to commit to a two-way deal.

Then he paused. Was Reaves sure?

Reaves grabbed the phone and sent the message himself.

That August, Reaves played for the Lakers' summer league team. A few games in, Lakers coaches told friends around the league that Reaves was a steal. A couple months later, Reaves impressed his new teammates at LeBron's mini-camp. The Lakers then converted his two-way contract to a standard deal. That December, he hit a game-winning three-pointer to beat the Mavericks in overtime. In April, he put up a triple-double in the Lakers' final game of the season. He came back the next year even better, and after the All-Star break became the Lakers' third-best player. He nearly doubled his scoring (10.5 points per game to 17.6), more than doubled his assists (2.2 to 5.5), and did all that while improving his efficiency. He was crafty with the ball and had an uncanny ability to draw fouls, but, more than that, he was fearless.

"AR YOU A BAD MUTHA . . . SHUT YO MOUTH!!! You tooooo TOUGH!! 🔥 🔥 🔥 😂 👑," LeBron tweeted after Reaves scored 35 points to lead the Lakers to a late-March win over the Magic.

Reaves had stepped up at the perfect time. The previous month LeBron tore a tendon in his right foot, sidelining him for 13 games. The injury was so severe that two doctors had told him that without surgery he wouldn't be able to play. He got a third opinion—"I went to the LeBron James of feet," he'd later say—who told him he could return to the court, and in late March he did. Despite the pain, he averaged 25.3 points, 7.6 rebounds, and 6.1 assists in the Lakers' final eight games. They won six of them, and 16 of their 24 after the All-Star break, a streak that propelled them back into the opening round of the play-in tournament. There, they knocked off the Timberwolves in overtime, 108–102. They then took down the second-seeded Grizzlies in six games, setting up a high-profile second-round matchup with Steph Curry and the Warriors. They took them down in six games, too. The Lakers had gone from 2–10 to the Western Conference finals. They were just four wins away from what would be one of the more improbable trips to the finals in league history.

But first, they'd have to once again go through the Nuggets. And unlike three seasons earlier, the Lakers would no longer have the best player on the floor. That moniker belonged to Nikola Jokić, who, in the years since their Western Conference finals matchup, had won two MVPs.

The Lakers had no answer for him. They tried guarding Jokić, straight up; he scored at will. They tried sending help; he'd find teammates for open dunks or threes. They tried mixing things up; he was always one step ahead, as if he had access to some sort of time machine that allowed him to see how and where the defense was moving before it did. The Lakers lost Game 1 by six points and Game 2 by five. They fell in Game 3 by 11 points but, despite being down 3–0, came out fighting two nights later. LeBron scored 31 points in the first half, and the Lakers led by 15 entering the break. Then Jokić took control. He scored 13 points in the third quarter to go along with 10 rebounds and three assists, and the Nuggets outscored the Lakers by 20.

Still, the Lakers kept fighting. With 5:02 left in the game, Davis tied the game with a dunk.

With four seconds remaining, the Lakers had the ball down just two. LeBron attacked the hoop coming out of a timeout. The Nuggets swarmed him and blocked the shot, bringing the Lakers' run to an end.

It was a disappointing finish, but the future once again looked bright. The late-season overhaul had injected life into the franchise. The Lakers had LeBron and Davis, as always, but also Reaves looked like a budding star, Ham looked like the right coach, and Pelinka looked like someone deserving of the keys to the franchise.

In the span of just a few months, the Lakers had gone from chasing mediocrity to competing for a title. They fell short of their goal, but they'd also accomplished more than anyone thought they could.

13

Not everyone in the Lakers organization appeared to be inspired by the team's late-season turnaround.

Addressing the media after the Game 4 loss to the Nuggets, LeBron, leaning back into his chair and, with hat brim pulled low, looked tired. He sounded tired, too, his voice softer and lower than usual. It was understandable. He was thirty-eight years old and had just played all but 40 seconds of a grueling playoff game, and had averaged nearly 43 minutes per game throughout the series, and had done it all with a torn tendon in his foot. And yet, despite it all, there remained something jarring about seeing the NBA's Superman looking defeated.

First, LeBron commended the Nuggets for being the best team he'd faced since joining the Lakers. Then, despite multiple reporters pointing out the team's incredible end-of-season surge, he declined to claim any sort of moral victory. "We had a great run," LeBron said, "but we fell short of our goal and our goal is to win championships." Then he demurred when asked how confident he was about the talent on the roster going forward. "I mean . . . I'm not quite sure what the roster will look like next year," he said. He pointed out that multiple players were on expiring deals.

The last question came from Fox Sports' Melissa Rohlin.

"On a personal level," she asked, "how would you evaluate the season that you had?"

"Um," he said.

He paused for a few seconds.

He rambled through some jumbled thoughts.

He paused again.

"It was a very challenging season," he said.

"It was pretty cool, a pretty cool ride . . . I don't know, it was okay."

The shield was coming down.

"I don't like to say it's a successful year because I don't play for anything besides winning championships at this point in my career," he added. "You know, I don't get a kick out of making a conference [finals] appearance. I've done it. A lot. And it's not fun to me to not be able to be a part of getting to the finals. But we'll see. We'll see. We'll see what happens going forward. I don't know. I don't know."

Then he dropped something unexpected.

"I've got a lot to think about, to be honest. Just for me personally going forward with the game of basketball, I've got a lot to think about."

The press conference concluded. Just about thirty minutes later, *Bleacher Report*'s Chris Haynes tweeted that, according to "league sources," retirement was "under consideration" for LeBron. Meanwhile, ESPN's Dave McMenamin had followed up with LeBron after the press conference and, not long after, published part of their conversation.

"When you say you got to think about stuff, what thread should we be pulling on that?" McMenamin had asked him.

"If I want to continue to play," LeBron replied.

"As in next year?"

"Yeah."

"You would walk away?"

"I got to think about it."

Few around the NBA, in the media, or in the public believed LeBron was actually done. He had spent the previous few years talking about his desire to play alongside his older son, Bronny, who was a year away from being draft eligible. Was he really willing to give up that dream after coming so close? And would he really walk away without a farewell tour?

Two months later, while accepting an award at the ESPYs, LeBron confirmed that he was indeed returning. "I don't care how many more points I score or what I can or cannot do on the floor," he said. "The real question for me is, 'Can I play without cheating this game?' The day I can't give everything on the floor is the day I'll be done. Lucky for you guys, that day is not today." But the fact that LeBron had suggested that he might step away, even if it was just a momentary reaction to a crushing loss and a taxing season, was telling. The end was close. He could feel it. It was time to prepare for life after basketball and write the final chapter of his career.

• • •

In early September, just about three months after saying that he was contemplating retirement, LeBron, Maverick Carter, and Randy Mims boarded a flight for Saudi Arabia. They spent multiple days there. LeBron visited a local basketball camp, but he also spent time with Badr bin Abdullah Al Saud, the kingdom's minister of culture and a member of the royal family. LeBron didn't post about it on social media, and the trip got little coverage in the United States. It didn't take much to connect the dots, though.

With an estimated net worth north of $1 billion—the first NBA player ever to cross that threshold while still playing, according to *Forbes*—there weren't many endeavors for which LeBron needed cash. He could buy real estate, invest in various apps and businesses, and launch a content company. What he wanted most, though, was to buy an NBA team, and with valuations skyrocketing past $4 billion—the valuation price at which the Suns sold for in 2022—he couldn't afford one without some help.

LeBron's pursuit of an NBA franchise had started nearly a decade earlier. "My dream is to actually own a team," he had said on a podcast in August 2016. The NBA prohibited active players from having equity in a franchise, but that didn't mean LeBron couldn't start preparing. Around that same time, people close to him began reaching out to moneymen in NBA ownership circles to build the necessary connections, and as the years went by, LeBron became more vocal about his goals. "Ain't no maybe about it," he told *The Athletic*'s Joe Vardon in the winter of 2019. "I'm going to do that shit." He even started analyzing the league from an owner's perspective. In 2023, the league and the NBPA finalized a new collective bargaining agreement. Soon after, the union set up individual meetings with every team to review the details of the deal. During the Lakers' session, LeBron expressed frustration about the difficulty teams would face in retaining their players. He thought teams that drafted well and made smart decisions—like the Thunder, whom he specifically mentioned*—should be rewarded. Or at least be given mechanisms to keep their rosters intact.

By the summer of 2023, LeBron had a target city in mind. Three

---

* LeBron sure does seem to love Sam Presti.

years earlier, Adam Silver had told reporters, "I think I've always said that it's sort of the manifest destiny of the league that you expand at some point," and it soon became accepted that Las Vegas would be a city receiving an NBA expansion team.

LeBron wasted no time planting his flag.

"I want a team in Vegas," he said during an episode of his YouTube show *The Shop* in June 2022.

"I would love to bring a team here at some point," he told reporters following a preseason game in Las Vegas that October.

"I think adding an NBA franchise here would just add to the momentum that's going on in this town," he said during another exhibition game in Vegas a year later. "I think it's only a matter of time, and I hope I'm part of that time."

But LeBron wasn't the only one gunning for an NBA franchise, and he wasn't the only one eyeing Vegas. Various sports bigwigs and financiers were laying the groundwork for potential Sin City proposals, and most of them had more money than LeBron. "It doesn't matter who he is," a team owner said. "If he gets outbid, he's not getting the franchise."

Many in ownership circles assumed this was the reason for his trip to Saudi Arabia. After all, it had come just a few months after LeBron, in response to reports that a Saudi Arabian football club had offered the French soccer superstar Kylian Mbappé nearly a billion dollars to come play for them, tweeted the Forrest Gump running GIF and wrote, "Me headed to Saudi when they call @RichPaul4 & @mavcarter for that 1 year deal! 🏃‍♂️👨‍👦😂." LeBron received some heat for his overtures to Saudi Arabia. A September 2023 column in *The Daily Beast* accused him of participating in "sportswashing"—a phrase used to describe the way some nations invest in sports to distract from ugly episodes or policies—but few others did. And anyway, LeBron by this point was no longer as concerned with being a vocal political force; in the lead-up to the 2024 presidential election, he stepped down as the leader of More Than a Vote, the nonprofit organization he'd launched during the tumultuous summer of 2020, and handed the reins to WNBA All-Star Nneka Ogwumike.

But Saudi Arabia wasn't just trying to convince athletes to come play in the Gulf. It had also, through its sovereign wealth fund, begun investing billions of dollars in Western sports teams and leagues. These offerings were welcomed with open arms; in 2022, in response to the largesse from Saudi Arabia and other Gulf nations, NBA owners approved a rule change allowing sovereign wealth funds to purchase up to 20 percent of a tcam.

"The [Saudi government's public investment fund] would be the perfect partner for LeBron," said an NBA owner. "It would give him the cash, because he could still be the front man."

Over the next two years, LeBron would become an investor in a Saudi public investment fund–backed boat-racing league, while Carter and the same fund would both become strategic investors in a nascent international basketball league. For LeBron, though, taking the next steps toward NBA ownership would have to wait. All he could do in the meantime was prepare and take advantage of any opportunity he had on the Vegas stage.

• • •

Lakers management took LeBron's retirement comments to heart. No one within the organization believed he was actually stepping away, but everyone recognized that, by the end of the season, he felt worn down. Pelinka and Ham decided it was time to change their approach. LeBron was the oldest player in the league, just a few months away from turning thirty-nine and entering his 21st NBA season. They didn't believe they could ask him to carry them anymore, even if he had crossed into the realm of legends like Tom Brady and Roger Federer, age-defying greats whose careers seemed to break biology's rules.

Unlike in years past, the Lakers believed they now had enough talent and depth to limit LeBron's minutes. Pelinka, preaching the value of continuity, had brought back Russell, Reaves, Hachimura, and Vanderbilt, but he'd also bolstered the roster along the edges, adding a pair of (theoretical) 3-and-D wings in Taurean Prince and Cam Reddish; Christian Wood, a talented reserve center; and Gabe Vincent, one of the league's better backup point guards. The moves were widely praised, with many analysts listing the Lakers as one of the "winners" of the 2023 offseason.

In the lead-up to the 2023–24 season, Pelinka and Ham huddled with LeBron's inner circle, a group that included Paul and Mike Mancias, LeBron's trainer. They decided they'd start limiting LeBron to between 28 and 32 minutes every game, a steep drop from the previous season, when he averaged 35, but one they thought would ensure that he was fresh come playoff time. LeBron never joined in on the chats, but he passed along his approval.

"Everyone agreed on it," a person with knowledge of the conversations said.

The plan was kept under wraps until the Lakers' first game of the season. That night, against the Nuggets, who had gone on to win the title the previous June, LeBron played just 29 minutes in a 119–107 loss.

"I know you got me on fucking old-man time percentages and shit. Play eight minutes and shit," he said to the coaching staff during one stoppage in play. "Two shots in eight minutes, just getting cardio. I hate this shit already. This shit's garbage."

Speaking to reporters after the game, LeBron acknowledged that he and the team had agreed on a minutes limit, but it was evident he wasn't happy. Two nights later, LeBron played 35 minutes, including the entire fourth quarter, when he scored 10 of his 21 points, leading the Lakers to a 100–95 comeback win over the Suns. He played 39 minutes the next game and 42 two after that. Less than a week into the season, and just five months removed from him claiming that he was contemplating retirement, the minutes restriction was scrapped, the latest offseason plan put together by the Lakers and LeBron on which they'd fail to follow through.

This time, at least, doing so made sense. LeBron was playing at an All-NBA level, and feeling good and energized. On December 9, the Lakers were 14–9, good for fourth in the Western Conference. They were a bottom-10 offense, but with Davis healthy, they owned the league's seventh-best defense. That night, they faced the Pacers in the championship game of the inaugural NBA Cup, an in-season tournament introduced to juice up the regular season. The game took place in Vegas, and while Davis led the way with 41 points and 20 rebounds, it was LeBron who set the tone. The Lakers attacked the rim, controlled the paint, and used their size and length to hound the Pacers' guards en route to a 123–109 win. No one was confusing this accomplishment with a deep playoff run, but the intensity of the tournament games had surprised many observers. Winning it seemed to carry some weight.

LeBron, after playing some of his best games of the season during the tournament, was named MVP.

"The only thing I can say is," Silver said while presenting the award,

"I'm sorry, but it doesn't come with a franchise." ESPN's Malika Andrews then asked LeBron what it meant to win.

"I don't think it's even about the MVP, I think it's about us coming together to win this thing," LeBron said. "Records will be broken, but one thing that will never be broken is to be the first to do something . . . and it's great to do it with a historical franchise and just a great cast of funny, engaged, competitive men over here."

Standing among his smiling teammates, LeBron looked happy.

•　　•　　•

The tweet was posted late at night, just hours after an embarrassing 138–122 late-January loss to Atlanta, dropping the Lakers to 24–25. It was just a single emoji. No words, no hashtags, no context, and yet, no translation was needed, not when this was coming from LeBron at 2:26 a.m. with the trade deadline just nine days away.

"⌛."

His frustration had been building since the in-season tournament. What was supposed to serve as a building block had turned out to be, to that point, the peak of the season. After the win over the Pacers, the Lakers won just five of their next 17 games, killing all the momentum they had gained in Vegas. "We just suck right now," LeBron told reporters after an early-January defeat at the hands of the Grizzlies.

The issues were familiar. The wings Pelinka had added in the offseason were struggling. Vincent and Vanderbilt couldn't stay healthy, leaving Ham with a dearth of two-way players. Every lineup he deployed represented a choice between offense and defense.

In search of an answer, Ham cycled through numerous groupings. He tried playing Russell and Reaves together, like he had during the previous season's playoff run, but didn't like that neither could contain opposing ballhandlers. He tried providing the pairing with cover by replacing Hachimura in the starting lineup with Prince, who was a stronger defender, but doing so just weakened the offense without providing enough of a defensive boost. He tried using Reddish as a glue guy, but he was ineffective on offense and not consistent enough on defense. At the urging of LeBron—who believed he still had enough in his tank to carry an offense by himself—Ham tried surrounding him and Davis with the big, defense-first trio of Vanderbilt, Reddish, and Taurean Prince, but that unit couldn't score enough to survive.

The incessant changes prevented any of the lineups from building chemistry. They also aggravated the players, who, more than anything else, craved defined roles. During one airing of grievances in which Ham was chastising the group, Russell asked, *You mean there's nothing wrong with the rotations?* Stories about Davis going rogue on the court, and LeBron taking control of timeouts, and players mocking the way Ham always stuffed his hands into his pockets on the sidelines, started making the rounds in NBA circles. In early January, the knives came out. "Lakers Coach Darvin Ham's Standing in Question amid Locker Room Disconnect," read a headline in *The Athletic*. LeBron, never one for subtlety, then spent the next week going out of his way to praise Heat coach Erik Spoelstra ("Worth Every Single Cent of that contract!!!" he tweeted in response to news that Spoelstra had signed an eight-year, $120 million extension) and Clippers coach Tyronn Lue ("It don't take T. Lue long to make sure shit get right," he said when asked about the Clippers' midseason turnaround).

Not even two months had passed since the NBA Cup title game, and LeBron's entire demeanor had changed. He started coasting on defense. He'd slump his shoulders whenever Hachimura chucked up a contested shot, which happened often. He'd look over to Ham whenever Russell made the wrong pass or blew a defensive assignment, both frequent occurrences. He'd yell at Wood whenever he allowed a guard to finish around him at the rim, a regular result whenever Wood was in the game.

"And when LeBron's doing that stuff, the other guys can all see it," a Lakers coach said. "It created a fucked-up vibe in the locker room."

The January loss to the Hawks appeared to break him. LeBron scored 20 points in nearly 36 minutes and added in nine rebounds and eight assists, but a sore left hip and an Achilles issue had sidelined Davis, and without him, the defense looked helpless. Russell had also gone cold, hitting just three of his 11 shots, all while having to contend with Hawks fans chanting, "We don't want you!"—a response to recent reports that the Lakers were interested in sending him to Atlanta in exchange for point guard Dejounte Murray, a 2022 All-Star who also happened to be a Klutch client.

After the loss, a reporter asked LeBron what his message would be to his teammates to help the team get back on track.

"I don't have any message for my teammates," he said. "Just go out and do your job. I mean—"

Ta'Nisha Cooper, a Lakers flack who in the years since LeBron's arrival had appointed herself his handler, jumped in.

"Thanks, LJ," she said.

"Way to cut me off," LeBron said. "Because I was about to . . ."

He trailed off.

Next up was a nationally televised game in Boston. Davis remained out, and LeBron, nursing a sore foot, decided to take the evening off, too. It was the Lakers' third game in four nights, but Ham, sensing LeBron's frustration, wondered if LeBron's goal was for the Lakers to get crushed on national TV and Ham be blamed. And so before the game, Ham gave the players who were suiting up a rousing speech.

"When I look around this locker room, I see a bunch of young, hungry, talented pit bulls. And the only mistakes we can make is to not give multiple efforts and not have a next-play mentality," he recalled saying. "Go to the basket, miss a layup? Fuck it. Next play. Referee calls a bullshit foul? Fuck it. Next play. Play great defense, they got an offensive rebound? Fuck it. Next play."

Behind 32 points from Reaves, the Lakers pulled off one of their best wins of the season, a 114–105 upset. The trade deadline was now just a week away, and next up was a battle with the Knicks at Madison Square Garden, where there'd be even more media attention on LeBron than usual. This, LeBron believed, was an opportunity to turn up the heat on Pelinka. The Lakers had just one first-round pick available to trade, and LeBron, just like the previous year, wanted them to use it to improve the team. The difference this time around was that his contract gave him some leverage. He had a $51.4 million player option for the following season; if he declined, he'd be a free agent in the summer. His camp had already started wielding this weapon by spreading rumors around the NBA that LeBron was open to leaving LA.

The morning after the Celtics win, Paul called ESPN's Brian Windhorst. "LeBron won't be traded, and we aren't asking to be," he told him. Notably, though, he didn't pass along any on-the-record updates about LeBron's plans beyond the season. The next day, during a Lakers practice at Nike's New York headquarters, LeBron spoke to reporters for the first time since his hourglass tweet. Leaning against a fence with his shoulders hunched, a white knit cap on his head and a sullen look on his face, LeBron fielded questions.

"There was a lot of speculation about what your tweet meant . . . Do you want to clarify?" Woike asked.

"No," LeBron said softly.

"You have an option this summer with the Lakers, do you know what you're gonna do?" McMenamin asked.

"No," LeBron mumbled.

LeBron's frustration was so evident that, in the lead-up to the trade deadline, two teams even called the Lakers to see if he was available. The first was the Sixers, whose top executive, Daryl Morey, never missed an opportunity to try reeling in a star. In fact, this wasn't the first time that Morey had gone after LeBron despite knowing his odds of acquiring him were slim.

Back in the summer of 2014, when LeBron opted out of his contract with the Heat, Morey was running the Rockets. Like most of the NBA world, he was all but certain that LeBron would be signing with the Cavs. Yet even if he had only a one percent chance of landing LeBron, he figured it was still worth taking a swing.

That same summer, Morey was chasing free-agent point guard Kyle Lowry. Lowry was spending his summer in his hometown of Philadelphia; Morey's plan was to show up at his door at midnight, when free agency officially started. Morey arrived in Philadelphia the day before and, instead of spending the evening in a hotel, camped out at the house of his close friend Sam Hinkie, the general manager of the 76ers. Morey was preparing his Lowry pitch when, at around 11 p.m., he heard from Rockets head coach (and Hall of Fame player) Kevin McHale.

I forgot to tell you, McHale told Morey. *We got our time with LeBron.*

It turned out that the reason Morey hadn't yet heard from Klutch was because McHale, who was longtime friends with Mark Termini, already had. McHale had just neglected to pass the information along.

It's at 2:30, McHale told Morey.

Not in the afternoon but in the morning, meaning Morey had less than four hours to prepare. With Hinkie laughing in the background, and while picking at cookies baked by Hinkie's wife, Morey scrambled to scribble down notes. When the time arrived, he and McHale hopped on a conference call with Paul and Termini. They were told LeBron was present and listening, but they were dubious; he never said a word.

This time around, however, Morey didn't even get to speak with anyone from Klutch. Pelinka told him that the Lakers weren't dealing LeBron, then countered with a question of his own: Were Morey and the Sixers interested in trading their own star, Joel Embiid? Morey said he was not.

The other call came from the Warriors. On February 7, four days after LeBron's comments in New York and the day before the trade deadline, Draymond Green, the team's star forward and a Klutch client, encouraged team owner Joe Lacob to contact the Lakers. Everyone could see how despondent LeBron looked; perhaps, the Warriors thought, linking up with Green and Steph Curry would be an opportunity that reinvigorated him. Lacob reached out to Jeanie. She said the Lakers had no desire to trade LeBron; what she didn't say was that they *wouldn't* trade him. She told Lacob to speak to Paul and find out what LeBron wanted, the implication being that if LeBron was indeed interested in a deal, she'd consider it. It was a stunning, out-of-character reply. This was the daughter of Dr. Jerry Buss, the steward of the Lakers, someone who prided herself on catering to stars and who believed that nothing in the sports business was more important than doing so. Sure, at a recent league meeting she had mentioned to some peers that she was growing tired of the partnership with Klutch and LeBron. But grumbling behind closed doors was one thing. Being open to a breakup with LeBron was another. (The Lakers dispute this interpretation of the events. "Saying that [Jeanie] had no desire to trade James certainly does not mean that she would consider trading him—it means the opposite," the team representative said. "To claim that her statement somehow meant that she would consider trading him is false.")

Paul told Lacob that LeBron wasn't looking to change teams. The Lakers had called LeBron's bluff. He didn't want to leave LA. He never did. What he wanted was for the Lakers to prioritize the present, to show more urgency in surrounding him with a championship-caliber team. Jeanie and Pelinka wanted that, too, but doing so was no longer their sole goal. After all, LeBron was now thirty-nine years old. It was time to start planning for life without him, whether he liked it or not.

The trade deadline passed without the Lakers making a single move.

"You can't buy a house that's not for sale," Pelinka told reporters. Just like the previous year, he wasn't interested in marginal upgrades and didn't feel the need to capitulate to LeBron. He was looking for needle-movers, and he was prepared to wait until one became available. If it meant possibly wasting the final few years of LeBron's career, that was a risk he was willing to take.

•   •   •

All-Star weekend arrived. LeBron was voted as a starter for the 20th time, an NBA record. Before the game, though, he would have to answer more questions about his future with the Lakers. Leading up to the weekend, ESPN published a story revealing the talks between Buss, Lacob, and Paul, and the NBA world wanted to know where LeBron stood.

"It never even got to me," he told TNT's *Inside the NBA* when asked about the trade discussions. "I heard it when the reports dropped."

Later, during a pregame press conference, he was asked if he knew how many more years he planned on playing and if he planned on spending those years playing for his current team.

"I don't have the answer to how long it is or which uniform I'll be in," he said. "Hopefully it is with the Lakers. It's a great organization and so many greats. But we'll see. I don't know how it's going to end, but it's coming. It's coming, for sure."*

The Lakers reconvened after the All-Star break and, just like the previous season, caught fire. Russell and Hachimura found their shooting strokes, Reaves found his rhythm, and, most importantly, the team's two stars remained healthy. LeBron missed just four games after the break, Davis missed just two, and both played more than 70 games, each player's first time doing so since the 2017–18 season. The Lakers won 12 of their last 15 games and finished the season 47–35, four wins

---

* Later, LeBron was asked a question by *USA Today*'s longtime NBA writer, Jeff Zillgitt, who had undergone cancer surgery the year before. "First of all, it's fucking great to see you. It's so great to see you, Jeff," he said while smiling and pointing at him. "Love this. And the fact that you got the last question is even greater. You tried to hide in the back, I love that as well. Love you, man. Wow, it's great to see you."

better than the season before, good for seventh in the Western Conference. They earned a spot in the play-in tournament and advanced to the playoffs with a 110–106 win over the Pelicans.

Their reward? Yet another date with the Nuggets.

This was a nightmare matchup for the Lakers. The last time they had beaten Denver was December 16, 2022, a nearly 500-day stretch that had encompassed eight games. Entering the series, they projected confidence, but they knew the odds were against them. "We have to play mistake-free basketball," LeBron told reporters before the series. The Lakers dropped Game 1, 114–103, but came out in Game 2 looking like a different team. LeBron controlled the action, Davis dominated the paint, Russell caught fire, and the defense forced the Nuggets into misfires from deep.

The Lakers built up a 20-point lead.

By the midway point of the fourth quarter, it was down to four.

The two teams traded baskets.

With 30 seconds left, Jamal Murray drilled a pull-up jumper over LeBron, tying the game.

LeBron missed an open step-back three.

With seven seconds on the clock, Murray jogged across halfcourt, used a Jokić screen, drove to the right baseline, and, while fading away, flicked the ball high over Davis's outstretched arms. The buzzer sounded, and the ball fell through the hoop, giving the Nuggets the win. Speaking to reporters after the game, Davis blamed the loss on Ham. "We have stretches where we just don't know what we're doing on both ends of the floor," he said.

"I'll agree to disagree on that," Ham told reporters two days later.

The series returned to LA for Game 3. No NBA team had ever come back from a 3–0 playoff deficit. This was the Lakers' last chance.

They lost 112–105.

They avoided a sweep with a 119–108 Game 4 win, but the most memorable image from the night was LeBron throwing a tantrum in the fourth quarter after Ham and the coaching staff had declined to challenge a questionable call. Two nights later, the Lakers found themselves back in familiar territory.

A pair of free throws from LeBron with 26 seconds left tied the game at 106.

Murray walked the ball up the floor.

Jokić set a screen.

Murray attacked.

With 3.6 seconds left, he hit a floater, giving the Nuggets a 108–106 lead.

Out of timeouts, Davis inbounded the ball to LeBron, who kicked the ball ahead to Prince, who fruitlessly hurled the ball toward the hoop from halfcourt as the clock hit 0:00.

After the game, everyone's attention turned toward LeBron. The year before, a playoff loss had led to him publicly contemplating retirement for the first time. "Tonight," a reporter asked him, "was there any thought at all that this could have been your last game with the Lakers?"

"Um, I'm not going to answer that," LeBron said. He stood up to end the press conference. "Appreciate it."

The focus then turned to Ham. ESPN and *The Athletic* both published postmortems of the Lakers' season featuring anonymous Lakers officials framing the year as a failure and laying the blame for that failure at Ham's feet. "The job of a coach is to make the best out of what you have, and he wasn't doing that," ESPN's McMenamin quoted a team source as saying. Ham had already lost his stars. And the fan base, which loathed his stoic demeanor, had been out on him for a while, too. But now it was evident Ham no longer had the backing of the team's C-suite, either. It might not have been fair—and, given that he'd gone 90–74 in two seasons and won nine playoff games, a good argument could be made that it wasn't—but there was no way he could return.

Four days after the Nuggets loss—why the Lakers strung him along for that long was unclear—Pelinka informed Ham that he was being let go. It was the third coach Pelinka had fired in five years. Yet another season had ended with an early playoff exit, broken relationships, and jobs lost. In the eyes of Jeanie and Pelinka, the time had arrived to close the book on one era and begin working on the next.

14

MIND THE GAME

Pelinka was in no rush to find a new head coach. He knew this was a hire he had to get right, for his own job security and for the sake of the organization he cared so much about. He also knew finding the right candidate would be complicated. He needed a coach capable of leading the Lakers into the post-LeBron future, someone with the skills and patience to connect with Zoomers fresh into the league, but also someone with enough gravitas and tactical expertise to command a locker room full of veterans. It was like hiring for two jobs at once.

The Lakers opened their search by putting together a list of candidates. Some were former head coaches, like James Borrego, who had led the Magic and Hornets and was serving as the lead assistant for the Pelicans. Some were longtime assistants looking for their first head-coaching gig, like Denver's David Adelman. Some were former players turned assistants, like Sam Cassell and Chris Quinn.

One candidate was straight out of central casting. JJ Redick was young. He was smart. He was a former player. He was good with the media. And it just so happened that, in March, he had begun hosting a podcast with LeBron, during which they would dive deep into X's and O's over bottles of very expensive wine. At times, *Mind the Game* felt like an audition.

Redick had never done any coaching before—other than leading his son's fourth-grade travel team—but he was one of those players whose coaches always believed could thrive in the profession. "JJ's greatest strength is that he's incredibly focused on improving, learning more about the game and figuring things out," said Stan Van Gundy, who coached Redick for five seasons in Orlando and one in New Orleans. "His intelligence, his attention to detail, his discipline is what allowed him to have the career that he had . . . He certainly wasn't a guy who was getting by in the NBA based on athleticism. So he really had to know what was going on." After Redick retired in 2021, multiple teams spoke to him about coming on as an assistant. He was intrigued but wanted to give broadcasting a try. It paid more and offered a better work-life balance, and he was good at it, too. He had started a podcast while playing, which grew into a major hit, and in retirement became one of ESPN's most prominent analysts.

Redick loved his media jobs. But he wasn't feeling fulfilled. "What I really miss is the juice," he said during a media interview a week after Ham was fired. "I miss the action, I miss the competition, I miss leadership, I miss being on a team." After speaking with his "performance coach,"* Redick decided that coaching could be the solution. Not only would it reintroduce those things that he was missing back into his life, but, as a detail-obsessed grinder who loved learning and working with a group, it also felt like a profession tailor-made for his personality. He wasn't going to be an assistant, though. Doing so would represent a significant pay cut, and he was confident that his playing career more than qualified him to jump straight into the top chair. Instead, he'd spent his time compiling notes and picking the brains of other coaches until the right job came along.

His first interview came in May 2023 with the Raptors. Nearly a year later, in April, he had informal talks with the Hornets. A few weeks after that, he met with Pelinka in Chicago during the draft combine. The two chatted for about ninety minutes. Redick was excited. "He always told me that when it came to coaching, there were a handful of teams that, if the opportunity comes, you just say, 'Yes,' and figure it out later," Jason Gallagher, the head of production at Redick's podcast company, said. "And the Lakers were absolutely one of those teams." The assumption around the league was that the deal was done. Redick checked every box. He was the kind of candidate who felt like a Lakers hire but also, given the podcast, clearly had LeBron's vote, too.

On May 21, two days after the conclusion of the combine, Shams Charania and Jovan Buha of *The Athletic* reported that the Lakers were "infatuated with Redick's potential" as a coach and viewed him as "a Pat Riley–like coaching prospect."

"The Lakers are zeroing in on Redick as the front-runner to be the franchise's next head coach," they wrote, using a phrase that had become

---

* This is the title Redick used to describe this person.

sports insider code for *the move is done; it's just not official yet.* Coming from a reporter as connected as Charania, the update carried weight.

What only a handful of people knew, though, was that Pelinka was actually chasing someone else.

•　　•　　•

Dan Hurley was coming off one of the greatest runs in college basketball history. His UConn Huskies had become the first Division I men's basketball team to win back-to-back championships in seventeen years. More impressive, though, was the way they had pummeled their opponents; their average margin of victory during the NCAA Tournament was 23.3 points, the highest mark since 1967.

The son of a legendary high school coach and the younger brother of an all-time great Duke guard, Hurley had spent ten years coaching high school ball in New Jersey before landing his first college job. He was a brilliant tactician who cared deeply about his players. He was also known for chewing them out during practices and berating referees during games. He was a bit manic and a bit eccentric—he wore the same pair of red boxers under his suit every game; they had cartoon dragons on them—but he was revered as a coach. His teams worked hard on defense. They moved the ball on offense. They were well prepared. The more time his players spent with him, the better they seemed to get; two were drafted the previous year, and two more were projected to go in the top 10 in 2024.

UConn's ascension had attracted the attention of NBA teams, and while scouting for the draft over the previous few years, Pelinka became enamored with everything Hurley had established. From the offensive playbook to the player development program to the overall culture, it all seemed to be top-notch and precisely what Pelinka was looking to inject into the Lakers with his next hire. Unlike his previous coaching searches, this time around Pelinka wasn't looking for a subordinate. He wanted a star, someone who could come in, imprint his DNA on the organization, and lead the Lakers for the next decade.

In April, after turning down overtures from Kentucky, Hurley told an interviewer that the only way he'd ever leave UConn was for an NBA job. Pelinka saw the story and took note. A few weeks later, he was on the phone with Bret Just, Hurley's agent at WME. They were going over Just's client list and discussing whether any might be a good fit to replace Ham. Pelinka, however, told Just he had his eyes on one person in particular.

Would Dan Hurley consider leaving? he asked.

Hurley, upon hearing about Pelinka's interest, was intrigued. "If your whole life has been basketball and the LA Lakers call, it's an exciting moment," he'd later recall. "Your imagination goes wild." Just passed along Hurley's answer to Pelinka. He was open to the idea but needed time to think it through. In the meantime, Just told Pelinka, the Lakers needed to keep these discussions quiet. The moment it got out that Hurley was willing to even consider a current NBA opportunity, he'd have only a few days to make a final call. And if Hurley was forced to decide before he was ready, it was unlikely that he'd leave UConn.

Pelinka was fine with that. He believed Hurley was special, a potential "legacy coach"—a phrase he used often during his recruitment—someone who could one day have his own era in Lakers history, just like Pat Riley and Phil Jackson. Pelinka shared nothing with his executives or staff. Rich Paul and LeBron were kept out of the loop as well.

Hurley spent the next few weeks contemplating the opportunity. On the one hand, taking the job would mean leaving behind everything he knew. He had never coached in the NBA, never lived west of New Jersey, never had a head-coaching job where he wasn't the most powerful person in the building. He'd also be trading some of the best job security in the country—he was the king of men's college basketball, and his agent and UConn were putting the final touches on a new contract that would make him one of the highest-paid coaches in the sport—to take a job with an organization that seemed to view coaches as disposable.

On the other hand, this was the Lakers, the franchise of Riley and Jackson and Kareem and Magic and Shaq and Kobe and now LeBron. And if Hurley were to succeed in the NBA, he'd cement his legacy as one of the greatest coaches in the history of the sport, a goal he had openly discussed with friends and colleagues.

Hurley and Pelinka first spoke at the combine, but the chats were informal. A couple weeks later, around Memorial Day, the conversations grew more serious. Hurley started asking Pelinka all sorts of questions. Some were basic ones about the NBA, like what the calendar looked like for a head coach. Others were more specific to the Lakers: What were Pelinka's expectations for the team? What were his plans for the roster? How did he envision the partnership between the two of them working? Would Pelinka be okay with roster decisions being collaborative? How could Hurley take what he had built at UConn and adapt it to the Lakers? What was LeBron like? Would Hurley be able to coach him hard? How many more years did he plan on playing?

Pelinka, using the recruiting skills he'd honed over the years, was more than happy to address Hurley's concerns.

The reason he wanted Hurley was because he was looking for a partner, someone who could help revamp the basketball side of the organization.

He didn't know how many years LeBron had left.

What he did know was that he wanted Hurley to be there once LeBron did retire.

What he also knew was that Hurley would have no issues coaching LeBron. LeBron, Pelinka said, respected coaches who were prepared and put in the work, and no one had any doubt that Hurley would always be the former and do the latter. More than that, LeBron was a basketball savant, someone whom Hurley wouldn't merely enjoy being around but from whom he'd also be able to learn.

The more Hurley heard, the more torn he became. This wasn't the first time a job offer had left him paralyzed. The same thing had happened in 2012 when Rhode Island pried him away from Wagner, and again six years later when UConn came to poach him from Rhode Island. Change wasn't in Hurley's DNA. "Just look at his dad," a friend of Hurley's said. Hurley's father had spent forty years coaching at St. Anthony High School in New Jersey, turning down multiple college offers along the way.

Hurley took as much time as he could to assess the situation, but, after a few weeks, recognized that he was running out of time. Whether staying or leaving, he had to make a decision; he owed it to UConn, to his players, to his recruits, and to the Lakers. Around the start of June, Just informed the school that Hurley was talking to the Lakers about their head-coaching job. With UConn now in the loop, the pursuit was no longer a secret. Soon after, Hurley told the Lakers he was ready to formalize the interview process. Early in the morning on Thursday, June 6, about thirteen hours before Game 1 of the finals tipped off, ESPN's Wojnarowski broke the news: "The Los Angeles Lakers are targeting Connecticut's Dan Hurley to become the franchise's next coach and are preparing a massive, long-term contract offer," he wrote. The report sent shock waves throughout the basketball world.

Hurley met with his players that day. He could see their stress. "I explained this was the equivalent of the NBA wanting them as a top-five pick in their draft," he later recalled. "I'm gonna consider it, that's what I would tell you to do." That night, he flew out to LA with Just; his wife, Andrea; and their two sons. The Lakers put them up at Shutters on the Beach in Santa Monica. On Friday, Hurley met with Pelinka and Jeanie at the facility. They showed him around and told stories about Magic and Kobe and Kareem. Jeanie told him that, despite being a massive global brand, at their core, the Lakers were a family business, and that if Hurley joined the organization, his family would become part of theirs. They ate dinner at the facility, too. Kurt and Linda Rambis attended, as did Jay Mohr, a comedian and actor whom Jeanie had married the previous summer.

"I just couldn't believe that my husband was wanted for this job," Andrea recalled. "The fact that he climbed his way from where we were to here, that the Lakers want him, holy God."

Hurley flew home the next day. He had tickets to see Billy Joel at Madison Square Garden on Saturday night and didn't want to miss the show. "Billy is older, and you just don't know how many more times you'll be able to see him," he later told CBS Sports' Matt Norlander. Before that, the Lakers presented him with an offer: six years, $70 million. Compared to some of the contracts handed out to NBA coaches over the previous year, it wasn't an eye-popping figure—it would have made him the sixth-highest-paid coach in the league—but it dwarfed every other contract Jeanie and Pelinka had ever offered a coach (this was the pair who just five years earlier had lowballed Tyronn Lue). The Lakers were open to negotiating but didn't want to present Hurley with an offer he couldn't refuse only for him to later wish that he had. They hoped he would choose the Lakers because he wanted to, not because he felt like he had no choice.

Hurley returned home as conflicted as ever. Everything he heard from the Lakers was great. But did he really want to uproot his family and leave UConn? He looked for guidance wherever he could. His dad, his brother, his coaching friends, including Billy Donovan, who had made the jump from college to the NBA in 2015. But in the end he recognized that this decision was one that only he could make.

To help do so, he went dark. He stopped responding to Pelinka after returning from LA. He started ignoring his agent's calls. "I put the phone away," he later said. He gave himself a deadline: UConn was scheduled to practice Monday afternoon; Hurley wanted to have an answer for his team by the time he walked into the gym. He agonized over the decision throughout the weekend before reaching out to Pelinka on Sunday night. He had one more set of questions he wanted answered.

Pelinka responded. Hurley liked what he heard. He texted Pelinka that he appreciated how he and Jeanie had handled everything throughout the process, and he appreciated that this was a once-in-a-lifetime opportunity they were offering him. He said he needed one more night to think things over. Pelinka understood. He went to sleep that night believing he was close to closing the deal.

Hurley, however, was once again having doubts. He kept thinking about a conversation he'd recently had with one of his players who'd come to him looking for advice. Alex Karaban was a star forward for UConn who couldn't decide whether he was better off leaving for the NBA or returning to school for one more year.

"If a decision is really hard, whether you should stay in a place or leave a place, and you're torn, you probably should never go," Hurley recalled telling him. "You should only probably leave a place if it's a clear thing to do."

Karaban had elected to stay at UConn. Hurley and his wife were now ready to do the same.

The next day, he informed the Lakers that he was passing on the job. Soon after, Wojnarowski broke the news.

"In the end, it was pretty simple," one of Hurley's friends said. "He felt like he'd be betraying the guys that had committed to play for him, and he liked the setup he had at UConn."

The Lakers had missed out on their primary target. It was now time to move on to plan B.

•　　•　　•

Redick had thought his initial chat with Pelinka in Chicago went well. It also clarified for him that he wanted the job.

In the weeks since the combine, however, he hadn't heard anything from Pelinka. The radio silence, he told an NBA friend, confused him. His agent asked around in search of an update, yet despite all the reports claiming he was close to getting hired, no one seemed to know anything. Meanwhile, Redick remained a regular presence on TV.

"It was a hard time period to compartmentalize because there was so much overlap with everything," he recalled. His frustration with the process seemed to bubble to the surface during a June 5 interview on the *GoJo and Golic* show.

"The Shams report comes out yesterday," host Mike Golic Jr. said, referring to Charania saying the Lakers were "zeroing in" on Redick. "Is there any truth to the reports out there?"

"I would say this: My focus right now is on calling the NBA Finals," Redick replied. "In terms of Shams [Charania], that will be addressed once the season is over. I'll just say that."*

Even before the Hurley news, the narrative about Redick and the Lakers had spiraled out of control. One misconception was that he and LeBron had spoken about the job. "I know no one believes it, but they never did," Gallagher, Redick's podcast producer, said. "We had the cameras rolling on them for hours at a time. Not once did we hear it discussed." Another was that LeBron was pushing for Redick to get the gig. "I know LeBron and JJ have the podcast," Rich Paul told *Bleacher Report*'s Chris Haynes in late May. "But just because they have a podcast—the Lakers have to make a decision for now and later." Paul raised similar questions in private. *JJ's never coached before,* he told an associate in May. *If the Hornets didn't want him, why would we?* Davis told at least one person that he wanted the Lakers to hire Borrego, the Pelicans assistant.

But just like during the 2019 coaching search, the Lakers weren't interested in Klutch's opinion. "The fact that certain confidential information is not disclosed to somebody does not mean that you do not trust them," the Lakers representative said. "Some things are intended to or, for various reasons, must be kept confidential, and whether somebody is trusted has nothing to do with whether or not it is appropriate to disclose certain confidential information to them." Not long after

---

* Charania declined to comment.

receiving Hurley's rejection, Pelinka got back to Redick. An official interview was scheduled. Later that week, while out to dinner with friends, Redick couldn't stop smiling or talking about the job.

"He was giddy the whole time," Gallagher said.

Between Games 4 and 5, Redick flew out to LA. He met with Jeanie, Pelinka, and others. A few days later, the Celtics won the title. A few days after that, the Lakers offered Redick a four-year contract for around $8 million per year.

Redick was visiting his alma mater, Duke, and having lunch with his dad when he got the news. He was thrilled. But, before accepting, he wanted to make one call. A few minutes later, he and LeBron were chatting about the job for the first time. LeBron might not have pushed for Redick during the search, but he respected Redick's intelligence—it was what had drawn him to Redick when the idea for a podcast was first discussed—and knew that Redick was a worker. The conversation went well. Redick told the Lakers that he was in.

Four days later, the Lakers held a press conference to celebrate the hire. As Pelinka explained to the assembled media why the Lakers had hired Redick, he repeatedly returned to a single theme.

When he and Redick had first talked at the combine, he said, it was clear that the two "shared a basketball philosophy that was very similar . . . It was based on a certain way of communicating with players and teaching them. And probably most importantly, prioritizing player development."

Pelinka referenced the NBA's new collective bargaining agreement, which was set to go into effect and designed to limit big-spending teams. "At the core of that," Pelinka said, "is going to be the importance of a great franchise like the Lakers modernizing and leaning into development."

Pelinka said that during the interview process, one of the attributes that had stuck out most to him was "JJ's passions [for] bringing some of the incredible things he's done in basketball thinking and basketball content to player development." He added that he and Redick had already had "some really robust conversations around innovation and sort of even gamifying player development. If you think about a twenty-year-old basketball player today and maybe a twenty-year-old basketball player, I don't know, ten, fifteen, twenty years ago, the mediums of learning are completely different."

Only three years had passed since Jeanie had brought Russell West-brook into her office to talk about the importance of titles and catching the Celtics, yet here was her GM, not even a month removed from Boston winning championship No. 18, sounding like a small-market executive. There was nothing wrong with proclaiming a desire to emphasize player development, but coming from Jeanie Buss's Los Angeles Lakers, the team employing the modern NBA's most preeminent star, it was stunning to hear.

The Lakers had entered a new era. LeBron may still have been part of the team, but the days of the team being his had come to an end.

Before moving on, though, they decided to give him one more gift.

15

JR.

Opening night for the 2024–25 season had arrived, and the Lakers looked great. The defense was aggressive and on point. The new offense installed by Redick—featuring more ball and player movement—created easy looks. Davis was dominating on both ends.

Around the midway mark of the second quarter, LeBron, having been subbed out for a brief break, found a seat on the bench alongside a new teammate.

"You about ready?" he asked.

The teammate nodded.

"You see the intensity, right?" LeBron asked.

The teammate nodded some more.

"Just play carefree, though," LeBron said.

The teammate remained silent.

"Don't worry about mistakes," LeBron added. "Just go out and play hard."

The two watched the next three minutes of action side by side. Seated across the court were Ken Griffey Sr. and Ken Griffey Jr., the first and only father-son duo ever to play in a Major League Baseball game together. LeBron's seventeen-year-old son, Bryce, and his ten-year-old daughter, Zhuri, sat on the baseline. LeBron's wife, Savannah, watched from the stands.

With just over four minutes left in the half, LeBron and the teammate popped out of their seats. An energy surged through the arena. The clock stopped at 4:00. Both players shed their warm-up shirts. The crowd cheered. Thousands of phones were lifted into the air.

Together, LeBron and the son who shared his name walked onto the court.

•   •   •

In February 2022, LeBron returned to Cleveland for the NBA All-Star Game. This was Westbrook's first season with the Lakers, and, desperate for the Lakers to make a move, LeBron had elected to put some pressure on Pelinka. "I don't play mid-level basketball," he told *The Athletic*'s Jason Lloyd, after saying that he was open to the idea of one day returning to the Cavaliers. But, he told Lloyd, there was one thing he was willing to prioritize more than winning.

"My last year will be played with my son," he said. "Wherever Bronny is at, that's where I'll be. I would do whatever it takes to play with my son for one year."

Twenty years earlier, LeBron had met a girl from a rival high school. Soon after, he took her to an Outback Steakhouse for a date. In October 2004, the beginning of LeBron's second NBA season, Savannah Brinson gave birth to the couple's first child, a boy. LeBron had a name ready to go.

"When I was younger, I didn't have a dad," he later said. "So my whole thing was when I have a kid, not only is he gonna be a junior, I'm gonna do everything that this man didn't do."

Eventually, LeBron James Jr. started going by Bronny. Like his father, Bronny loved basketball, and LeBron watched Bronny play as much as he could. When at the games, he'd celebrate Bronny's plays by leaping out of his seat. Sometimes he'd join Bronny's team in layup lines. Sometimes he'd get into good-natured arguments with the parents of opponents. The footage often went viral. Those who disliked LeBron would hold these clips up as proof that he was a self-centered, attention-craving phony. But many saw them as something else: a man who had no relationship with his own father delighting in the opportunity to be one himself.

Savannah gave birth to LeBron's second son in June 2007. The couple married in September 2013, and their daughter was born one year later. After LeBron signed with the Lakers, the whole family moved to LA. Bronny enrolled at Sierra Canyon, a prestigious private school with an elite basketball program. He wasn't a star, but he flashed enough promise for LeBron to begin thinking about a possible NBA future. During the Lakers' unofficial pre-bubble workouts in 2020, he brought Bronny to train with him and his teammates. Bronny went through all the drills and played in the scrimmages. "If he messed up or made a mistake, Bron would be like, 'They're not gonna play with you,'" Talen Horton-Tucker said. "He didn't want anyone taking it easy on him, either." No one did, and Bronny held his own. "It didn't feel like a Make-A-Wish kid or anything," recalled an attendee. "He fit in." During one run, Bronny caught an outlet pass and spotted LeBron streaking toward the hoop, pointing toward the sky. Bronny fired a lob from near halfcourt. LeBron caught the ball in the air and slammed down a reverse dunk.

LeBron was still chasing championships. And he still hoped to pass Kareem's scoring record. But he was now ready to add two new items to his list of goals.

The first was guiding his son to the NBA. The second was becoming the first NBA player to share the court with his son. Two years later, during that All-Star weekend in Cleveland, he decided that it was time to go public. "I put it in the air because I like to talk to the basketball gods out there and see if things can come to fruition," LeBron later told *Sports Illustrated*'s Chris Ballard. "I've always set out goals in my career, talked to the basketball gods, and they've listened to all of them. Hopefully they can listen to this last one, too."

LeBron's quote to *The Athletic* catapulted Bronny into the spotlight, and by his senior year, the hype had reached overdrive. LeBron and Savannah didn't exactly embrace it, but they didn't pull Bronny out of the spotlight, either. Their strategy was to do what LeBron had done throughout the back half of his career: Use the media as a tool but try to control the message. Uninterrupted, LeBron's content company, produced a documentary about the Sierra Canyon basketball team, and the James family had full creative control. Unlike his teammates, Bronny never gave interviews; any reporter who approached was shooed away by a security guard employed by the family. Still, everyone on the team and around it loved him.

"If I had another son, I'd want that son to be like Bronny," Ed Estavan, a Sierra Canyon assistant coach and the head of Bronny's AAU team, said.

Bronny's game mirrored his personality. He was unassuming, selfless, and content in a supporting role. He loved playing defense. He loved passing the ball. "A lot of times he was too passive," Luca Evans, who covered Bronny at Sierra Canyon for the *Los Angeles Times,* said. "The hype off his name is so contrary to how he plays." Everything about Bronny—from his game to his personality—was quiet and understated. The only time that ever changed was when LeBron stepped in.

"Man Bronny definitely better than some of these cats I've been watching on league pass today," LeBron tweeted in March 2023, near the end of Bronny's senior year of high school. "Shit lightweight hilarious 🤣🤣🤣🤣."

At that point, few around the NBA agreed. Scouts and analysts liked Bronny's game and appreciated how, despite growing up in a fishbowl, he appeared to be a pretty normal, humble, even-keeled teenager. But in the eyes of most evaluators—the lone exception being ESPN's Jonathan Givony, who, in a February 2023 mock draft projected him as a top-10 pick—Bronny was nothing more than a borderline draft pick.

In May 2023, Bronny accepted a scholarship to USC. The family's plan was for him to play one season and then declare for the 2024 NBA draft. Whether or not the rest of the world believed Bronny was ready didn't matter. To LeBron, there was no doubt.

All that got pushed to the back burner on one July morning. While doing some cardio drills in the USC gym, Bronny blacked out and fell to the floor. He had suffered cardiac arrest. Trainers performed CPR, and an ambulance rushed Bronny to the hospital. He was later diagnosed with a congenital heart defect.

Bronny returned to the court in January but struggled finding his footing, averaging just 4.8 points off the bench. People close to him pointed to the cardiac episode he'd suffered over the summer, and many talent evaluators were sympathetic to the impact of suffering such a traumatic event. But the reality remained that Bronny was an undersized wing shooting an ugly 26.7 percent from deep. It wasn't that scouts and analysts were rooting against him. They just didn't see him becoming a legitimate NBA player. LeBron, however, remained resolute. "He could play for us right now, easy," he told Austin Reaves after one game in January, loud enough for all the reporters in the locker room to hear.

As the 2024 draft approached, Klutch got to work. The good news was that LeBron and Kluch weren't the only ones interested in seeing Bronny wear a Lakers uniform. As the Bronny storyline had picked up steam over the previous year, Jeanie spoke often in public about how she remembered watching a hockey game as a teenager featuring her family's LA Kings and the Hartford Whalers. That night, the Whalers put out a lineup featuring the future Hall of Famer Gordie Howe and one of his sons. "It was just one of those great moments and a great thing to watch," Jeanie said on *The Rich Eisen Show* in October 2022.

The Lakers weren't going to waste their first-round pick on Bronny, but they also owned pick No. 55. Players selected there rarely made the NBA. Maybe Bronny could defy the odds; if not, the Lakers would still make history and, at the same time, appease LeBron, who had a player option.

In the meantime, Klutch was doing everything it could to push Bronny to the Lakers. When speaking with other teams, Rich Paul insisted that Bronny was a first-round talent. When asked whether Bronny would be open to spending time in the G League, he would say yes but qualify that by adding that only when the NBA team had a day off. All of it seemed to be a way of scaring off other potential suitors. Later, Paul doubled down on this approach. *If you take him, he's going to play in Australia,* he'd told inquiring teams. He then gave former Warriors GM Bob Myers, who was working the draft for ESPN, permission to share that message on the air during Day 2 of the draft.

No one knew whether Paul was bluffing. But based on his threats, no team was willing to draft Bronny hoping LeBron would leave the Lakers to join him.

The 54th pick was announced. The Lakers were now on the clock. Pelinka, seated next to Redick, called Paul, who put Bronny on the phone.

"Bronny, you got Rob Pelinka here, Coach Redick," he said. "I think first and foremost, you've worked incredibly hard, man. You've put in a ton of work . . . that means a lot to us.

"I think second to that, you're a player of high character, and a person of high character, and that is valued at the Lakers. And so, it's important for Coach Redick and I to let you know that those qualities really stand out. And so, the Lakers are gonna draft you with the 55th pick in the draft, and I just wanted to let you know."

Redick leaned over.

"Bronny, this is JJ. I just wanted to say congrats, man. Your hard work has paid off, you're gonna have a long NBA career, and I can't wait to coach you, man. Congrats."

"Thank you, Coach," Bronny said. "Appreciate it, Coach."

"We'll see you soon, Bronny," Pelinka said. "The work begins."

"Yes, sir," he said.

Pelinka hung up. Everyone in the room applauded.

After hearing NBA deputy commissioner Mark Tatum announce the pick on TV, LeBron's family and closest friends, watching together in Manhattan, did the same. Savannah handed Bronny a Lakers hat. Tears streamed down his cheeks.

One week later, LeBron, after declining his player option, signed a new one-plus-one deal with the Lakers.

• • •

During training camp, LeBron looked happier than he had in years. He made Bronny wear a holographic backpack as part of the team's rookie hazing. After practices, he and Bronny worked together, getting up extra shots.

"Just pure joy, to be honest," LeBron told reporters in September. "To be able to come to work every day, put in the hard work with your son every day and see him continue to grow."

LeBron and the Lakers decided that the best course of action would be to have him and Bronny play together in the first game of the season and then move on. The NBA, recognizing the magnitude of the moment—and level of interest in the LeBron-Bronny storyline—slotted the Lakers onto its opening-night schedule, which featured two games on national TV. The evening started with the Celtics raising a banner representing title No. 18, which they had won in June, breaking their tie with the Lakers, to the rafters. They then throttled the Knicks, 132–109. In a stark contrast, the Lakers were on TV for a reason that had nothing to do with winning. And yet, like so many other nights throughout NBA history, the spotlight belonged to them.

On Bronny's first possession, the Timberwolves set a screen to isolate him on Julius Randle; Randle backed him into the paint and buried a jumper. On the other end of the court, Bronny missed a tip-in chance and a catch-and-shoot three off a feed from his dad. After two and a half minutes of action, Redick subbed Bronny out.* The highlight of the stint had been LeBron beating his man backdoor on the baseline

---

* My favorite part of the whole thing was how, when LeBron and Bronny entered the game, TNT cameras panned over to Bryce to show his reaction. He looked up, smiled, and then, seemingly unimpressed by his dad and older brother doing something literally no one in history had ever done before, returned to scrolling TikTok.

for a thunderous, one-handed slam, a mind-boggling feat, considering the dunk was thrown down by someone so old that his son was on the court.

In the locker room after the game—a 110–103 Lakers victory—the players doused Redick in water to celebrate his first career win. The room had quieted by the time the media was let in, but the mood remained upbeat. Davis and LeBron talked football with a group of reporters. The Minnesota Vikings were coming to LA, and LeBron said he was thinking about going to the game. "So I can see [Justin] Jefferson," he said, referring to the team's star wide receiver. He talked about how Usher had recently held a concert at the nearby Intuit Dome. ESPN's Malika Andrews mentioned that Billy Joel had performed there, too.

"Hell nah!" LeBron said. "I ain't listening to no Billy Joel."

Ta'Nisha Cooper, the Lakers flack, came by to ask LeBron which family photos the team could post from its official social media accounts.

"Yeah, that's beautiful," LeBron said, looking at one.

"What about the one with Savannah?" she asked.

"You have to ask her," he said.

A few stalls over, Bronny was getting dressed. He and his father didn't look at each other until it was time to head to the media room for their postgame press conference.

Bronny followed LeBron out.

Speaking to reporters, LeBron tried putting the evening's emotions into words. He talked about how special it was to begin his day by wishing his daughter a happy tenth birthday before she went to school; and how incredible it was to then come in to work and see his son; and how the moment that he and Bronny checked in together would be one he'd never forget, "no matter how my memory may fade as I get older"; and how incredible it was for a day featuring all that to then also end with a win.

"Everything was just great today," LeBron said. "Everything."

16

THE LUKA LAKERS

They might have had a new coach in place, but as the 2025 trade deadline approached, the Lakers' season was, to quote a famous baseball legend, feeling like déjà vu all over again. Once again, Pelinka, seemingly content to wait out LeBron and then rebuild after he retired, was holding on to future draft picks instead of using them to upgrade the roster. Once again, LeBron and Klutch were annoyed and trying to pressure Pelinka into making a move.

They had started the campaign in mid-January when, after a loss to the Clippers, LeBron was asked about the team's margin for error. "That's not how our team was constructed," he told reporters. "We have to play close to perfect basketball." Later that week, during a sit-down interview with ESPN's Shams Charania, Davis took the baton. "I think we need another big," he told Charania, noting that the Lakers had won the 2020 title with him playing alongside true centers like Dwight Howard and JaVale McGee.

What Davis failed to point out, though, was that the Lakers' best lineups featured him at center. And what LeBron seemed to be ignoring was that, despite his gaudy numbers, his own play had been holding the team back. Considering he was forty, it was understandable, but his defensive effort was at an all-time low and some of his teammates felt that at times he was hijacking the offense. For the first time in his career, LeBron's team was statistically better with him off the court.

Pelinka had addressed some of these issues a month earlier in a savvy trade with the Nets. Out went D'Angelo Russell and his inefficient gunning. In came Dorian Finney-Smith, a versatile forward and stout defender. After the trade, despite Davis's and LeBron's comments, the team's play had improved. Redick had the group moving the ball, playing hard, and defending at an elite level. Entering a Saturday-night showdown in New York City with the Knicks, the Lakers had won eight out of nine. A championship still seemed unlikely, but at the least LeBron would spend his 22nd NBA season competing for a team that felt like it had a purpose.

What neither he nor almost anyone else knew was that Pelinka was working on something even bigger. A deal that, if completed, would solidify his legacy and give LeBron, Jeanie, and Lakers fans everything they wanted.

• • •

A few weeks earlier, Pelinka had traveled with the Lakers to Dallas. While there, an old friend reached out. Pelinka had first met Nico Harrison in the early 2000s. Harrison was a junior executive with Nike at the time and trying to sign Kobe to a shoe deal. He attended every Lakers home game during the 2002–03 season and, that summer, landed Kobe with a five-year, $40 million offer. The contract was negotiated by Pelinka. From that point on, Harrison was Kobe's primary contact and closest confidant at Nike. Through that relationship, he and Pelinka developed a connection of their own.

In 2021, the Mavericks hired Harrison to be their GM. He took over a team that had one of the league's premier players, Luka Dončić, a Slovenian prodigy entering just his fourth NBA season and already widely considered one of the five best players in the league. Dončić was a brilliant passer who could bury shots from any spot and any angle. He was also 6-foot-6 and thick, which made him nearly impossible to guard. Those defenders quick enough to keep up with him were usually too small to handle his size. Those defenders big enough to handle his size were usually too stone-footed to keep up. Dončić had spent his first six NBA seasons dominating opponents in a way few players ever had and was coming off one in which he had led the league in scoring (33.9 points per game), finished third in MVP voting, nearly averaged a triple-double (9.8 assists and 9.2 rebounds), and carried the Mavericks to the finals. He was universally recognized as a once-in-a-generation talent.

Not by Harrison, though. He'd become fixated on Dončić's flaws, on the way he'd coast on defense and argue with referees mid-play and always seemed to put on weight during breaks. Despite the recent trip to the finals, Harrison no longer believed that Dončić could serve as the cornerstone of a championship team, not after seeing him respond to a disappointing finals performance—the Mavericks fell to the Celtics in five games—by reporting to training camp the following fall out of shape and then, during the Mavericks' Christmas Day game, suffering his fourth calf strain in three years. Which was why, when the Lakers came to town, Harrison had asked Pelinka about getting a coffee.

The two met up at a café about a half mile from American Airlines Center, where the Lakers were set to face the Mavericks that night. Pelinka wore a black hoodie; Harrison, dressed in a black beanie and dark zip-up vest, opted for a more incognito look. Which made sense. He was about to propose what would become one of the most shocking, controversial, and, eventually, ridiculed trades in sports history, one that broke every cardinal rule about team-building in the NBA. Superstars like Dončić were the most valuable commodity in the sport. NBA history had shown that without one, winning a title was nearly impossible. And yet here Harrison was, preparing to ask Pelinka whether the Lakers would be open to a Dončić for Anthony Davis swap.

Over coffee, Harrison explained the situation. He told Pelinka that the Mavericks weren't shopping Dončić—he needed to keep things quiet and preserve the relationship in case he failed to complete a deal—and that he was reaching out to the Lakers and no one else.[*] Harrison wanted to turn the Mavericks into an elite defensive team and believed Davis, one of the league's top defensive players, could help him do so. That Davis was thirty-one and had a long injury history didn't seem to matter.

The two executives went back and forth. Pelinka told Harrison he was intrigued and that he'd be in touch. After the meeting, he called Jeanie and relayed the conversation. "She was extraordinarily excited and hopeful that we could get to the end," Pelinka recalled. He and Harrison spent the next three weeks hammering out the details. What other players would be included? How many first-round picks would the Lakers have to give up? Which assets could the Lakers hold on to? All the while, Pelinka, utilizing the same playbook he'd used during the

---

[*] At some point, Harrison did call Timberwolves president Tim Connelly about Anthony Edwards, the team's twenty-three-year-old All-NBA wing. But Connelly didn't believe Harrison was actually interested in dealing Dončić and the talks went nowhere.

Hurley recruitment, kept the circle tight, out of respect for Harrison's request, but also understanding that a closed auction worked to his advantage. There were numerous teams out there with the ability to top the Lakers' package, and who no doubt would if they learned that Dončić was available.

By January 31, a Friday night, the Lakers and Mavericks had agreed on the outline of the deal. In addition to Davis, the Lakers would send Dallas one of their two tradeable first-round picks along with Max Christie, a young and talented 3-and-D wing. Considering that players far less talented and accomplished than Dončić had fetched packages of four first-round picks *plus* other assets, Pelinka was getting a steal. He'd somehow convinced Harrison that, since the Mavericks were preventing Pelinka from discussing Dončić's future with his agent, the Lakers were taking on too much risk to part with another asset, be it a first-round pick, Austin Reaves, or rookie Dalton Knecht.

For salary cap reasons, though, the Lakers had to first complete a separate trade with the Jazz. But before the Jazz could do that, they had to complete yet a different deal with the Clippers. And for that, the Clippers needed to receive sign-off from the agent of Patty Mills, whom they were getting from Utah.* The problem was that Mills's agent, CAA's Steven Heumann, was observing Shabbat and offline. This meant that all parties had to wait until an hour after sundown on Saturday night, when the Lakers were taking on the Knicks. In the meantime, Pelinka and Harrison agreed to keep the details quiet. Neither side wanted to risk anything leaking until all the necessary paperwork was completed.

•   •   •

The Lakers stepped onto the Madison Square Garden floor the next night and put on one of their best performances of the season, cruising to a 128–112 win. LeBron, energized by the Broadway stage, looked explosive and spry. In yet another turn-back-the-clock performance, he dropped 33 points and recorded his 10th triple-double of the season.

In the locker room afterward, LeBron talked about how excited he

---

* When players are traded in the final season of their contract, the NBA requires their registered agent and the team acquiring them to certify that no future contract has been agreed to under the table.

was to go out to dinner with his wife, who was waiting for him in the hallway. Beside her was Rich Paul, laughing with various reporters and Klutch COO Fara Leff and unaware that one of his top clients was on the verge of being traded. Pelinka, meanwhile, had remained in LA, where he was finalizing the deal. At around 9 p.m. on the West Coast, Dončić's agent, Bill Duffy, was informed that Dončić was headed to the Lakers. A few minutes later, the details reached ESPN's Charania. "I thought my phone was hacked," he'd later say. Soon after, he broke the news. Most people around the NBA, upon seeing Charania's post and finding it inconceivable that the Mavericks would actually trade Dončić, also assumed it was some sort of prank. Charania was forced to send out a follow-up post confirming the report.

Davis, who had stayed back in LA to nurse an abdominal strain, was settling in to watch a movie with his wife when Pelinka called to share the news. Pelinka then called LeBron, who was out to dinner in New York City with his wife and others, including Paul. Bronny, meanwhile, who was not with his dad, shared Charania's post in the players' group chat and asked if it was real. Davis then jumped in. "Did these n****s just trade me?" he wrote. He wished the group good luck and left the chat.

"WTF," LeBron wrote. That night, he FaceTimed Davis. "It was definitely a weird, uncomfortable truth moment for us," LeBron later recalled. "Just knowing that he was gonna be gone, it was very difficult. Very challenging. I could see how in shock he was."

Around the NBA, speculation swirled: Would LeBron, after watching the Lakers trade his closest friend on the team and a fellow Klutch client, request a move before the deadline? Those questions were put to rest the next day when ESPN's Dave McMenamin and NBA reporter Chris Haynes—both known to have close ties to Klutch—reported that LeBron intended to stay in LA.

The Lakers officially welcomed Dončić to LA later that week. "I think Luka Dončić joining forces with the Los Angeles Lakers is a seismic event in NBA history," Pelinka, wearing a fitted leather bomber jacket that Bill Simmons would later say made him resemble a *Fast and Furious* villain, said. "The reason I say that is because we have a twenty-five-year-old global superstar that's going to get on the stage of the most popular, influential basketball brand on the globe."

There was no talk about player development or the limitations of the league's new collective bargaining agreement this time around. The Lakers were back to being about stars. "When we make decisions around superstar players, we partner and collaborate with them," Pelinka said, after shouting out Duffy. He commended Jeanie and "her vision, which falls in line with the great and late Dr. Buss, to always make sure the brightest and best basketball superstars play for the Los Angeles Lakers, she's clearly carried that vision on from her dad." Dončić was honest about not having wanted to leave Dallas and the shock that had swept over him upon learning about the trade. But, he added, "I'm just very happy to be here, for this opportunity. This is the Lakers—one of the best clubs in history, so I'm excited to be here." The nearly twenty-seven-minute press conference was both a victory lap and a commercial for Lakers exceptionalism.

With the trade deadline that week, Pelinka took time to huddle with Dončić. The two talked about what could be done to improve the team, both over the ensuing days and in the future. In Dallas, Dončić had thrived playing alongside bouncy centers who could catch lobs, and both he and Pelinka knew the Lakers needed to find one of their own. They circled Mark Williams, a twenty-three-year-old seven-footer with the Hornets. Williams was loaded with talent but often injured, and yet, both Pelinka and Dončić believed he was their man. The day before the deadline, Pelinka and the Hornets agreed to a trade. The Lakers would send out Knecht, an unprotected first-round pick, and a pick swap and, in return, get Dončić the pick-and-roll partner he craved.

That Pelinka had been open to parting with a future first-round pick to help Dončić—something he had refused to do for LeBron and Klutch over the previous two years—spoke volumes. It didn't matter that the trade was later rescinded after Williams failed the Lakers' physical.* The Lakers, it was clear, were now preparing for life after LeBron.

---

* Williams's agent later released a statement asserting that "the overwhelming sentiment, after conferring with multiple, nationally recognized doctors, is that the Los Angeles Lakers should not have failed Mark Williams on his physical," the implication being that the team had simply changed its mind about the deal and then engaged in an act of bad faith. The Lakers' response? "To claim that the Lakers backed out of the Mark Williams trade for reasons other than on the basis of the results of the physical examination they conducted on him in connection with the trade is a lie," the representative said.

LeBron was still on the team, but the days of the team being his had come to an end.

In previous years, LeBron might have bristled at the keys of his franchise being handed to someone else. But at this stage of his career, his priorities had shifted. "If I had any concerns, I would have waived my no-trade clause and got up out of here," he told reporters a few days after the trade deadline. He and Dončić quickly jelled.

"I've never seen [LeBron] as happy as he [looks] playing the game right now," Carmelo Anthony, a close friend of LeBron's, said on a podcast that March. With Dončić by his side, LeBron was suddenly playing some of the best all-around basketball of his career, not just scoring but, in the words of Redick, guarding "at an All-NBA defense level," too. The Lakers finished the regular season with 50 wins, the third most in the Western Conference. They fell to the Minnesota Timberwolves in the playoffs' first round, but the season had been a rousing success. Entering the summer of 2025, the Lakers looked to be one of the most well-positioned teams in the league.

Seven years earlier, LeBron and the Lakers had come together for a simple reason: Each party needed something from the other. Now, with that partnership entering its final stage, it was clear that, despite all the bumps along the way—the resignations and firings and botched hirings and bad trades and passive-aggressive swipes—the decision to merge their respective brands had paid off for both sides.

Pelinka, after pulling off what many experts hailed as one of the greatest trades in NBA history—and delivering the franchise a new cornerstone for the post-LeBron era—was rewarded in April with another contract extension. He also had the "vice" stripped from his title, making him the Lakers' first president of basketball operations since Magic Johnson.

Rich Paul had become not just the most famous sports agent in the country but a brand unto himself. He'd become bigger than his field, his name so synonymous with success among the public that, in June 2025, the e-learning platform MasterClass added him as an instructor. His course—*win deals like the NBA's No. 1 negotiator*—was offered alongside those taught by visionaries like Bob Iger, Neil deGrasse Tyson, and Martin Scorsese.

Jeanie had brought the Lakers back from the abyss and, in doing so, succeeded in casting herself as the savior of everything her father had built. In February 2025, Netflix released *Running Point*, a sitcom that Jeanie, who worked as an executive producer along with Linda Rambis, helped create. The show, starring Kate Hudson, chronicles the inner workings of a pro basketball team called the Los Angeles Waves as the protagonist and her siblings battle for control. Hudson's character is framed as the only member of the family who is both competent and likable. The show was a hit and renewed for a second season.

A few months later, the Lakers announced that the Buss family had agreed to sell a majority stake in the franchise to billionaire Mark Walter, already a minority owner of the team and the controlling owner of the Los Angeles Dodgers. The deal came at a record-setting $10 billion valuation. All these years later, Jeanie, Johnny, Jimmy, and Janie had finally found something they could agree on. Instead of letting their two younger half-siblings inherit the franchise in the future, they decided to exercise their majority vote and cash out. Jeanie, however, negotiated that she'd remain in place as governor of the franchise "for the foreseeable future," ensuring that the Buss name would remain inextricably tied to the Lakers.

Meanwhile, sitting at the center of it all, as was always the case, was LeBron. He'd won his title, he'd made his movie, he'd broken the scoring record, he'd shared an NBA court with his son. He'd saved the Lakers, giving everything he had to them and the league, and, in doing so, achieved more than he ever could have dreamed. LeBron James had come to Hollywood, won in Hollywood, and become part of Hollywood. All that remained was a ride off into the sunset.

ACKNOWLEDGMENTS

The three years it took me to write this book were the hardest of my life. (On a related note: If you ever sign a book contract, maybe don't do it right before your spouse is due with your third kid. Not an ideal combo.) There were so many people who helped me reach the finish line with this. What follows is my attempt to thank them all.

First up is my brilliant agent, Anthony Mattero. I don't think it's possible for an agent to support an author or value journalism more than Anthony does. I consider myself blessed to have him in my corner.

Next up is my wonderful editor, Khari Dawkins, and not just because he's a Sixers fan who likes mocking the franchise. Khari believed in this project from the jump and was an incredible sounding board throughout. His insight and input made the book better. I couldn't ask for a better editor. Here's to the first of many.

To the amazing team at Doubleday: Mike Collica, Kirsten Eggart, Andrea Monagle, Kathryn Ricigliano, Vimi Santokhi, and the entire production crew: Thank you for your meticulous copy editing and fact-checking. To Sara Hayet and Anne Jaconette: Thank you for the tireless work on publicity and marketing. To Dan Novack: Thank you for standing up for my journalism while having my back on all things legal (and also all the great NBA takes!). I couldn't have dreamed up a better group to work with.

I'll deny it if he ever tries taking credit, but, between us, the idea for this book actually belongs to Mike Vorkunov, the fantastic NBA reporter at *The Athletic* whom I feel fortunate to count as a close friend and whose edits and feedback I have come to rely on. While on that subject: The NBA media world is a tough ecosystem, one that would be impossible to navigate without having true friends in your corner. Over the years, I've met so many great people from this profession whom I'm lucky to consider friends, but three in particular—Howard Beck, Stef

Bondy, and Michael Pina—have gone above and beyond. Whether it's advice, a phone number, or a much-needed laugh, they've always come through. I'm so grateful to have you all in my corner.

The same must be said about James Herbert, my incredible friend who, for reasons I will never fully understand (it's probably because he's Canadian), edited this book as if it were his own. And thank you to his wife, Becca Laurie, whose fact-checking and copy editing were the best I've ever seen (if you're writing a book, you should hire her!!!). I've said this to you both privately, but let me say it here, too: I wouldn't have made it to the finish line without you, and there's no way to fully express how much better this book became because of everything you both did.

To Jeff Pearlman, Jonathan Tropper, and Ben Osborne, I wrote this last time, but it still holds true: This career wouldn't exist for me if not for everything each of you has done for me over the years. I am forever grateful. Same goes for Lou Oppenheim. Not many people are able to seek professional guidance from their former Little League coach, but I feel so lucky to have mine back in my life.

Thank you to Sam Kinches for the help with research and transcription—I couldn't have done it without you. And to Michele Souli, your investigative work left me in awe.

To every source who participated—especially those who let me come back again (and again) to double-, triple-, even quadruple-check things—you know who you are. I don't take your time, trust, or honesty for granted. This book would not have been possible without you. Thank you for your willingness to help me tell this story accurately and responsibly. And on that note, to Bill Oram, the rare journalist who roots for others to succeed and someone who is an even better person than he is a reporter (low bar, I know) and whose help and guidance on this project were invaluable. Also, he sends the best IG screenshots.

Now onto the personal side of things.

To all our friends in the YIS community who have become family, thank you for the carpools and playdates and sleepovers and, more than that, emotional support.

To Rabbi Eli Ciner, who was one of the first to ever be in my corner and has always been in my corner even when others have not, thank you for, well, everything.

To my siblings-in-law, Rebecca, Corey and Dalia, Marielle and "Steven," Sammy and Klara, just know that every single thing you do for our family—whether coming by with a pizza or dropping everything to go pick up a kid from school in the middle of a workday because your sister and I needed to drive two hours to a hospital—is something that we are truly grateful for. To Marla and Avri—or, as I like to call them, Dad and Mrs. Horowitz—I hope by this point you know how I feel. Our life—let alone this book—would not be possible if not for all the support you both give. I used to worry about living in the same town as you guys. Now I consider it one of my life's greatest blessings.

To my brother, Ilan, blah blah blah, and, despite the fact that you can somehow hit a softball three hundred feet farther than me, I guess I kind of appreciate everything you do for me and all the ways you're always there for me.

To my parents, I know I can (occasionally) give you both grief, but your belief in me and never-ceasing encouragement are what laid the foundation for this life. It's also what keeps me going. That, and all that babysitting.

To Maayan, Lior, and Matan, I'm going to be honest: I'm not sure you belong in the category of people who tried making this project easier for me. Case in point: Before you all came along, I never knew how much writing could get done on three hours of sleep. Life with you guys is never boring. That used to scare me. Now it's something I'm thankful for every day.

Last but certainty not least, Micole. I'm writing this the day after our AC went out in the middle of a heat wave in a week where you're working two jobs and where one of our sons got strep and then, somehow, passed it on to me. In other words, it's just another Thursday night for us. At least that's how it feels, and the reason it feels that way is because of everything you do. Whether it's as a wife, a mom, or a friend, your blend of compassion, intelligence, and determination (one could even say *grit*) leave me in awe. None of this—this book, this life—would be possible without the support you give me and belief you have in me. Last time I wrote that if there was a draft of wives, you'd be one I'd tank for, so now let's tweak it. If you were a free agent, I'd spend years clearing cap space just for a chance at a meeting, and then I'd have Magic Johnson deliver the pitch.

NOTES

The book draws primarily from interviews I conducted with nearly three hundred people. In lieu of direct interviews with LeBron, I relied on other interviews he participated in—especially longform podcast interviews—and other statements he has made throughout his public career. For background information and perspective on the Lakers and the Buss family, I relied heavily on *Legacy: The True Story of the LA Lakers,* the Hulu documentary executive produced by Jeanie Buss. Most of the quotes from her and other members of the Buss family are sourced from that series. Additional material came from press conferences archived on NBA.com and YouTube, as well as reporting from ESPN, *The Athletic,* the *Los Angeles Times,* and *The Orange County Register.* In particular, the journalism conducted by Lakers beat writers Jovan Buha, Tania Ganguli, Kyle Goon, Dave McMenamin, Bill Oram, and Dan Woike was invaluable. Same goes for the work done by national writers like Sam Amick, Shams Charania, Baxter Holmes, Ramona Shelburne, and Adrian Wojnarowski.

Details and quotes pulled from outside sources include, by chapter:

1. Too Many Buss Drivers

7 "It'd be good to know that guy": Tania Ganguli, "Lakers' Signing of LeBron James Began with a Jerry Buss Dream," *Los Angeles Times,* July 21, 2018.

8 Setting bowling pins: Jeff Pearlman, *Showtime: Magic, Kareem, Riley, and the Los Angeles Lakers Dynasty of the 1980s,* 22.

9 "The Lakers belong to my children": *Legacy: The True Story of the LA Lakers* (Hulu, 2022), Episode 3.

10 A baby would derail his plans: *Legacy,* Episode 10.

10 "[I'm] too busy getting": Lee Klose, *Late for the Buss: An Adoption Story.*

10 "I remember asking a lot": *Legacy,* Episode 1.

11   "It left us confused": Frank Lidz, "She's Got Balls," *Sports Illustrated*, November 2, 1998.

11   "We'd vie for his attention": *Legacy*, Episode 1.

11   Johnny had quit: Lidz, "She's Got Balls."

11   "I think we were 8–40": *Legacy*, Episode 2.

11   "Being the son of a famous man": Lidz, "She's Got Balls."

12   "I didn't like being in the limelight": *Legacy*, Episode 2.

12   She read DC Comics: Thomas Golianopoulos, "Family Business," *Grantland*, April 3, 2015.

12   "always trying to please my dad": Lidz, "She's Got Balls."

12   "Yes, I already told him": *Legacy*, Episode 2.

12   "I want you to know what it feels like": Jeanie Buss and Steve Springer, *Laker Girl*, 217.

13   Buss showed up to the wedding reception: Buss and Springer, *Laker Girl*, 186.

13   "I was homesick": *Legacy*, Episode 5.

13   "I felt such a sense of relief": *Legacy*, Episode 5.

13   enticed tennis stars: Buss and Springer, *Laker Girl*, 132.

13   "I didn't take it as much as a sexual advance": *Legacy*, Episode 5.

14   He reduced the team's annual losses: *Legacy*, Episode 5.

14   "We were probably best friends": *Legacy*, Episode 2.

14   "all they did was blame me": Lidz, "She's Got Balls."

15   "With a colt": Lidz, "She's Got Balls."

15   "I wouldn't mind Jeanie having control": Lidz, "She's Got Balls."

15   "We all understood that": Tania Ganguli, "Johnny Buss Distances Himself from Siblings and the Lakers," *Los Angeles Times*, June 18, 2017.

16   "I had never seen him like that": Buss and Springer, *Laker Girl*, 302.

16   Kobe visited him three times: Buss and Springer, *Laker Girl*, 302.

16   he wanted to repay his former star: Bill Plaschke, "To Magic Johnson, Jerry Buss Was Friend, Mentor and 'Second Father,'" *Los Angeles Times*, February 19, 2013.

16   "I love you": *Legacy*, Episode 9.

17   "None of us really knew": *Legacy*, Episode 9.

18   "I think [Dr. Buss] kept it to himself": *Legacy*, Episode 9.

18   "Are you kidding?": Buss and Springer, *Laker Girl*, 220.

18   "get the fuck out": *Legacy*, Episode 9.

21   "I think Mike was in over his head": *Legacy*, Episode 9.

21   *Where's Jeanie?*: Buss and Springer, *Laker Girl*, 293.

22   "I thought things would be different": Buss and Springer, *Laker Girl*, 294.

22   Jeanie left with her dog: Buss and Springer, *Laker Girl*, 294.

22   "He told us he didn't want to coach": *Legacy*, Episode 9.

22   Jackson . . . thought the meeting went great: Buss and Springer, *Laker Girl*, 296.

23   "It was clear to me": Buss and Springer, *Laker Girl*, 296.

23   *Okay. All right. Okay*: Buss and Springer, *Laker Girl*, 296.

23   "I wonder where all that came from?": Golianopoulos, "Family Business."

23   "A great farter": Andrew Sharp, "Dwight Howard Was Great at Farting," *SB Nation*, October 2, 2012.

23 "Did you kick me?": Baxter Holmes, "Kobe's Career Is Ending, but His Playing Days Ended Long Ago," ESPN, April 11, 2016.

24 Nash showed up: Henry Abbott, "Is Kobe the Reason for the Lakers' Downfall?," ESPN, November 29, 2015.

24 *You have to learn how it's done:* Adrian Wojnarowski, "Kobe Bryant Challenges Dwight Howard in Meeting," Yahoo Sports, July 3, 2013.

24 "They would've probably had": Ramona Shelburne, "Lakers VP Jeanie Buss Says Her Dad Could Have Wooed Dwight Howard to Stay in L.A.," ESPN, August 8, 2013.

2. Klutch Time

26 he set up a holding company: Tim Arango, "LeBron Inc.," *Fortune,* December 10, 2007.

26 "He tells me what socks to buy": "Buffett Sits Courtside to Watch Buddy LeBron Play," Associated Press, March 26, 2007.

27 "There's no way": "Michael Jordan on LeBron James' Decision: I Wouldn't Have Called Larry Bird, Magic Johnson," Associated Press, July 19, 2010.

27 "narcissistic": Maureen Dowd, "Miami's Hoops Cartel," *New York Times,* July 10, 2010.

28 "When I'm done [playing]": S. L. Price, "The King Maker: Why Rich Paul Will Own the NBA Summer," *Sports Illustrated,* June 12, 2019.

28 waiting to board a flight: Rich Paul, *Lucky Me,* 228.

28 "The minute I met Rich": Paul, *Lucky Me,* vii.

28 setting up Paul and his mother: Paul, *Lucky Me,* 22.

29 He gave them cash: Paul, *Lucky Me,* 59.

29 "I felt more alone": Paul, *Lucky Me,* 191.

30 a salary of $48,000: Paul, *Lucky Me,* 234.

30 "He was really stuck": Uninterrupted, *More Than an Athlete* (ESPN, November 2018), Episode 5.

31 "He was in a lot of places": *More Than an Athlete,* Episode 5.

31 "I learned nothing at CAA": Isaac Chotiner, "LeBron James's Agent Is Transforming the Business of Basketball," *New Yorker,* May 31, 2021.

32 "I knew he had put in time": *More Than an Athlete,* Episode 5.

32 "another Master P situation": Chris Broussard, "The Chosen's One," *ESPN The Magazine,* December 25, 2012.

34 Ritz-Carlton: Joe Drape, "LeBron James's Representative Completes His Own Journey," *New York Times,* August 17, 2014.

35 "I said, 'Mr. Carter' ": "Ex-Mav Jim Jackson Divulges Details of His 1992 Holdout, Explains Why 'Three Js' Era Never Panned Out," *Dallas Morning News,* January 26, 2014.

36 "Finally, the Mavericks came in": "Ex-Mav Jim Jackson Divulges Details of His 1992 Holdout."

36 "In the NBA": Mark Termini, *Words to Negotiate By.*

36 "I knew what I didn't know": Rich Paul, interview by JJ Redick, *The JJ Redick Podcast,* October 2023.

38 "I'm not the beautiful mind": Mark Termini, interview by Brian Windhorst, *The Hoop Collective,* August 2023.

39 "Bled felt antsy": Paul, *Lucky Me,* xvii.

39 "doesn't do any work": Paul, *Lucky Me,* xviii.

39 "That was the first real money": Paul, *Lucky Me,* xviii.

3. The Mother of Dragons

40 *When will we be back in the playoffs?: Legacy: The True Story of the LA Lakers* (Hulu, 2022), Episode 9.

40 "Nobody understands the pressure": *Legacy,* Episode 9.

40 "A year": *Legacy,* Episode 9.

40 *Why would you say that?: Legacy,* Episode 9.

41 "There's no way that's going to happen": *Legacy,* Episode 9.

41 "Just so you know": *Legacy,* Episode 9.

41 "You have to have a real superstar": *Legacy,* Episode 10.

41 "Basically we put everything": Kevin Ding, "Ding: LeBron to Lakers? Jim Buss Excited by Free-Agent Possibilities," *Orange County Register,* October 18, 2012.

41 no interest in taking a pay cut: Serena Winters, "Kobe Bryant Discusses Financial Future with Lakers," *Lakers Nation,* July 11, 2013.

41 "We never got an opportunity": Eric Pincus, "Jeanie Buss Says Kobe Bryant Deserves Farewell Tour and His Extension," *Los Angeles Times,* March 19, 2014.

41 "we don't have Carnival Cruises": Dave McMenamin, "Q&A with Jim Buss, Part 1," ESPN, April 18, 2012.

42 "I've had a lot of clients": Henry Abbott, "Is Kobe the Reason for the Lakers' Downfall?," *ESPN The Magazine,* October 20, 2014.

43 "I never talked to Jeanie": Ramona Shelburne, "The Inside Story of the Lakers' Family Drama," ESPN, March 8, 2017.

43 *This is theirs to lose:* LaMarcus Aldridge, interview by Matt Barnes and Stephen Jackson, *All the Smoke,* December 28, 2023.

43 "I don't give a shit about trending": Aldridge, interview by Barnes and Jackson.

44 "It was a miscalculation": Aldridge, interview by Barnes and Jackson.

45 "The vibe of understanding": Aldridge, interview by Barnes and Jackson.

47 "was far too proud of her career": Shelburne, "The Inside Story of the Lakers' Family Drama."

48 a naked Jerry Garcia: John Gustafson, "Son King," *ESPN The Magazine,* November 12, 2002.

48 "People would walk in": Luke Walton, interview by Richard Jefferson and Channing Frye, *Road Trippin',* December 2018.

48 a restored 1970 yellow Cadillac: Bud Withers, "Here Comes the Son: Luke Walton and Arizona Coming to Town," *Seattle Times,* February 5, 2003.

49 "If there was a recruit": Walton, interview by Jefferson and Frye.

49 "I think Phil [Jackson] saw": Ethan Strauss, "Luke Walton, the Golden State Warriors' Winless Wonder," ESPN, November 24, 2015.

49 chart statistics from the bench: Ohm Youngmisuk, "How Luke Walton's Coach-

ing Style Was Influenced by the Major NBA Championship Figures in His Life," ESPN, December 6, 2017.

50 "I think he is our best": William Weinbaum and Steve Delsohn, "Los Angeles Lakers Dynasty Derailed," ESPN, October 21, 2016.

51 "Looking back at some of the decisions": *Legacy,* Episode 9.

51 *Offer them something to drink:* Jeanie Buss, interview by Rich Kleiman, *The Boardroom Podcast,* November 2021.

51 "It was this smile": Buss, interview by Kleiman.

51 *You're not gonna believe what he said:* Buss, interview by Kleiman.

52 *As soon as he puts on a Lakers uniform:* Buss, interview by Kleiman.

52 they sat down for dinner: Ramona Shelburne, "Los Angeles Lakers Co-Owner Jeanie Buss Meets with Magic Johnson," ESPN, January 18, 2017.

52 "You have four boys": Shelburne, "The Inside Story of the Lakers' Family Drama."

53 "Earvin and I were basically raised": Bill Oram, "Jeanie Buss Is Lakers' Wonder Woman," *Orange County Register,* July 23, 2017.

53 "I was worried": Jeanie Buss, *The Boardroom Podcast,* November 2021.

54 "Go all in or don't do it at all": Sam Amick, "Landing LeBron: How Jeanie Buss Became the 'Mother of Dragons' with an Assist from Kobe and Spawned a New Lakers Golden Era," *The Athletic,* September 26, 2020.

54 she stayed in LA: Shelburne, "The Inside Story of the Lakers' Family Drama."

54 "That's when I knew something was up": *Legacy,* Episode 9.

54 Magic was at the gym: Shelburne, "The Inside Story of the Lakers' Family Drama."

55 Jeanie was in her office: Shelburne, "The Inside Story of the Lakers' Family Drama."

56 "We were trying to figure out": *Legacy,* Episode 9.

56 "just [making] sure": *Legacy,* Episode 9.

56 "They tried to disregard": *Legacy,* Episode 9.

57 room 629: Nathan Fenno, "It Was 16 Months Ago When Jeanie Buss Made a Daring Move to Seize Control of the Lakers," *Los Angeles Times,* July 4, 2018.

58 "nondescript concrete bunker": Bill Oram: "Lakers' Move to New Headquarters Means 'Bittersweet' Goodbye to Longtime Home," *Orange County Register,* July 30, 2017.

4. Call the Lakers

59 In fact, his agent had already: "Los Angeles Lakers Fined $500,000 for Tampering by NBA," Associated Press, August 31, 2017.

60 dreamed of playing for the Lakers: Dave McMenamin, "How Jayson Tatum and the 2017 NBA Draft Fuels the Boston Celtics and Los Angeles Lakers Rivalry," ESPN, January 23, 2025.

60 visited the Ball family's Chino Hills home: Tania Ganguli, "A Look Behind the Scenes as the Lakers Prepared to Draft Lonzo Ball," *Los Angeles Times,* June 25, 2017.

61 a $21 million, ten-thousand-square-foot home: Dave McMenamin, "LeBron James of Cleveland Cavaliers Purchases Los Angeles Vacation Home for Nearly $21 Million," ESPN, November 11, 2015.

62 *How about PG?:* Dahntay Jones, interview by Paul George, *Podcast P,* February 2024.

62 "He was selling like a motherfucker": Jones, interview by George.

62 *You're both cool:* Jones, interview by George.

62 *I'm gonna try to make this happen:* Jones, interview by George.

63 he urged the Cavs: Jason Lloyd, "As Tensions Mount, the Distance Between LeBron James and the Cavaliers Is Growing," *The Athletic,* February 6, 2018.

64 *Do not trade Kyrie:* Joe Vardon, "LeBron James: Cavaliers' Trading of Kyrie Irving Was 'Beginning of the End for Everything,'" *New York Times,* November 19, 2018.

64 "At that point in time": Vardon, "LeBron James."

65 "All I want us to do": Tania Ganguli, "Lakers Looking Mostly for Growth in Ultra-Competitive Western Conference," *Los Angeles Times,* September 26, 2017.

65 Dr. Buss had always intended: Tania Ganguli, "Johnny Buss Distances Himself from Siblings and the Lakers," *Los Angeles Times,* June 18, 2017.

65 spent countless hours: Mike Trudell, "Jesse Buss Q and A," NBA.com, September 19, 2022.

68 "I think Koby did": Dave McMenamin, "New-Look Cavaliers Provide Reason for Optimism, but Questions Remain," ESPN, February 22, 2018.

70 LeBron and his family left: Lee Jenkins, "Inside LeBron James's Third Free-Agency Decision," *Sports Illustrated,* July 1, 2018.

71 "I wanted to help Jeanie": LeBron James, X, October 5, 2024.

71 Maria Shriver and Gavin Newsom: Jenkins, "Inside LeBron James's Third Free-Agency Decision."

71 boarded a private plane: Jenkins, "Inside LeBron James's Third Free-Agency Decision."

71 "Call the Lakers": Jenkins, "Inside LeBron James's Third Free-Agency Decision."

71 Paul texted Jeanie one word: Ramona Shelburne, "How LeBron James' Decision Instantly Changed Los Angeles Lakers, Cleveland Cavaliers and NBA," ESPN, July 11, 2018.

72 "I love the young guys": Rachel Nichols, "LeBron: 'I've Always Been a Part of Beating the Odds in Life,'" ESPN, July 30, 2018.

72 *You have to have a superstar: Legacy: The True Story of the LA Lakers* (Hulu, 2022), Episode 10.

5. "LeBron's Gonna Trade You"

79 "I thought it was the best thing": Dave McMenamin, "How a Busted Trade Request Got Anthony Davis to Los Angeles," ESPN, October 8, 2019.

80 since attending his basketball camps: Adam Zagoria, "The Bond Between LeBron James and Anthony Davis Began at LeBron's Camp a Decade Ago," *Forbes,* October 2020.

80 "We were dogshit": Anthony Davis, interview by D'Angelo Russell, *The Backyard Podcast*, February 2024.

85 "That would be amazing": Dave McMenamin, "LeBron James: Los Angeles Lakers Getting Anthony Davis Would Be 'Amazing,'" ESPN, December 19, 2018.

85 "I don't really care": Zach Lowe, "Anthony Davis, Though Flattered by LeBron James' Comments, Says Focus Is on New Orleans Pelicans," ESPN, December 20, 2018.

85 reports surfaced that Davis had dinner: Chris Haynes, "Sources: LeBron James, Anthony Davis Meet for Postgame Dinner," Yahoo Sports, December 22, 2018.

85 Paul informed the Pelicans: Tania Ganguli and Broderick Turner, "Lakers' Trade Offer for Anthony Davis Now Includes Veterans and Two First-Round Picks," *Los Angeles Times*, February 4, 2019.

88 spent the week urging Demps: Adrian Wojnarowski, "Magic Johnson, Lakers Competing with Pelicans Desire to Wait on Anthony Davis," ESPN, February 5, 2019.

6. Can You Feel the Magic?

90 "'Can you do this for me?'": *Legacy: The True Story of the LA Lakers* (Hulu, 2022), Episode 5.

90 "He was hard, man": *Legacy*, Episode 5.

90 "Teach the Lakers what it was like": Scott Howard-Cooper, "Me-Me-Me-Me Turned Out to Be a Sour Note to Magic: Lakers: Attitude of the Players Was a Key Factor in His D," *Los Angeles Times*, April 17, 1994.

90 Fans welcomed him back: Jay Privman, "Johnson's Victorious Lakers Bring Life Back to Forum," *New York Times*, March 26, 1994.

91 talking about drag-racing: Danny Schayes, "Schayes: Divorce Court for Coaches and Players; a Magic Johnson Tale," *Sheridan Hoops*, March 9, 2015.

91 *You motherfuckers*: *Legacy*, Episode 5.

91 *Vlade, give me the beeper*: Schayes, "Divorce Court."

92 "Everybody cares about me, I, I, I": Howard-Cooper, "Me-Me-Me-Me Turned Out to Be a Sour Note to Magic."

92 "Coaching requires a tremendous": Scott Howard-Cooper, "Magic Passes a Last Time, Won't Coach Next Year: Lakers: After a 105-100 Defeat by the Trail Blazers Eliminates L.A., He Says Losing Is Too Hard to Take," *Los Angeles Times*, April 16, 1994.

92 "I have 1,000 résumés": Baxter Holmes, "Lakers 2.0: The Failed Reboot of the NBA's Crown Jewel," ESPN, May 29, 2019.

93 a seventy-three-meter-long, $680,000-per-week yacht: TMZ Staff, "Magic Johnson Entering 18th Day on $700,000-Per-Week Yacht!," *TMZ*, August 18, 2017.

95 "Just to kind of do a deep dive": Uninterrupted, *More Than an Athlete* (ESPN, November 2018), Episode 2.

95 "2018–19: CORE PILLARS": *More Than an Athlete*, Episode 2.

97 "admonished" Walton: Adrian Wojnarowski and Dave McMenamin, "Magic

Johnson Admonishes Luke Walton After Los Angeles Lakers' Slow Start," ESPN, November 2, 2018.

100 "Quit making this about": "Magic: Don't Treat Lakers 'Like Babies' After Davis Trade Talk," Associated Press, February 11, 2019.

100 "you're always going to be": Dave McMenamin, "Lakers' Magic Johnson Says Pelicans Didn't Act in Good Faith," ESPN, February 10, 2019.

100 "How am I supposed to answer that?": McMenamin, "Lakers' Magic Johnson Says Pelicans Didn't Act in Good Faith."

100 "I almost look at Bullock": Dave McMenamin, "GM Rob Pelinka Hopes Los Angeles Lakers Rally Like New England Patriots," ESPN, February 8, 2019.

102 the players met alone: Dave McMenamin, "How the Lakers Wasted Year 1 of LeBron," ESPN, April 10, 2019.

102 "I tried to get LeBron": Rajon Rondo, interview by Matt Barnes and Stephen Jackson, *All the Smoke,* December 2020.

102 That July afternoon: Ramona Shelburne, "How LeBron James' Decision Instantly Changed Los Angeles Lakers, Cleveland Cavaliers and NBA," ESPN, July 11, 2018.

102 "The rhythm is the answer": Shelburne, "How LeBron James' Decision Instantly Changed Los Angeles Lakers."

103 Even NBA commissioner Adam Silver: Holmes, "Lakers 2.0."

104 some street murals celebrating: Matt Bonesteel, "The LeBron James Mural in Los Angeles Got Vandalized Again, and Now It's Gone," *Washington Post,* July 12, 2018.

105 "pursed his lips": McMenamin, "How the Lakers Wasted Year 1 of LeBron."

107 *You guys knew Magic was stepping down: Legacy,* Episode 10.

107 *Magic just stepped down:* LeBron James, *The Shop,* HBO, May 2019.

107 "I was like, 'Man'": James, *The Shop.*

7. A Rob Pelinka–Type

109 they would not be hiring someone: Ramona Shelburne, "Source: Lakers Will Not Hire Replacement for Magic," ESPN, May 17, 2019.

110 It wasn't until: Paul Sullivan and *Chicago Tribune,* "Lake Forest Star Getting Noticed," *Chicago Tribune,* February 8, 1988.

111 a "Rob Pelinka–type": Mitch Albom, *Fab Five: Basketball, Trash Talk, the American Dream,* 255.

112 in his rusty Jeep: Rob Pelinka, interview by Adrian Wojnarowski, *The Woj Pod,* May 2018.

112 had worked as a stringer: Dan McQuade, "Arn Tellem and Franz Lidz Are Going to the Hall of Fame," *Philadelphia,* May 17, 2015.

112 That she was Mexican American: Jeff Pearlman, *Three-Ring Circus: Kobe, Shaq, Phil, and the Crazy Years of the Lakers Dynasty,* 185.

113 take whatever business card: Mike Bresnahan, "Bryant Not Working with a Secret Agent," *Los Angeles Times,* July 14, 2004.

113 "I looked at it as a challenge": John Heuser, *Ann Arbor News,* March 8, 2004.

115 "I'd resign immediately": "Pelinka and Client Criticized After Jazz Deal," ESPN, July 12, 2004.

116 first-ever televised ad: "Kobe's First TV Ad for Nike Debuts," Associated Press, February 8, 2006.

117 "He just asked me": Andre Iguodala and Carvell Wallace, *The Sixth Man: A Memoir* (New York: Blue Rider Press, 2019), p. 93.

118 Pelinka called up Duke: Bresnahan, "Bryant Not Working with a Secret Agent."

118 "I need somebody who": Lee Jenkins, "Lakers' Rebuild Could Be Ready for Showtime," *Sports Illustrated,* April 17, 2018.

118 "I know how you work": Pelinka, interview by Wojnarowski.

121 He'd pop into coaches' meetings: Baxter Holmes, "Lakers 2.0: The Failed Reboot of the NBA's Crown Jewel," ESPN, May 29, 2019.

121 Kobe being wowed by: Holmes, "Lakers 2.0."

124 "Shut the fuck up": Ken Berger, "In Taking Control of LeBron, Tyronn Lue Has Created a Monster in Cleveland," CBS Sports, May 18, 2016.

125 frustrated with LeBron's passive play: Lee Jenkins, "Crowning the King: LeBron James Is Sports Illustrated's 2016 Sportsperson of the Year," *Sports Illustrated,* December 2016.

125 Lue met with Pelinka: Kyle Goon, "Report: Lakers Meet with Ty Lue, Looking for Follow-Up Interviews Including Jeanie Buss," *Orange County Register,* April 20, 2019.

125 how he'd succeeded with LeBron: Joe Vardon, "Tyronn Lue Spelled Out How His Cavaliers' Blueprint for LeBron James Applied to Lakers—Now What?," *The Athletic,* May 9, 2019.

125 "almost every day": TMZ Staff, "Magic Johnson Says He's Still Working for Lakers, Loves Team and LeBron," *TMZ,* April 21, 2019.

125 That Friday, after learning: Tania Ganguli and Broderick Turner, "Lakers Open Talks with Tyronn Lue to Become Their Next Head Coach," *Los Angeles Times,* May 3, 2019.

125 three-year, $18 million contract: Adrian Wojnarowski and Dave McMenamin, "Lakers, Lue End Talks Without Deal, Sources Say," ESPN, May 8, 2019.

127 Lue was angry and offended: Ty Lue, interview by Stephen A. Smith, *The Stephen A. Smith Show,* December 6, 2024.

128 Lue's representatives informed the Lakers: Wojnarowski and McMenamin, "Lakers, Lue End Talks Without Deal."

128 they had decided to move on: Tania Ganguli, Twitter, May 8, 2019.

128 "He said, 'What do I gotta do?'": Lue, interview by Smith.

131 *I'm gonna get all these questions:* Frank Vogel, interview by Zach Lowe, *The Lowe Post,* October 2020.

133 ESPN published a story by reporter Baxter Holmes: Holmes, "Lakers 2.0."

133 "We can hold on": Zach Lowe, "What Happened at the Wildest NBA Lottery Ever Seen," ESPN, May 15, 2019.

135 "Ultimately, it was my decision": *Legacy: The True Story of the LA Lakers* (Hulu, 2022), Episode 10.

135 the Lakers had made a mistake: Ben Rohrbach, "Report: Lakers Had to Call Peli-

cans Back About Cap Space After Anthony Davis Deal," Yahoo Sports, June 20, 2019.

8. A Lion's Pride

139 usually on trips organized by Nike: Dave McMenamin, "Inside LeBron James' and Adam Silver's Make-or-Break Moments in China," ESPN, October 16, 2019.

140 Sponsors pulled their support: Tania Ganguli, "Lakers in China: How the Team and NBA Navigated the Crisis amid Tumultuous Week," *Los Angeles Times,* October 15, 2019.

140 Adam Silver called a meeting: McMenamin, "Inside LeBron James' and Adam Silver's Make-or-Break Moments in China."

140 LeBron, annoyed, raised his hand: McMenamin, "Inside LeBron James' and Adam Silver's Make-or-Break Moments in China."

141 "That was a big moment": Kevin Arnovitz, "How Frank Vogel Won Over the Lakers and Their Superstars," ESPN, January 17, 2020.

146 "You just sensed that": *The Redeem Team* (Netflix, 2022).

146 "Kobe's a[n] asshole": *Club 520 Podcast*, "Dwight Howard REGRETS Leaving Magic, LeBron vs. Kobe, Derrick Rose MVP Battle | Jeff Teague Club 520," YouTube, June 2, 2025.

146 "I understand Kobe is": *The Redeem Team.*

146 That meant imitating: *The Redeem Team.*

147 "Yo, Coach": Ian O'Connor, *Coach K: The Rise and Reign of Mike Krzyzewski,* 273.

148 Davis was watching *Avengers:* Dave McMenamin, "The Longest Flight in Los Angeles Lakers History: When the Team Learned of Kobe Bryant's Death," ESPN, January 26, 2021.

148 *Man, Kobe died:* McMenamin, "The Longest Flight in Los Angeles Lakers History."

148 *Man, y'all stop playin':* McMenamin, "The Longest Flight in Los Angeles Lakers History."

148 *It's true:* McMenamin, "The Longest Flight in Los Angeles Lakers History."

150 Over a two-hour lunch: McMenamin, "The Longest Flight in Los Angeles Lakers History."

150 *You're going to have to play:* McMenamin, "The Longest Flight in Los Angeles Lakers History."

150 "It helped us out a lot": Jared Dudley, interview by Zach Lowe, *The Lowe Post,* February 2020.

151 "After that": Alex Caruso, interview by JJ Redick, *The JJ Redick Show,* November 2020.

9. Bubble Boys

153 By the end of the call: Baxter Holmes and Tim MacMahon, " 'He's Got It': An Oral History of the NBA's COVID-19 Shutdown—and How It Changed Sports Forever," ESPN, March 11, 2025.

155 "The CBA was not built": Adrian Wojnarowski, "Adam Silver Prepares NBA Players for Challenges Ahead," ESPN, May 9, 2020.

155 the union started polling: Broderick Turner, "Coronavirus: Union Asks NBA Players If They Want to Restart," *Los Angeles Times,* May 12, 2020.

156 "You know who I'm voting for": Dan Labbe, "James, Jay-Z Energize Rally at the Q for Obama," *Cleveland Plain Dealer,* October 30, 2008.

156 at the behest of Jay-Z: Jeff Benedict, *LeBron,* 313.

156 "You want to keep athletics and politics separate": Eli Saslow, "LeBron the Activist vs. LeBron the Athlete," ESPN, May 3, 2016.

156 LeBron had appeared reluctant: Chris Strauss and Nate Scott, "LeBron James Wears 'I Can't Breathe' Shirt before Cavs Game," *USA Today,* December 8, 2014.

156 "I haven't really been on top": Saslow, "LeBron the Activist vs. LeBron the Athlete."

157 "I think it's quite sad": "Samaria Rice: LeBron James, Athletes Should Make a Statement for Black People," NewsOne, January 5, 2016.

158 "I realized that they were dead set": Will Leitch, "The Athletes Have More to Say," *New York,* March 2, 2021.

161 "I don't support going into Orlando": Shams Charania, "Sources Reveal Details of Call Among 80 NBA Players Led by Kyrie Irving," *The Athletic,* June 13, 2020.

161 "Once we start playing basketball again": Adrian Wojnarowski, "Sources—Kyrie Irving Plays Key Role in Friday Call with Players," ESPN, June 13, 2020.

161 met on the tarmac: JaVale McGee, *Life in the Bubble* (YouTube, 2020), Episode 1.

161 It was dark when they arrived: McGee, *Life in the Bubble,* Episode 1.

162 Each player was greeted: McGee, *Life in the Bubble,* Episode 1.

162 made a group toast: McGee, *Life in the Bubble,* Episode 1.

162 "Mike Budenholzer would always": Kyle Kuzma, interview by Adrian Wojnarowski, *The Woj Pod,* January 2023.

164 "all you heard": LeBron James, interview by Richard Jefferson and Channing Frye, *Road Trippin',* December 2020.

165 *Is this really your typical:* Rob Pelinka, interview by Adrian Wojnarowski, *The Woj Pod,* October 2020.

166 sixteen boxes: McGee, *Life in the Bubble,* Episode 16.

166 LeBron woke up: James, interview by Jefferson and Frye.

166 "No one knew what was going on": James, interview by Jefferson and Frye.

166 "We're tired of the killings": Marc Spears, Twitter, August 26, 2020.

167 bacon and tangerine juice: Taylor Rooks, "Inside the Great NBA Bubble Experiment," *GQ,* November 24, 2020.

167 Giannis Antetokounmpo joined them: Rooks, "Inside the Great NBA Bubble Experiment."

167 LeBron worked the phones: James, interview by Jefferson and Frye.

167 The three were annoyed: James, interview by Jefferson and Frye.

168 "When it hits in your backyard": James, interview by Jefferson and Frye.

169 *Are you going home to work:* Zach Lowe et al., "Inside the Hectic Hours Around a Historic NBA Boycott," ESPN, August 27, 2020.

169 "Everybody was giving their opinions": Austin Rivers, *Off Guard with Austin Rivers,* The Ringer, May 2023.

169 *Hey, yo, bro:* Rivers, *Off Guard with Austin Rivers.*

170 "We sat there and talked": James, interview by Jefferson and Frye.

170 "I thought it was 70–30": Jared Dudley, interview by Bill Simmons, *The Bill Simmons Podcast,* October 2020.

170 Use it, Obama said: Barack Obama, interview by LeBron James and Maverick Carter, *The Shop,* HBO, October 29, 2020.

174 "Fuck it, bring out the cards": Rajon Rondo, interview by Matt Barnes and Stephen Jackson, *All the Smoke,* December 2020.

174 fired a bottle of Vitamin Water: NESN Staff, "Rajon Rondo Flips Out During Heat Playoff Series, Throws Bottle That Breaks Video Screen, Says New Report," NESN, December 13, 2011.

175 Kendrick Perkins had started calling him: Jackie MacMullan, "The Rehabilitation of Rajon Rondo," ESPN, October 4, 2020.

175 "I just did not see them losing": James, interview by Jefferson and Frye.

176 "I couldn't believe it": James, interview by Jefferson and Frye.

176 "It was a 'wing it' play": Danny Green, *Inside the Green Room,* September 2020.

177 "That was Mamba right there": McGee, *Life in the Bubble,* Episode 17.

178 "I watched him a lot in New Orleans": James, interview by Jefferson and Frye.

178 black and blue: James, interview by Jefferson and Frye.

178 "One thing about dogs": McGee, *Life in the Bubble,* Episode 17.

10. Seventy-One Days

184 "Mama, Mama!": Scott Gleeson, "LeBron James Pays Tribute to His Mother on FaceTime Following Championship: 'I Hope I Continue to Make You Proud,'" *USA Today,* October 12, 2020.

185 the sixteenth and final "X": JaVale McGee, *Life in the Bubble* (YouTube, 2020), Episode 18.

185 "She came running down": Rob Pelinka, interview by Adrian Wojnarowski, *The Woj Pod,* October 2020.

185 "You ever see the movie": Jared Dudley, interview by Bill Simmons, *The Bill Simmons Podcast,* October 2020.

185 Covid had already cost: Ben Golliver, "Coronavirus Could Cost NBA $1 Billion, Bring About Record Salary Cap Drop," *Washington Post,* March 21, 2020.

187 "We absolutely can [repeat]": LeBron James, interview by Jefferson and Frye, *Road Trippin',* December 2020.

188 "It's a business": Kevin Gray Jr., "Exclusive: Klutch Sports CEO Rich Paul on Anthony Davis/Luka Dončić Trade," *DLLS Sports,* February 7, 2025.

188 the importance of diversifying portfolios: Rich Paul, interview by Bloomberg, Bloomberg Power Players Summit, August 2022.

191 "It's a hard pill to swallow": Dan Woike, "Marc Gasol: Lakers Signing Andre Drummond Hard to Accept," *Los Angeles Times,* April 3, 2021.

194 "I wanna see you win one": DeMar DeRozan, *Above the Noise: My Story of Chasing Calm* (Harmony, 2024), 197.

194 having lunch on the patio: DeRozan, *Above the Noise,* 198.

194 "The next episode of my career": DeRozan, *Above the Noise,* 198.

195 cut middle school classes: Melissa Rohlin, "How Russell Westbrook's Lakers Tenure Changed His Career Trajectory," Fox Sports, March 1, 2023.

195 end up back in LA: Dan Woike, "Lakers' Russell Westbrook Back in L.A. with a Story to Tell," *Los Angeles Times,* October 19, 2021.

195 He called up Leonard: Ramona Shelburne, "How Two Phone Calls Two Years Apart Led to the Los Angeles Lakers Landing Russell Westbrook," ESPN, August 2, 2021.

195 Leonard listened to Westbrook's pitch: Shelburne, "How Two Phone Calls Two Years Apart Led to the Los Angeles Lakers Landing Russell Westbrook."

198 Kuzma began preparing: Kyle Kuzma, interview by Gilbert Arenas, *No Chill with Gilbert Arenas,* Fubo Sports Network, September 7, 2021.

200 "I'm so happy that you're here": Brian Windhorst, "LeBron James, Russell Westbrook and the Los Angeles Lakers' Tumultuous Season, in Their Own Words," ESPN, April 11, 2022.

200 "We know what we need to do": Windhorst, "LeBron James, Russell Westbrook and the Los Angeles Lakers' Tumultuous Season."

11. Russ Being Russ

201 The players found seats: *Backstage: Lakers* (Spectrum SportsNet, September 2021).

201 "You could say this room": *Backstage: Lakers.*

204 had a specialist examine his hands: Ramona Shelburne, "Why This Los Angeles Lakers Season Was Doomed from Their First Team Outing in October," ESPN, April 8, 2022.

206 "I need to get as much money": Alex Caruso, interview by JJ Redick, *The JJ Redick Show,* November 2021.

206 Caruso set up shop: Bill Oram, "Gone in a Blink: The Inside Story of Alex Caruso's Departure from the Lakers," *The Athletic,* November 15, 2021.

207 "So I said, 'Okay' ": Caruso, interview by Redick.

208 force Indiana wing Caris LeVert: Dave McMenamin, "Los Angeles Lakers Star Russell Westbrook Benched Late in Loss; Coach Frank Vogel Had Green Light, Sources Say," ESPN, January 20, 2022.

209 being applied by Kurt Rambis: Sam Amick and Bill Oram, "Sources: Lakers Coach Frank Vogel's Job in Serious Jeopardy Despite Jazz Win," *The Athletic,* January 18, 2022.

209 a frequent presence in Vogel's meetings: Amick and Oram, "Sources: Lakers Coach Frank Vogel's Job in Serious Jeopardy Despite Jazz Win."

212 A meeting was called: Adrian Wojnarowski, "Sources: LeBron James' Agent Meets with Los Angeles Lakers, Denies Any Push to Shake up Front Office," ESPN, February 25, 2022.

213 Oram would later write: Bill Oram, "I Survived a Media Feud with LeBron James and All I Got Was This Column," *The Oregonian,* March 28, 2025.

12. The Pursuit of Happiness

218 "I wanted to make sure": Jeanie Buss, interview by Rich Eisen, *The Rich Eisen Show,* October 2023.

219 spent eleven days in the hospital: Dan Woike, "Darvin Ham Survived the Streets, a Bullet and Grief to Coach Lakers," *Los Angeles Times,* December 11, 2022.

219 "I had great parents": Marc J. Spears, "Darvin Ham Is Bringing His Philosophy and a Saginaw Toughness to the Lakers," *Andscape,* July 7, 2022.

228 "He gets this, 'Oh, he's controlling the team'": *Starting 5* (Netflix, 2024–), Episode 1.

233 He skipped parties and school dances: Austin Reaves, interview by Andre Iguodala and Evan Turner, *The Point Forward,* March 2023.

233 "It was all about playing the long game": Austin Reaves, interview by Matt Barnes and Stephen Jackson, *All the Smoke,* July 2023.

13. ⧗

238 boarded a flight for Saudi Arabia: Corbin Smith, "LeBron James' Visit to Saudi Arabia Is Sportswashing at Work," *Daily Beast,* September 10, 2023.

238 "My dream is to actually own": Dave McMenamin, "Cleveland Cavaliers Star LeBron James Says His 'Dream' Is to Own an NBA Team," ESPN, August 17, 2016.

241 "I know you got me": *Starting 5* (Netflix, 2024–), Episode 1.

244 "When I look around": Dave McMenamin, "The Lakers' Inconsistent, Injury-Filled Season Leaves Two Massive Questions," ESPN, April 30, 2024.

244 Paul called ESPN's Brian Windhorst: Brian Windhorst, "LeBron James Won't Ask for Trade or Be Traded by Lakers, Agent Says," ESPN, February 2, 2024.

245 two teams even called the Lakers: Adrian Wojnarowski and Ramona Shelburne, "Sources: Dubs Made Bid for LeBron at Deadline," ESPN, February 14, 2024.

246 encouraged team owner Joe Lacob: Wojnarowski and Shelburne, "Dubs Made Bid for LeBron at Deadline."

246 Lacob reached out to Jeanie: Wojnarowski and Shelburne, "Dubs Made Bid for LeBron at Deadline."

14. Mind the Game

250 a list of candidates: Jovan Buha and Shams Charania, "JJ Redick, James Borrego, Sam Cassell Emerge as Early Top Targets for Lakers' Coaching Job: Sources," *The Athletic,* May 14, 2024.

250 "JJ's greatest strength": Stephen Noh, "Former NBA Coach Says Lakers Expectations for JJ Redick Are 'a Little Bit Crazy,' Laments Los Angeles' Roster," *Sporting News,* October 18, 2024.

251 "What I really miss": Tyler Conway, "Lakers Rumors: JJ Redick Eyed by Insiders as HC Front-Runner, Job Is 'His to Lose,'" *Bleacher Report,* 2024.

251 coaching could be the solution: Josh Rosenberg, "JJ Redick Is Putting the NBA Through Therapy, One Podcast at a Time," *Esquire,* December 22, 2022.

251 in May 2023 with the Raptors: Adrian Wojnarowski, "JJ Redick Interviews for Raptors' Coaching Job, Sources Say," ESPN, May 10, 2023.

251 chatted for about ninety minutes: Adrian Wojnarowski, "Sources: Lakers to Interview JJ Redick for Coaching Job," ESPN, June 13, 2024.

252 the same pair of red boxers: Kirsten Fleming, "UConn Coach Danny Hurley Won't Change Any of His Clothes, Including His Lucky Dragon Underwear, Until Huskies Lose," *New York Post,* March 29, 2023.

252 the only way he'd ever leave UConn: Pete Thamel, "Hurley Plans to Stay at UConn, Chase a Dynasty," ESPN, April 9, 2024.

253 "If your whole life has been": Matt Norlander, "Why Dan Hurley Stayed at UConn: Texts with LeBron James, Billy Joel Concert Lead to Decision to Spurn Lakers," CBS Sports, 2024.

255 "I explained this was": Dan Hurley, interview by Graham Bensinger, *In Depth with Graham Bensinger,* September 2024.

255 "I just couldn't believe that my husband": Hurley, interview by Bensinger.

255 He looked for guidance: Michael Cohen, "'One, Two, Three, Stay': Inside Dan Hurley's Choice to Pass on 'Once-in-a-Lifetime' Job," Fox Sports, June 14, 2024.

256 "I put the phone away": Norlander, "Why Dan Hurley Stayed at UConn."

256 "If a decision is really hard": Norlander, "Why Dan Hurley Stayed at UConn."

257 "It was a hard time period": JJ Redick, interview by Zach Lowe, *The Lowe Post,* September 25, 2024.

258 was visiting his alma mater: Dave McMenamin, "How Coach JJ Redick, LeBron James and the Lakers Got Here," ESPN, September 30, 2024.

258 he and LeBron were chatting: McMenamin, "How Coach JJ Redick, LeBron James and the Lakers Got Here."

15. Jr.

260 "You about ready?": Tom Dierberger, "Mics Caught LeBron's Message to Bronny James on Lakers' Bench Before NBA Debut," *Sports Illustrated,* October 23, 2024.

261 he took her to an Outback Steakhouse: "LeBron and Savannah James Mourn the Closing of Their 'First Date' Spot—an Outback Steakhouse in Akron, Ohio," *People,* 2024.

261 "I didn't have a dad": "LeBron James of Los Angeles Lakers Says He Regrets Naming Son LeBron Jr. Due to Pressure," ESPN, July 27, 2018.

262 "I put it in the air because": Chris Ballard, "LeBron James Wants to Play with His Sons, Bronny and Bryce. Got a Problem with That?," *Sports Illustrated,* August 30, 2022.

262 had full creative control: Ballard, "LeBron James Wants to Play with His Sons."

263 Bronny blacked out: Luca Evans, "'Like He Was Trapped in a Box': The Oral

History of Bronny James' Heart Scare," *Orange County Register,* January 23, 2024.

263 "He could play for us": Erin Walsh, "LeBron James Reportedly Heard Saying Bronny Could Play for Lakers 'Right Now. Easy.'," *Bleacher Report,* 2025.

263 "It was just one of those great moments": Jeanie Buss, interview by Rich Eisen, *The Rich Eisen Show,* October 2023.

264 *If you take him:* Ryan Glasspiegel, "Rich Paul Threatening Teams Bronny James Will Play in Australia If Picked in NBA Draft: Bob Myers," *New York Post,* June 27, 2024.

264 "Bronny, you got Rob Pelinka here": Los Angeles Lakers, "Behind the Scenes: Lakers Make the Call to Draft Bronny James," YouTube, June 28, 2024.

16. The Luka Lakers

267 "We have to play close to perfect": "Anthony Davis Says Lakers 'Right There' but Need to Add Center," ESPN, January 24, 2025.

268 a five-year, $40 million offer: Ramona Shelburne and Tim MacMahon, " 'Unfathomable': How This Stunning Luka Doncic–Anthony Davis Trade Came Together for Los Angeles Lakers and Dallas Mavericks," ESPN, February 3, 2025.

268 Not by Harrison, though: Shelburne and MacMahon, " 'Unfathomable.' "

269 The two met up at a café: Shelburne and MacMahon, " 'Unfathomable.' "

269 Over coffee: Shelburne and MacMahon, " 'Unfathomable.' "

271 "I thought my phone was hacked": Joseph Zucker, "Shams Charania: 'I Thought My Phone Was Hacked' When I Got Luka-AD Trade Details," *Bleacher Report,* February 3, 2025.

271 Pelinka called to share the news: Dave McMenamin, X, February 2, 2025.

272 took time to huddle with Dončić: Dave McMenamin, "Inside the Most Chaotic, Transformational NBA Trade Deadline in Lakers History," ESPN, February 10, 2025.

273 "I've never seen [LeBron] as happy": Brigid Kennedy, "Carmelo Anthony Says LeBron James Looks Happier Than Ever After Luka Doncic Trade," *Sports Illustrated,* March 6, 2025.

SOURCES

The following is a list of the sources that I drew upon most.

Abbott, Henry. "Is Kobe the Reason for the Lakers' Downfall?" ESPN, November 29, 2015.

Abrams, Jonathan. *Boys Among Men: How the Prep-to-Pro Generation Redefined the NBA and Sparked a Basketball Revolution.* Three Rivers Press, 2017.

Adande, J. A. "Kobe Bryant Gets Shots in During Last Game with LeBron James." ESPN, March 12, 2016.

Albom, Mitch. *Fab Five: Basketball, Trash Talk, the American Dream.* Grand Central Publishing, 1994.

———. "Two Worlds Conquered: Fifth-Year Seniors Pelinka, Voskuil Excel on the Court, in the Classroom." *Detroit Free Press,* November 21, 2008.

Amick, Sam. "Absent a 'System,' the Pressure and Angst Is Being Turned Up on These Lakers." *New York Times,* November 3, 2018.

———. "Jeanie Buss Unplugged: On Lakers Power Structure, LeBron's Future, Russell Westbrook and More." *The Athletic,* August 30, 2022.

———. "Lakers Coach Luke Walton Adjusting to New Landscape in Los Angeles." *USA Today,* March 5, 2017.

———. "Landing LeBron: How Jeanie Buss Became the 'Mother of Dragons' with an Assist from Kobe and Spawned a New Lakers Golden Era." *The Athletic,* September 26, 2020.

———. "Magic Johnson Reveals Details About Meeting That Sealed LeBron James to the Lakers." *USA Today,* July 13, 2018.

Arango, Tim. "LeBron Inc." *Fortune,* December 10, 2007.

Associated Press. "Jeanie Buss, Fearing Brothers' Takeover of Lakers, Briefly Takes to Court." *New York Times,* March 4, 2017.

Ball, Lonzo. Interview by JJ Redick. *The JJ Redick Podcast,* April 2020.

Ballard, Chris. "LeBron James Wants to Play with His Sons, Bronny and Bryce. Got a Problem with That?" *Sports Illustrated,* August 30, 2022.

Benedict, Jeff. *LeBron.* Simon & Schuster, 2023.

Bergeron, Elena. "Kentucky's Anthony Davis Is Next." *ESPN The Magazine,* December 26, 2011.

Beverley, Patrick. *The Pat Beverley Show.* Episodes on January 10, 2023; October 18, 2020; and February 14, 2023.

Beverley, Patrick, and D'Angelo Russell. Interview by Patrick Beverley. *The Pat Beverley Show*, August 2, 2023.

Boyd, Flinder. "Luke Walton's Road to Coaching: Hippies, Hoops . . . and Hazing?" *Bleacher Report*, 2017.

Bresnahan, Mike. "Bryant Not Working with a Secret Agent." *Los Angeles Times*, July 14, 2004.

———. "How the Lakers Lost LaMarcus Aldridge." *Los Angeles Times*, July 1, 2015.

Broussard, Chris. "The Chosen's One." *ESPN The Magazine*, December 25, 2012.

Bryant, Kobe. Interview by Rich Eisen. *The Rich Eisen Show*, August 2018.

Buha, Jovan. "Inside the Lakers' Recent Draft Success and Their Preparation for the No. 22 Pick." *New York Times*, July 28, 2021.

Buha, Jovan, and Sam Amick. "A Lakers Dream Turned to Nightmare: Inside the 'Toxic' End of the Russell Westbrook Era." *The Athletic*, February 9, 2023.

Buss, Jeanie. Interview by Danny Green. *Inside the Green Room*, September 2020.

———. Interview by Graham Bensinger. *In Depth with Graham Bensinger*, October 2024.

———. Interview by Rich Eisen. *The Rich Eisen Show*, October 2023.

———. Interview by Rich Kleiman. *The Boardroom Podcast*, November 2021.

———. Interview by Zach Lowe. *The Lowe Post*, January 2019.

Buss, Jeanie, and Steve Springer. *Laker Girl*. Triumph Books, 2013.

Caruso, Alex. Interview by Danny Green. *Inside the Green Room*, December 2019.

———. Interview by JJ Redick. *The JJ Redick Show*, November 2020; November 2021.

———. Interview by Zach Lowe. *The Lowe Post*, May 2020.

Clarkson, Jordan. Interview by Zach Lowe. *The Lowe Post*, March 2021.

Chotiner, Isaac. "LeBron James's Agent Is Transforming the Business of Basketball." *New Yorker*, May 31, 2021.

Cohen, Ben. "Alex Caruso: The LeBron of Playing with LeBron." *Wall Street Journal*, October 18, 2020.

———. "How LeBron, Magic and the Lakers Failed." *Wall Street Journal*, April 10, 2019.

———. "LeBron James and the Golden Age of Geezer Athletes." *Wall Street Journal*, December 22, 2019.

Connally, C. Ellen. "Book Review: Cleveland's 21st-Century Horatio Alger by C. Ellen Connally." CoolCleveland.com, October 16, 2023.

Cook, Quinn. Interview by Danny Green. *Inside the Green Room*, October 2019.

Davis, Anthony. Interview by D'Angelo Russell. *The Backyard Podcast*, February 2024.

Dawson, Brett. "The Summer When a Skinny Anthony Davis Had Chicago 'Buzzing About Him.'" *The Athletic*, February 15, 2020.

Ding, Kevin. "A Family Divided: Unrest Growing in Buss Family as Lakers Struggle to Rebuild." *Bleacher Report*, June 8, 2018.

Drape, Joe. "LeBron James's Representative Completes His Own Journey." *New York Times*, August 17, 2014.

Dudley, Jared. Interview by Adrian Wojnarowski. *The Woj Pod*, July 2019.

———. Interview by Bill Simmons. *The Bill Simmons Podcast*, October 2020.

———. Interview by Danny Green. *Inside the Green Room*, January 2021.

———. Interview by Richard Jefferson and Channing Frye. *Road Trippin',* October 2019.

———. Interview by Ryen Russillo. *The Ryen Russillo Show,* November 2019.

———. Interview by Zach Lowe. *The Lowe Post,* February 2020.

Dudley, Jared, and Carvell Wallace. *Inside the NBA Bubble.* Amazon Original Stories, 2021.

Elliott, Helene. "Elliott: Lakers Made Right Choice in Hiring Frank Vogel." *Los Angeles Times,* September 27, 2020.

Evans, Luca. "'Like He Was Trapped in a Box': The Oral History of Bronny James' Heart Scare." *Orange County Register,* January 23, 2024.

Fader, Mirin. "The Summer of Austin Reaves." *The Ringer,* October 17, 2023.

———. "The Wait and Weight for Bronny James." *The Ringer,* March 6, 2024.

Fenno, Nathan. "In Court Papers, Jeanie Buss Says Brother Was 'Completely Unfit' to Run Lakers' Basketball Operations." *Los Angeles Times,* March 5, 2017.

———. "It Was 16 Months Ago When Jeanie Buss Made a Daring Move to Seize Control of the Lakers." *Los Angeles Times,* July 4, 2018.

Fischer, Jake. *Built to Lose: How the NBA's Tanking Era Changed the League Forever.* Triumph Books, 2021.

Frydenlund, Zach. "Rich Paul and the Art of Building a Powerhouse Sports Agency from Scratch." *Complex,* December 7, 2016.

Fuqua, Antoine. *Legacy: The True Story of the LA Lakers.* Hulu, 2022.

Ganguli, Tania. "Jeanie Buss Believes Luke Walton Can Be the Lakers Coach for 10–15 Years, 'as Long as We Don't Kill Him.'" *Los Angeles Times,* March 30, 2017.

———. "Johnny Buss Distances Himself from Siblings and the Lakers." *Los Angeles Times,* June 18, 2017.

———. "Lakers Championship Was a Real Coup for Jeanie Buss." *Los Angeles Times,* October 14, 2020.

———. "Lakers Coach Frank Vogel Is Positively Just Being Himself." *Los Angeles Times,* December 22, 2019.

———. "Lakers in China: How the Team and NBA Navigated the Crisis amid Tumultuous Week." *Los Angeles Times,* October 15, 2019.

———. "Lakers! What Winning the NBA Championship Meant to Each Laker." *Los Angeles Times,* October 16, 2020.

———. "Lakers' Frank Vogel Has Won Over His Players, Including LeBron." *Los Angeles Times,* December 3, 2019.

———. "When an NBA Dad's Love for His Family Comes Bubble-Wrapped." *Los Angeles Times,* August 15, 2020.

———. "How LeBron James and NBA Players Decided to Resume Season." *Los Angeles Times,* August 28, 2020.

———. "How Magic Johnson's Late-Night Meeting Sealed the Lakers' Deal for LeBron James." *Los Angeles Times,* July 2, 2018.

Gold, Jon. "Jeanie Buss Is Laughing Through Her Pain." *New York Times,* July 12, 2021.

Golianopoulos, Thomas. "Family Business." *Grantland,* April 3, 2015.

Goon, Kyle. "In His Coaching Journey, Lakers' Darvin Ham Has Learned to Weather the Storm." *Orange County Register,* November 19, 2022.

Gregory, Sean. "LeBron James Is TIME's 2020 Athlete of the Year." *Time,* 2020.

Greif, Andrew. "The Inside Story Why Chris Paul's Trade to Lakers Was Vetoed." *Los Angeles Times,* December 13, 2021.

Golliver, Ben. *Bubbleball: Inside the NBA's Fight to Save a Season.* Abrams, 2021.

Ham, Darvin. Interview by Marc Stein and Chris Haynes. *The Stein and Haynes Podcast,* July 2023.

Haynes, Chris. "Inside the Emotional 48 Hours That Saved the NBA's Bubble." Yahoo Sports, August 28, 2020.

Heisler, Mark. "Life Gets up Close and Very Personal." *Los Angeles Times,* December 15, 2004.

Hernández, Dylan. "Column: Frank Vogel Shows Ability to 'Roll with the Punches' During Lakers Intro." *Los Angeles Times,* May 20, 2019.

Holmes, Baxter. "Lakers 2.0: The Failed Reboot of the NBA's Crown Jewel." ESPN, May 29, 2019.

Howard, Dwight. Interview by Danny Green. *Inside the Green Room,* November 2019.

James, LeBron. Interview by Richard Jefferson and Channing Frye. *Road Trippin',* March 2020.

———. Interview by Richard Jefferson and Channing Frye. *Road Trippin',* December 2020.

James, LeBron, and Buzz Bissinger. *Shooting Stars.* Penguin Press, 2009.

Jenkins, Lee. "Inside LeBron James's Third Free-Agency Decision." *Sports Illustrated,* July 1, 2018.

———. "Lakers' Rebuild Could Be Ready for Showtime." *Sports Illustrated,* April 17, 2018.

———. "LeBron James and the Lakers Form Hollywood's Ultimate Marriage." *Sports Illustrated,* July 11, 2018.

———. "Pelicans Forward Anthony Davis Emerges as NBA's Latest Phenom." *Sports Illustrated,* December 2, 2014.

Jackson, Phil, and Michael Arkush. *The Last Season: A Team in Search of Its Soul.* Penguin Press, 2005.

Johnson, Magic. Interview by Maverick Carter. *Kneading Dough,* July 2018.

Keown, Tim. "Isolation Play." ESPN, September 2003.

Klose, Lee. *Late for the Buss: An Adoption Story.* Bookbaby, 2022.

Kupchak, Mitch. Interview by Adrian Wojnarowski. *The Woj Pod,* October 2017.

Kuzma, Kyle. Interview by Adrian Wojnarowski. *The Woj Pod,* January 2023.

Lazenby, Roland. *Showboat: The Life of Kobe Bryant.* Hachette, 2016.

Lee, Michael. "How Athletes Built a Voter-Turnout Machine for 2020 and Beyond." *Washington Post,* December 4, 2020.

Leff, Fara. Interview by *Comebacks Show. Comebacks Show,* October 2020.

Leitch, Will. "LeBron James Doesn't Talk About Politics Anymore." *New York,* October 26, 2022.

———. "The Athletes Have More to Say." *New York,* March 2, 2021.

Lidz, Frank. "She's Got Balls." *Sports Illustrated,* November 2, 1998.

Lloyd, Jason. *The Blueprint: LeBron James, Cleveland's Deliverance, and the Making of the Modern NBA.* Penguin, 2017.

————. "The Cavs' Last Dance Had the Same Moves as the One by the Bulls." *The Athletic*, May 6, 2020.

Los Angeles Times. "Rob Pelinka on Magic Johnson's Comments: 'They're Simply Not True.'" May 20, 2019.

Lowe, Zach. "LeBron vs. MJ, This Lakers Season and a Great NBA What-If." ESPN, March 12, 2019.

————. "The Cavs' Imperfect Deadline Was the Best They Could Do." ESPN, February 9, 2018.

————. "Why Brandon Ingram's Superstar Potential Matters." ESPN, January 19, 2021.

————. "Do Anthony Davis and the Pelicans Still Need Demarcus Cousins?" ESPN, April 24, 2018.

————. "Lakers' Dilemma: Search for a Superstar or Keep It Together?" ESPN, December 22, 2016.

Mahoney, Rob. "The Rebirth of Thunder Basketball: Paul George's Return Provides Hope in OKC." *Sports Illustrated,* October 15, 2018.

McGee, JaVale. *Life in the Bubble.* YouTube, 2020.

McMenamin, Dave. "How the Lakers Wasted Year 1 of LeBron." ESPN, April 10, 2019.

————. "How Year 2 of LeBron and the Lakers Turned into a Roller Coaster." ESPN, July 30, 2020.

————. "Inside Anthony Davis and the Lakers' Vision for Their Latest Big-Man Trio." ESPN, November 13, 2023.

————. "Inside LeBron James' and Adam Silver's Make-or-Break Moments in China." ESPN, October 16, 2019.

————. "Lakers Players Say There's Still Time to 'Figure Things Out' ahead of Restart." ESPN, June 14, 2020.

————. "Lakers' Magic Johnson Says Pelicans Didn't Act in Good Faith." ESPN, February 10, 2019.

————. "LeBron James: Los Angeles Lakers Getting Anthony Davis Would Be 'Amazing.'" ESPN, December 19, 2018.

————. "Q&A with Jim Buss, Part 1." ESPN, April 18, 2012.

————. "Q&A with Jim Buss, Part 2." ESPN, April 18, 2012.

————. "Sources: Los Angeles Lakers Feel Urgency to Make Changes as Trade Deadline Nears." ESPN, February 9, 2022.

————. "The Longest Flight in Los Angeles Lakers History: When the Team Learned of Kobe Bryant's Death." ESPN, January 26, 2021.

McMenamin, Dave, and Malika Andrews. "NBA Finals: The Scenes of a Lakers Title Celebration like No Other." ESPN, October 12, 2020.

McMenamin, Dave, and Ohm Youngmisuk. "Who's Running the Show? Inside the Lakers' Hierarchy." ESPN, May 10, 2019.

Medina, Mark. "Why Warriors' Andrew Bogut Remains Upset with the Los Angeles Lakers." *Mercury News,* April 4, 2019.

Miller, James Andrew. *Powerhouse: The Untold Story of Hollywood's Creative Artists Agency.* HarperCollins, 2016.

Morris, Markieff. Interview by Danny Green. *Inside the Green Room,* 2020.

Needelman, Joshua. "In the World of Wrestling, a Heavy Hitter Steps into the Ring." *New York Times,* December 15, 2022.

O'Connor, Ian. *Coach K: The Rise and Reign of Mike Krzyzewski.* HarperCollins, 2022.

Oram, Bill. "Dwayne 'The Rock' Johnson Motivates Lakers with Stories of Life Experiences, Overcoming Disappointment." *Orange County Register,* March 14, 2018.

———. "From Kobe Bryant's Agent to Magic Johnson's GM: Can Rob Pelinka Save the Lakers?" *Orange County Register,* March 2017.

———. "How the Lakers Won the LeBron Sweepstakes but Ended up Back in the Lottery." *The Athletic,* April 9, 2019.

———. "Inside Locker Room, Lakers Players See and Feel the Same Problems as Everyone Else and Also Want Change." *The Athletic,* February 9, 2022.

———. "Jeanie Buss Is Lakers' Wonder Woman." *Orange County Register,* July 23, 2017.

———. "Luke Walton's Last Days? How the Lakers Strayed from Their Values and Are Now Set to Betray Their Coach." *The Athletic,* March 11, 2019.

———. "Michigan Judge Orders Lakers' Kentavious Caldwell-Pope to Remain in California, Costing Him at Least Three Road Games." *Orange County Register,* December 17, 2017.

———. "Oram: Lakers' Willingness to Make D'Angelo Russell a Casualty of Trade Is Fitting End to Flawed Tenure." *Orange County Register,* June 21, 2017.

———. "Oram: Lakers' Move to New Headquarters Means 'Bittersweet' Goodbye to Longtime Home." *Orange County Register,* July 30, 2017.

———. "Oram: Magic Can Question the Coaching, but Who Is Holding the Front Office Accountable for This Roster?" *The Athletic,* November 3, 2018.

———. "Signing LeBron James Would Catapult Lakers up Standings, Redirect Course for Young Stars." *Orange County Register,* March 11, 2018.

———. "Will Lakers' 'Kids' Test the Patience of LeBron James and the Veterans?" *The Athletic,* September 26, 2018.

———. "With Magic Gone, Jeanie Buss Must Hire the Best—Not Her Best Friends." *The Athletic,* April 10, 2019.

Oram, Bill, and Sam Amick. "Lakers Coach Frank Vogel's Job in Jeopardy with Team Seventh in West: Sources." *The Athletic,* January 18, 2022.

Paul, Rich. *Lucky Me.* Random House, 2024.

———. Interview by Bloomberg. Bloomberg Power Players Summit, August 2022.

———. Interview by Chris Haynes. *Bleacher Report,* February 2024.

———. Interview by *Comebacks Show. Comebacks Show,* October 2022.

———. Interview by JJ Redick. *The JJ Redick Podcast,* October 2023.

———. Interview by *Rap Radar. Rap Radar Podcast,* June 2018.

Pearlman, Jeff. *Showtime: Magic, Kareem, Riley, and the Los Angeles Lakers Dynasty of the 1980s.* Penguin, 2014.

———. *Three-Ring Circus: Kobe, Shaq, Phil, and the Crazy Years of the Lakers Dynasty.* Mariner Books, 2020.

Pelinka, Rob. Interview by Adrian Wojnarowski. *The Woj Pod,* May 2018; October 2020.

———. Interview by Danny Green. *Inside the Green Room,* September 2020.

Pina, Michael. "Jared Dudley Talks About What Really Happened When the NBA Went on Strike." *GQ,* September 2020.

Pincus, Eric. "How LA Lakers Mismanaged Their Way from Champs to Chumps." *Bleacher Report,* July 26, 2022.

Plaschke, Bill. "A Memorial Service Perfectly Suited to Jerry Buss: Glitz, Grace and Some Goofiness." *Los Angeles Times,* February 21, 2013.

———. "Column: Lakers' Coaching Search Is More Proof Jeanie Buss' Team Is Lost Without a Leader." *Los Angeles Times,* April 24, 2019.

———. "Column: Magic Johnson Was Never All In, So Now He's All Gone." *Los Angeles Times,* April 10, 2019.

———. "L.A. Times Exclusive: Jeanie Buss Tells Bill Plaschke She Isn't Happy and Vows 'I've Got to Make It Better.'" *Los Angeles Times,* May 10, 2022.

———. "Lakers Go Back to a Sweet Spot with Hiring of Luke Walton." *Los Angeles Times,* April 30, 2016.

———. "Rob Pelinka Is Force Behind Lakers' Rise as Title Contenders." *Los Angeles Times,* September 29, 2023.

Pluto, Terry. "Cleveland Cavaliers Have Terry Talkin' About Why LeBron James Felt Comfortable to Sign New Deal." *Cleveland,* August 13, 2016.

Presti, Sam. Interview by Adrian Wojnarowski. *The Woj Pod,* December 2019.

Price, S. L. "The King Maker: Why Rich Paul Will Own the NBA Summer." *Sports Illustrated,* June 12, 2019.

Randle, Julius. Interview by Paul George. *Podcast P,* June 2023.

Reaves, Austin. Interview by Andre Iguodala and Evan Turner. *The Point Forward,* March 2023.

———. Interview by Matt Barnes and Stephen Jackson. *All the Smoke,* July 2023.

———. Interview by Ryen Russillo. *The Ryen Russillo Show,* October 2023.

Rohlin, Melissa. "How Russell Westbrook's Lakers Tenure Changed His Career Trajectory." Fox Sports, February 10, 2023.

Rondo, Rajon. Interview by JJ Redick. *The JJ Redick Podcast,* October 2024.

———. Interview by Matt Barnes and Stephen Jackson. *All the Smoke,* December 2020.

Rooks, Taylor. "Inside the Great NBA Bubble Experiment." *GQ,* November 24, 2020.

Rosman, Katherine. "Lady of the Lakers." *New York Times,* January 2, 2021.

Russell, D'Angelo. Interview by Adrian Wojnarowski. *The Woj Pod,* July 2017; October 2016.

Shelburne, Ramona. "A Los Angeles Lakers Sequel That Failed to Live Up to the Original." ESPN, June 4, 2021.

———. "Anthony Davis Sr. Doesn't Want Son in Boston, Cites Treatment of Isaiah Thomas." ESPN, February 2, 2019.

———. "How LeBron James and Jeanie Buss Squashed Lakers Drama." ESPN, September 17, 2020.

———. "How LeBron James and the Los Angeles Lakers Made Their Biggest Statement Yet." ESPN, March 8, 2020.

———. "How LeBron James' Decision Instantly Changed Los Angeles Lakers, Cleveland Cavaliers and NBA." ESPN, July 11, 2018.

———. "Inside the NBA's Return: How Adam Silver, Star Players and Owners Got Here." ESPN, June 4, 2020.

———. "Lakers Reminded of Ill-Fated 2021 Trade as They Trail Nuggets 3-0." ESPN, May 21, 2023.

———. "Los Angeles Lakers Coach Luke Walton Meets with LeBron James." ESPN, July 17, 2018.

———. "Los Angeles Lakers' Jeanie Buss Thwarts Coup Attempt of Brothers Johnny Buss, Jim Buss." ESPN, March 3, 2017.

———. "NBA Finals: Anthony Davis Walked in Kobe Bryant's Footsteps to Get to This Moment." ESPN, October 3, 2020.

———. "The Inside Story of the Lakers' Family Drama." ESPN, March 8, 2017.

———. "The Los Angeles Lakers and Russell Westbrook Are Stuck inside Their Own Grand Experiment." ESPN, January 25, 2022.

———. "The Massive Risks and Rewards Behind This Anthony Davis Trade." ESPN, June 16, 2019.

Shelburne, Ramona, and Tim MacMahon. "'Unfathomable': How This Stunning Luka Doncic–Anthony Davis Trade Came Together for Los Angeles Lakers and Dallas Mavericks." ESPN, February 3, 2025.

Shelburne, Ramona, Dave McMenamin, and Brian Windhorst. "Inside the Weeks of Dysfunction Surrounding Kyrie Irving's Trade Demand." ESPN, July 23, 2017.

Smith, J. R. Interview by Danny Green. *Inside the Green Room,* 2020.

Stein, Marc. "To Woo LeBron James, David Geffen Seeking 51 Percent of Los Angeles Clippers from Donald Sterling." ESPN, June 8, 2010.

Strauss, Ethan. "Klutch Lakers vs. CAA Knicks." *House of Strauss,* March 4, 2022.

———. "Luke Walton, the Golden State Warriors' Winless Wonder." ESPN, November 24, 2015.

Termini, Mark. *Words to Negotiate By: Axioms, Proverbs and Collected Wisdom from a Lifetime Operating in the Complex Worlds of Business and Sports . . . Compiled by the Multibillion-Dollar Sports Attorney and Agent.* MTA Publishing, 2023.

———. Interview by Brian Windhorst. *The Hoop Collective,* August 2023.

Thomsen, Ian. *The Soul of Basketball: The Epic Showdown Between LeBron, Kobe, Doc, and Dirk That Saved the NBA.* Houghton Mifflin Harcourt, 2018.

———. "Cavaliers Offer Boozer Chance to Redeem Reputation." *Sports Illustrated,* January 20, 2005.

Torre, Pablo. "LeBron James' Plan to Become King of Hollywood." ESPN, 2017.

Trudell, Mike. "Getting to Know: Rob Pelinka." NBA.com, April 10, 2017.

———. "Lakers | Dr. Jerry Buss: The Oral History of the Greatest Owner in Sports." NBA.com, February 10, 2020.

Tucker, Kyle. "'Vampire Hours' at Fazoli's with the Alien? Lakers' Anthony Davis 'Did It All in One Year' at Kentucky." *The Athletic,* May 21, 2021.

Turner, Broderick. "Anthony Davis Trade Saga: Magic Johnson to Meet with Lakers Players." *Los Angeles Times,* February 8, 2019.

———. "How the Lakers Pulled out Game 2 Win in the Last 20 Seconds." *Los Angeles Times,* September 21, 2020.

———. "Lakers Are in Trouble, and Many around NBA Think Rob Pelinka Must Go." *Los Angeles Times,* April 11, 2019.

Vardon, Joe. "Koby Altman Took Control of Cavaliers Roster to Begin Cleanup of Mess He, LeBron James and Tyronn Lue Made Together." *Cleveland,* February 16, 2018.

———. "LeBron James Experience Enters New and Perhaps Final Stage: 'When It's Over, You Will Respect Him More.'" *New York Times,* October 23, 2023.

———. "LeBron James Hears Magic Johnson and Kobe Bryant, but He Isn't Going to Listen." *New York Times,* December 5, 2018.

———. "LeBron James: Cavaliers' Trading of Kyrie Irving Was 'Beginning of the End for Everything.'" *New York Times,* November 19, 2018.

Vogel, Frank. Interview by Zach Lowe. *The Lowe Post,* October 2020.

Wade, Dwyane. Interview by Adrian Wojnarowski. *The Woj Pod,* February 2017.

Walton, Bill. *Back from the Dead.* Simon & Schuster, 2017.

Weinbaum, William. "Los Angeles Lakers Dynasty Derailed." ESPN, October 21, 2016.

Windhorst, Brian. "Truths About Anthony Davis and the Lakers." ESPN, December 19, 2018.

———. *LeBron, Inc: The Making of a Billion-Dollar Athlete.* Grand Central Publishing, 2019.

Windhorst, Brian, and Dave McMenamin. *Return of the King: LeBron James, the Cleveland Cavaliers and the Greatest Comeback in NBA History.* Grand Central Publishing, 2017.

Woike, Dan. "Anthony Davis Seems to Have Found His NBA Home with Lakers." *Los Angeles Times,* October 12, 2020.

———. "Austin Reaves: His Rise from Arkansas Farm to Lakers Fame." *Los Angeles Times,* June 13, 2022.

———. "Darvin Ham Survived the Streets, a Bullet and Grief to Coach Lakers." *Los Angeles Times,* December 11, 2022.

———. "How Bronny James's NBA Dream Is Complicated by Famous Father." *Los Angeles Times,* May 19, 2024.

———. "How LeBron James Claimed the NBA's Scoring Title." *Los Angeles Times,* February 8, 2023.

———. "How LeBron James, Anthony Davis Connect to Reach NBA Finals." *Los Angeles Times,* September 27, 2020.

———. "Kobe Bryant's Signature Shoes Keep His Memory Close to NBA Players." *Los Angeles Times,* September 30, 2020.

———. "Will Russell Westbrook Ever Be Happy? If He Is, Will Lakers?" *Los Angeles Times,* January 12, 2022.

———. "Will the Lakers Get Kyrie Irving? NBA Scouts and Execs Are Torn." *Los Angeles Times,* July 11, 2022.

Wojnarowski, Adrian. "Small-Market GMs Upset over LeBron James' Pitch for Anthony Davis." ESPN, December 21, 2018.

Wojnarowski, Adrian, and Malika Andrews. "Bradley, Coalition Seek NBA Plan for Black Causes." ESPN, June 16, 2020.

———. "New NBA Coalition Voicing Concerns of Players." ESPN, June 15, 2020.

Youngmisuk, Ohm. "How Luke Walton's Coaching Style Was Influenced by the Major NBA Championship Figures in His Life." ESPN, December 6, 2017.